DON'T
CALL
ME
BROTHER

DON'T CALL ME BROTHER

A Ringmaster's Escape from the Pentecostal Church

Austin Miles

PROMETHEUS BOOKS
Buffalo, New York

Library of Congress Cataloging-in-Publication Data

Miles, Austin, 1933-
    Don't call me brother.

    1. Assemblies of God—Controversial literature.
2. Pentecostal churches—Controversial literature.
3. Miles, Austin, 1933-   . I. Title.
BX8765.5.Z5M55   1989   289.9'4'0924 [B]   89-60074
ISBN 0-87975-507-5

This book is dedicated to Rose Marie,
who was right.

Acknowledgments

To the editor of this book, Edmund D. Cohen, whose sensitivity to the content and skillful surgery to the prose proved invaluable. The discipline and added dimension he contributed are manifest on every page.

To Shirley Ann, whose love, loyalty, and tremendous understanding encouraged me to go on during the most painful and trying time of my life.

To Shawn, Michael, and Cindy, for giving me the chance to be a Dad again, when I lost my daughter. Three for one is not a bad dividend.

I was a stranger, and ye took me in.

—Matthew 25:35

It was a mistake. I made a fool of myself. I was taken. Using and quoting the Bible, they twisted my mind so badly that I was motivated to do some pretty stupid things: things I would never even think of in my right mind. Regrettably, in my "born again" Christian piety, I said some cruel things that hurt and confused many decent people, including my own wife. What's worse, I was certain I had *all* the answers as a minister. Unfortunately, others will continue to make the same mistake.

—Austin Miles

Contents

Preface

The Assemblies of God is one of the fastest growing church denominations in the world.

In 1987, in the United States, the sect numbered:

1,879,182 members,
10,173 churches, increasing in number by 307 each year,
9 Bible colleges, a liberal arts college, and a graduate school of theology.

Overseas it listed:

233 Bible institutions,
1,220 foreign missionaries,
    and an annual missionary budget of $48,453,712.

The Assemblies of God produces an international radio program called "Revivaltime," which is heard on over 570 stations. It also produces a daily radio program called "Every Day with Jesus" on 42 stations. The denomination publishes *The Pentecostal Evangel,* which has a weekly circulation of 300,000. Most Christian television programs are Assemblies of God-oriented or backed.

The Assemblies of God is also a controversial, mysterious, and intriguing organization. The author of *Don't Call Me Brother* is the first ordained Assemblies of God minister to leave the denomination and write a book revealing the true character of this church whose "mission" is to take over the world.

The cast of characters reads like a *Who's Who* of Charismatic, Fundamental, Pentecostal circles. The reader will recognize many of the names, on both the national and local levels. The more than 133 prominent Christian personalities that appear in this book were a part of the author's life, and the portraits that evolved were drawn from personal relationships and encounters with them. The portrayals are honest ones, and above all, fair. All of the incredible events described are substantiated and documented.

Assumptions have been avoided altogether.

The reader will notice that, in all controversial situations, witnesses were present who corroborate the stories. In those instances where the author was not present, the scene and dialogue were carefully reconstructed from eyewitness accounts. Some of the steamier scenes described have been checked and verified by investigative reporter Art Harris of *The Washington Post,* who has used some of the material in his national articles. *Newsweek* has carried some of this material as well.

On legal matters, the previous law career of the editor, Edmund D. Cohen, was put to good use. One special reward of this collaboration was being able to exhume a scandal that the Assemblies of God would rather have left buried, along with the confusion they wrapped it in. At last, the full story about Reverend Thomas F. Zimmerman, the Assemblies of God hierarchy, and the Empire Bank of Springfield, Missouri, is out in the open.

Before writing this story, the author distanced himself from the material in order to give a responsible, balanced account of the experience. This proved to be a challenge considering the personal pain suffered by the author after becoming involved with the Charismatics and The Assemblies of God. According to those who read the pre-published manuscript with a critical eye, that goal was accomplished.

' Future historians will find that this work contains some of the most informative, accurate material ever published on The Assemblies of God, the televangelists, and the greatest religious scandal of all time. A scandal that will damage the credibility and effect of Christianity for many years to come.

So fasten your seat belts, and ". . . the grace of our Lord Jesus Christ be with you all. Amen."

Austin Miles
San Francisco, California
January 1989

Cast of Characters

THE GUARDIANS OF OUR SOULS

Jim Jones
Billy James Hargis
Bob Harrington
William Branham
Jack Coe
Kathryn Kuhlman
Oral Roberts
Charles Hunter
Frances Hunter
Pat Robertson
Eugene Profeta

Richard Dortch
John Wesley Fletcher
Ben Kinchlow
Russ Bixler
Dr. C. M. Ward
"Uncle" Henry Harrison
"Aunt" Susan Harrison
Leonard Evans
Paul Crouch
Mike Murdock
Robert Schuller

Marilyn Hickey
Marvin Gorman
Vicki Jamison
David Mainse
P. C. Nelson
Bob Gass
David Lewis
Rex Humbard
Ernest Angley
Jimmy Swaggart

Jim Bakker   Tammy Faye Bakker

CELEBRITY CHRISTIANS

Efrem Zimbalist, Jr.
Gary Paxton
Mickey Rooney
Howard Goodman
Vestal Goodman
Tino Wallenda Zoppe
The Singing Coal Miner

Donna Douglas
Miss America
Harold Hill
Dino Kartsonakis
Debbie Kartsonakis

Dexter Yaeger
Bobby Yerkes
Pat Boone
Dale Evans Rogers
Colonel Harland Sanders
Jessica Hahn
Donna Rice

and
J. Edgar Hoover?

THE HIERARCHY OF THE ASSEMBLIES OF GOD

Thomas F. Zimmerman
R. D. E. Smith
Joseph Flower

Riley Kaufman
Paul Markstrom

Arthur Shell
Don Shelton
Lee Schultz

MEMBERS OF THE PTL STAFF

Norman Bakker
Lyn McMann Robbins
Lee Robbins
Jim Moss
David Taggart
Jim Bakker's personal secretary

Raleigh Bakker
Harold Olshields
Bill Garthwaite
Don Hardister
Helen Headley
Thurlow Spurr
Jeanne Johnson

Reverend Russell Olson
Reverend Aubrey Sara
Martin Gutwerk
Jean Albuquerque
Melvin Stewart
Doug Odum

and Joy "Bambi" Christian

MEMBERS OF PAT ROBERTSON'S "700 CLUB" STAFF

"Reverend" Glenn McElwain   James Murphy   Barbara Johnson

MAINLINE MINISTERS AND PRIESTS

Reverend Addison Chapin
Reverend Don Theobald
Father John J. Johnston

Cardinal Terence J. Cooke
Bishop Fulton J. Sheen

THE PASTORS OF THE ASSEMBLIES OF GOD CHURCH WHO ALSO WERE A PART OF THE AUTHOR'S LIFE AND STORY

Coleman McDuff
Roger McDuff
Leon Cooke
Gerritt Kenyon
Robert Thom
Cameron Stanton
Edward G. Berkey
Vincent Terrenova
Robert Rosin
Richard Serro
Sam Peterson
Ray Rachels
Albert R. Fisher

Jack West
Ernie Eskelin
Ernest J. Moen
Almon Bartholomew
Hubert Morris
Irving Stevens
Calvin Bacon
Jack Piper
Joseph Sutera
James K. Barrett
Roland Buck
Donald Richardson

Stewart Robinson
Neil Eskelin
Ernest Steffensen
Frank Becker
Stanley Berg
Ellis Damiani
William J. Behr
Dan Raught
Martin Luther Davidson
Richard Orchard
John Bedzyk
E. R. Schultz
Winston Schmock

AND A CAST OF THOUSANDS . . .

"Ye shall know the truth..."

I

Anticipation filled the air as throngs of people crowded into the Heritage Village studio. The surrounding grounds resembled a small colonial Williamsburg, with a stately mansion and several offices housed in quaint little shop-like structures along winding streets. The grounds were neatly manicured.

Standing majestically, the Heritage Church dominated the charming early American setting. The church also housed the PTL studio, one of the most modern, state-of-the-art television facilities in North America. Even though young, the PTL (Praise the Lord) Club had already become firmly entrenched in the American television scene.

Jim Bakker checked his appearance in the lighted dressing room mirror. He turned his head from side to side. The puffy, dark hair that covered his ears was carefully styled in mid-seventies' fashion.

"Good," he said over his shoulder to the make-up girl. "Thank you."

Jim Bakker had a round, youthful face that conveyed an almost boyish innocence. He was short, and slightly on the pudgy side. His extra-wide, friendly mouth, tipped in a perpetual grin, looked as if it could have been borrowed from a ventriloquist's dummy.

He studied his reflection with satisfaction. Jim Bakker was fast becoming the most watched TV evangelist in America. His program was on two hours daily, and new stations were constantly being added. Faithful viewers gave their strong financial support. There was a surplus of money.

It had not been that long ago that the PTL Club was telecasting out of a converted furniture store on Independence Boulevard in Charlotte, North Carolina. Jim had opened the first bank account in the name of PTL with fifty-two dollars. His network consisted of three stations. But it was obvious to everyone that with his charisma and star-quality, he would rise rapidly.

He had recently moved his studio to this new location on Park Road. Being there was, in itself, a miracle. The way everything had fallen into place—for Jim to have acquired this property and built these new facilities with his limited budget—had to have been of God.

Bill Garthwaite, the producer of the program, looked the studio audience over. It was another overflow crowd. Next to him stood his assistant, Lyn McMann, clipboard in hand. Lyn's classic good looks reflected her former career as a model and actress.

"Looks like we've already outgrown this place," she said to Garthwaite. He nodded his head.

The floor director held up his hand dramatically, with five fingers outstretched. The studio audience suddenly became silent. The countdown to 10:00 A.M. began. Five—four—three—two—one! There was a timpani roll, and Thurlow Spurr, the orchestra leader, led the downbeat for the PTL theme, which had been composed by Gary Paxton. The live studio orchestra was a recent, sophisticated addition to the program. Previously, all music, including accompaniment for singers, had been taped.

The theme concluded with another timpani roll, over which "Uncle" Henry Harrison announced, ". . . and here is your host of the PTL Club— Jim Bakker!" The music built up to a final crescendo as Jim entered, to tumultuous applause. Jim tried to talk over the continuing applause. "My, my, my," he said with a broad smile. "Well, what another fine looking studio audience. You look so nice. Where is that group from Amway?"

A cheer from a section of the audience answered that inquiry.

"There are so many things happening here at PTL that I can't keep up with everything," Jim continued. "People are being saved and healed watching this program. We're getting hundreds of calls from all over the country. . . . Marriages are being put back together. Praise God, He is blessing us so much. More and more cities are being added to the PTL Network every day. I just found out before the telecast that PTL is now on in Washington, D.C."

The audience greeted that announcement with enthusiastic applause.

"Also, it looks very good that we will be on in—are you ready?— in New York City!" More applause broke out. "Remember now—all this is happening because of the faithfulness of your giving. Without your support we wouldn't be able to continue this ministry, so we are relying on you, our partners. If you're not already a partner of PTL, won't you call us today? For only fifteen dollars a month you will be helping this ministry stay on the air. You will receive a partnership card, our monthly newsletter, and you will be an essential part of so many exciting things, and God will bless you for it. So, call the number that's on the screen and say, 'Yes, I want to be a PTL partner.' "

The happy studio audience had come from all over. To them, the PTL Club and Jim Bakker represented the key link to their faith and to God. Jim's guests came from all walks of life, and included many celebrities. Their testimonies always came to the same conclusion: That without Jesus, life was nothing, empty, and the *only* way to happiness was to be "born again," to submit oneself to the precepts of the Bible and the discipline of a "Spirit-filled" church, to live only for Christ.

These testimonies served to validate and verify the superiority of the disciplined, self-sacrificing, Christ-centered life. More importantly, they were ironclad proof that the born-again Christians were absolutely right in their beliefs and in their decision to flee the world and its pleasures, and that everyone else should do the same.

It was mainly a middle-aged audience, with a scattering of older and younger people. Despite the wide age range and obviously varied backgrounds, these people all seemed to be poured from the same mold. A set radiance and ethereally happy expression carved on their faces displayed, on the surface, freedom from distress, which impressed those in "the world" who had their daily bouts with tension.

"It's going to be a very special program today," Jim went on. "Our guests include Dale Evans, Dr. C. M. Ward, and Austin Miles." The audience greeted each name with applause. "And let's open the show with Tammy Faye singing, 'We Are Blessed.' "

Tammy Faye was short like Jim, and together they looked like a pair of Kewpie dolls. One felt protective toward them. They seemed so huggable. They were ideally suited to one another, and blended together perfectly.

An emotional singer, Tammy belted out her songs with a torch-like quality, with a hint of country and western. She was indeed distinctive. By the time Tammy had finished singing, Jim was seated behind his desk with Uncle Henry Harrison next to him. There was a vacant colonial-style wing chair and a couch, both of them plushly upholstered in azure-colored cloth, next to the desk.

"Thank you, Tammy Faye," Jim acknowledged. "Our first guest today is Austin Miles, who was probably the greatest circus ringmaster in the world. He had fame and money but found life empty until he accepted the Lord Jesus Christ as his savior."

Scattered "amens" and "hallelujahs" ascended from the audience.

"Today he's a minister of the Gospel of Jesus Christ. He was one of my first guests when this ministry began. Would you please welcome— from Forest Hills, New York—the Show Business Chaplain—Austin Miles!"

"Okay Austin," said Bill Garthwaite behind the set, giving me a gentle nudge. I walked onto the set as the orchestra played the circus theme, "March of the Gladiators." I acknowledged the audience, walked over to the desk, shook Jim's hand, then Uncle Henry's, and sat down in the wing chair.

"Welcome back, Austin," Jim said warmly.

"Thank you, Jim," I answered. "And I have one thing to say to you and everyone in this audience." I began a sweeping movement with my hand and exclaimed, "You are special!" That phrase had become a trademark with me. The audience applauded it, as always. "You know, Jim, people can get into trouble if they forget how special they are. . . . If you don't mind, I'm going to tattle on a friend. Bobby Yerkes, as you know, is the one who led me to the Lord. He's a Hollywood stuntman now, and a great Christian witness. Well, he had a bad day at the studio, was on his way home, stopped at a stop sign, and no sooner had he stopped when the car behind him honked its horn. Well, that was the last straw. Bob got out of his car, stormed to the car behind him, pounded his fist on the roof, and said, 'Okay Buddy, if you've got anything to say to me, say it to my face!'

"The terrified driver said, 'But—you've got a bumper sticker that says "honk if you love Jesus!" ' "

A roar of laughter erupted from the audience. I immediately launched into another story.

*   *   *

Following the telecast I had lunch at the mansion with Uncle Henry and the other guests. "Oh, by the way, Austin," an aide interjected, leaning over me, "you're staying over tonight, aren't you?"

"Yes," I replied.

"I was told to tell you," he continued, "that if you like, you can use the health facility. We have an exercise room, whirlpool, steam room, and if you like, Melvin will give you a massage."

"Good," I said, "where is it?"

"On the other side of the studio in the basement."

After the elaborate lunch I retired to my room to read, and unexpectedly dropped off to sleep. It was evening when I got up from my chair. I stretched, and decided to go to the health club. Maybe it would still be open.

I found the right door and walked inside. The area was very quiet and looked deserted. Only a few lights were on. I walked between the pool and whirlpool, toward what I supposed must be the massage and steam room.

Putting my hand on the knob and turning it, I opened the door. As it opened, I stopped dead in my tracks. My feet felt nailed to the floor. I closed my eyes and opened them again in disbelief. There were Jim Bakker and three of his male staff members frolicking about in the nude.

The four were so absorbed in playing with and massaging each other that they did not see me by the door in the feeble light. Jim had one of the naked young men stretch out on the table and began massaging the prone man's legs, working his hands up over the knees and thighs.

The expression on my face probably revealed the rest of the story, as effeminate giggles and a falsetto "whoooeeeeee" filled the room. Suddenly, Jim looked up and saw me. There was a moment of deafening silence. Regaining his composure, Jim reached for a towel, wrapped it around him, and became very professional and formal.

"Austin, that was a wonderful show today." He turned to one of the nude young men. "I want you to book Austin on the program every month," he said in a commanding tone. The young man nodded his head, in agreement that Jim's will would be done.

Jim turned back to me. "You keep bringing me stories like you did today," he said.

"Right Jim," I said uncomfortably. "I'll see you later."

I retreated hastily. I stood outside the door for a few moments. Had I really seen what I thought I saw? Maybe I had misinterpreted the whole scene. It had probably all been innocent horseplay. But why had Jim booked me for monthly performances in that casual setting instead of upstairs, after the program? No, it all had to be innocent. I was getting too skeptical.

Hearing footsteps, I ducked into a shadowed area. I did not want anyone to see me. The approaching footsteps were heavy and determined. Tammy Faye was storming across the room, her face flushed with anger. She banged her fist on the steam room door.

"Jim Bakker, you come out of there right now! I know you're in there! Now, come out of there—I mean it!" As Tammy pounded on the door one of her false eyelashes fell off. This was the last straw. "Dammit!" she screamed while trying to recover the eyelash. "GODDAMMIT!" She leaned up against the door and started to cry.

I could hear footsteps coming from another direction. It was Lyn McMann. Lyn saw Tammy and walked over to her.

"What am I going to do?" Tammy sobbed. Lyn put her arm around Tammy understandingly. They walked off, leaving me alone in the dark corner.

What on earth had I gotten myself into? I really believed in these people and the church. They held themselves up to be superior to all others in morals and honesty. They raised money on that pretense. I had been in the full-time ministry for only a short time, but already I had seen enough shocking conduct among the ministers and evangelists to make me begin to wonder if I were taking part in a lie. Being a part of the Assemblies of God ministry had already taken a devastating toll on my family. Where was God in all of this?

But far worse would come out of the Pandora's box I had opened when I became a born-again charismatic Christian minister.

"In the beginning..."

II

It had started innocently enough. What harm could possibly have come of it? Even if it provided only a temporary relief, weren't the reassurance and inspiration that came from being "born again" worth desiring? To suggest an untoward end from something that seemed, at the start, so constructive would have been preposterous and absurd. In the passion of that moment, skepticism had no place.

It is always during a period of upheaval, tragedy, and insecurity that people reach most earnestly to God. The years following the Great Depression were no exception.

That spring Sunday in 1938 in Evansville, Indiana, was typical. Everything seemed to stop for the Lord's Day. All activities and transactions ceased, and there was a comforting peacefulness about that. This was a day when the entire citizenry was on their best behavior—a cherished time indeed!

The clang of a church bell broke the silence of the morning. Another, with its steady, mournful tones, joined in, and then another. Soon every church in the city had joined in the tintinnabulary concert that filled the heavens. It was, mind you, a pleasant sound that beckoned all the faithful to their various houses of worship.

Many families walked to church, others joining them along the way. It was an excellent time to catch up on the latest news. Everyone was dressed up in their "Sunday suits." The men were nattily attired in their seersucker suits with bow ties and straw boaters. The ladies, in their bonnets and flowing dresses, were well perfumed. The children were at their scrubbed best, with the little boys in their starched white shirts and ties, and the little girls in their Victorian collared dresses. All that decorum, however, could not hide the glint in some young eyes, foretelling mischief in the making.

The singing that filtered out of the various churches along the way indicated what particular approach to God those inside felt was essential for true worship. The Catholics chanted the somber tones of the liturgies. The "mainline" Protestants stiffly sang of pious gladness. In contrast, the uninhibited Pentecostals fairly shouted out their peppy, "Clap Your Hands All Ye People."

The Pentecostals were the least understood and least tolerated of all the churchgoers in town. The Assembly of God church, in a rather plain building with a bold sign in front proclaiming "Jesus Said Ye Must Be Born Again," was something of a curiosity to the people of Evansville. The Pentecostals were too emotional and exuberant for most people's comfort. "That church" was considered to be "on the other side of the tracks," and only for uneducated, strange fanatics who really didn't fit in anywhere else.

But the "mainline" Protestant church—that's where it was *at*. That was where the better people attended. Which of the various "mainline" Protestant churches was *the* church remained a matter of constant debate.

The North Park Presbyterian Church was filled, as usual. With reverently subdued joy, the congregation sang "In the Garden." The pastor, the Reverend Addison Chapin, waved his arms broadly as he led the final chorus in his deep, booming voice. With his black hair and square mustache, the Reverend Chapin looked like a composite of Adolf Hitler and Charlie Chaplin. There was always a twinkle in his eye. Even though he couldn't carry a tune in a bucket, he was so sincere that no one gave it a thought.

After Reverend Chapin had dismissed the congregation, a very lovely dark-haired young woman continued to sit for a few minutes. Her short hair was cut straight, with bangs over her forehead perfectly framing her pretty face. She was extremely well groomed, every hair in place. The tense lines in her face detracted only slightly from her beauty. She held her mouth rather tight, making it look smaller than it actually was. Her eyes communicated an unmistakable sadness.

Two women at the end of the pew where she was sitting got up to leave, never missing a word of their conversation. At one point, they glanced over at the dark-haired woman and continued their conversation in whispers. It was obvious who they were talking about. Becky Shanks Keeney pretended not to notice. After a few more moments, she scooted out of the pew, walked to the Sunday school class, and stood by the door.

Inside, seated around a low table in tiny chairs, the Sunday school children were singing, "Jesus loves me this I know, for the Bible tells me so. . . ." Becky's eyes scanned the group, settling on one little boy who seemed particularly to enjoy singing the words. I was that little boy.

An occasional parishioner leaving the small brick church would say with obvious effort, "Oh, good morning, Becky . . . and how are you, Alvie Lee?" Most of the time it came out "Avilee," a typical midwest verbal shortcut. I learned to hate that name from an early age. As we left, the dreaded moment came when I had to shake hands with Reverend Chapin. Purposefully or not, he always crunched my knuckles together.

Most of the congregation kept their distance from my mother and me. As we walked by, some conversations dropped to whispers and others stopped altogether. One congregant was heard to say, "There *she* is. . . . she's nothing . . . she's *divorced,* you know!" I suddenly looked up at a group of them. Their mouths—especially those of the church biddies—seemed to be going all at once, with their incessant cackling.

A flock of resident ducks in a pond at Garvins Park quacked loudly. As my mother and I walked alongside the pond, I watched the ducks closely and with fascination. My mother stopped. Her body tense, she began to tremble. Wheeling around at me, she said angrily, "You're like a clock around my neck ticking away the years. If it wasn't for you nobody would know." Her voice had now reached a crescendo. This had been building up for some time. "We did everything but strain you through a tea strainer to keep from having you," she screamed hysterically. She raised her hand—

"BECKY!"

The commanding tone of that voice stopped her in her tracks. A man came rushing over. It was Jim Stewart, who worked at the Southern Indiana Gas & Electric Company where my mother worked as a secretary. I had seen him on a few occasions. He was a friend. His front teeth protruded slightly. Those big teeth were displayed in all their glory when he smiled his frequent, broad, friendly smiles. Jim Stewart was a good man, who always put others before himself. He was not smiling now.

"Becky—you've got to get ahold of yourself," he said, taking her by the arm and walking her a few steps away. I could not hear the words that followed. I felt numb. Tears were rolling down my face as I stood there quietly. I wasn't sure exactly what it was that my mother was telling me. What does a five-year-old know about sex and birth control? But from the anger in her voice and the hatred in her eyes, I knew it was a rejection of the worst sort. What had I done?

"You have no idea what it's like, Jim," my mother was saying, almost frantic. "The church regards me as a—"

My mother could not quite say the word "whore." Well-bred people simply did not use such words.

"—as a *fallen woman,*" she said with emphasis, "a *Jezebel!* Because I am divorced, and I couldn't even help it—he left us! If it wasn't for *him*"—she pointed at me—"no one would have to know I am divorced and I could start a new life. But because of him I am going to be looked down on for the rest of my life."

My mother stiffened up, to keep from crying. To show further weakness by crying would only demean herself in her own eyes even more.

"Tell you what, Becky," Jim said understandingly, "you go on and do what you want to do today by yourself. . . . Relax, I'm taking your son with me. Come on, Avilee, I've got a surprise for you." He took me by the hand and walked me out of the park.

My mother sat down on a bench by the pond. Her face grew more and more tense until the lines suddenly seemed to burst, leaving in their place a relaxed expression as the tears began flowing down her face. That release was salutary and needed. A sweetness swept over her face as she sobbed.

My mother was a good woman, not given to hatred or mistreatment, and she loved me. But the hushed reproach of the Christian church was so all-pervasive that to love me completely and unreservedly would have seemed as if she were unrepentant of her "sin." Acceptance from the Christians seemed vitally necessary to her. She had to reject me for her own survival.

Her own youth had been troubled. Her mother had died at the age of fourteen, shortly after giving birth to her. My mother's father, William Shanks, worked at various traveling jobs, dragging his little girl with him. Most of the time, they lived in a tent. A constant diet of potatoes—all he could afford to provide—had damaged her complexion. In school—what few times they remained in one place long enough for her to attend—she was promptly labeled, "poor" or, rather, "right pore," because she had only one dress to wear to school every day. The other children made mean merriment over that fact. She finally had a permanent home, with Fanny and Perry Ladd, while she went to high school in Sturgis, Kentucky.

In her teens, she was swept off her feet by Al Keeney, a supervisor at the Shell Oil Refinery. He was tall, firmly built, and handsome, with wavy black hair, fine features including a sculptured Roman nose, and deep, penetrating bedroom eyes. There was an instant magnetism between them. They were married, and moved to Houston, Texas. Now, at last, she would have a real chance at life. But my father's womanizing and temper, combined with my mother's deeply ingrained insecurities from her childhood, clashed in a torrent of anger and jealousy on both sides, undermining the powerful love they nevertheless felt for one another. When I came along, the pressure cooker exploded, and each of them stormed off in a different direction.

My mother, crushed by the separation and ensuing divorce, and desperately wanting and needing love, status, identity, and respect above all other things, had turned to the Christian church for comfort. Now, she was in a worse state than ever.

Becky Shanks Keeney regained her composure. She wiped her eyes, took a mirror from her purse, powdered her face, and restored her make-up, to conceal that she had been crying. She got up from the park bench and walked away.

*   *   *

I looked wide-eyed out the front window of Jim Stewart's car as we approached the Memorial Coliseum. A crowd of smiling people were waiting to go in. Men in red sport jackets with funny round red hats with tassles were greeting the people coming in. There were even clowns.

"Here's your surprise, Avilee," Jim Stewart said, beaming. "I'm taking you to the Shrine Circus."

The inside of the coliseum looked like an assemblage from a giant erector set. Interesting looking props and apparatus were strung in all directions. There were huge, brightly colored rings on the floor, and everything glittered. Big balloons and cotton candy were everywhere. Jim Stewart bought me a balloon.

Gaiety and excitement filled the air. It was a happy place. Then, with authority and great dignity, the ringmaster walked to the center ring and blew his whistle. The lights went out, leaving him in the spotlight. He had an imposing black mustache and wore riding breeches, black boots, red tails, and a shiny black top hat that glistened in the spotlight.

"Ladeez and gentlemennn," he boomed into the microphone, "children of allll ages. Welcome to the Hadi Temple—Shurine CIRCUSSSSS." The bandmaster directed the downbeat and the music began. The arena came alive with dancing colored lights, and the elaborately costumed circus performers paraded around the track with big smiles, waving at the audience. Excited, I waved back.

There were floats, wagons, animals. The lively music stirred my very soul. There was no room to be downhearted here. One leaves all that outside. In this happy place, one becomes a part of a joyful excursion into a wonderful world of fantasy.

The circus people looked different from any people I had ever seen. Some indefinable quality in their faces radiated a firm but friendly self-assurance.

No experience on earth can compare to seeing a circus for the first time. One always cherishes that memory. I sat nervously on the edge of my seat as these people flirted with danger, even with death. I watched in disbelief as a performer hung from a trapeze bar suspended under a big metal airplane that was, itself, suspended by cables over our heads as it traveled in a wide circle. I laughed out loud at the antics of the chimpanzees and trained poodles. They seemed to be having the time of their lives.

The clowns delighted me, too, particularly Happy Kellems. But I pressed my hands over my ears uneasily when they got ready to explode a giant firecracker. I did not like that part at all!

I watched the family acts with special interest: the flying trapeze acts, the tumbling acts, and some of the animal acts. There was the father, the mother, and the kids working together, and they all seemed so happy. They *loved* one another. How wonderful that must be.

At five years of age, I had no idea who I was, or why I existed. Surely there must be something for me—somewhere. I found myself again focusing on the ringmaster. I was more fascinated by him than anyone.

III

It seemed to be a stock phrase: "Why, the high school years are the happiest years of your life!" I did not find that to be true at all. For me, it was an awkward and confusing time. I had acne. My voice was changing, and not for the better. Its awful, nasal quality made anyone glad to conclude a conversation with me.

I felt I had absolutely nothing in common with the other students. I could not relate to their ideas, their lifestyle, or their choice of music. Rock and roll was the craze, with Bill Haley and the Comets leading the latest trend. (Nobody guessed that rock and roll was here to stay.) I preferred quieter music, and when available, classical music. I did not really understand classical music, but found it somehow soothing.

I had absolutely no confidence in myself, and no social life. I felt ugly and undesirable. I was so shy that if I walked down a street and saw someone coming from the opposite direction, I would cross to the other side rather than meet the person face to face. My growing sexual awareness confused me. I had no idea how to deal with it, and no one to talk to about it.

The high school itself was dreadful. Central High, in the middle of Evansville, Indiana, was a dreary, run-down building that should have been condemned long ago. The students all seemed to have the same quality: bland. They had no drive, no ambition for their lives. The girls simply planned to get married and have kids. The boys talked of working at Chrysler, Servel, Seeger, or International Harvester—where they could retire at age sixty-five.

How can one even think of being sixty-five at age fourteen? Even the looks of my fellow students reflected that trudge-through-life attitude. Those who could have been attractive were just plain dull.

The teachers fit the atmosphere perfectly. They were arrogant, prissy, downright strange. One biology teacher was constantly asking the boys in his class if they were having "masturbation problems," eager to start up a conversation on the topic.

I especially detested gym class. I was never very strong, and proved to be a bomb when it came to athletics. Being a distinct liability to any team heightened my sense of rejection and insecurity.

The part of gym class I dreaded most was the compulsory weekly swim. The entire gym class would be taken to the YMCA pool next door to swim and play water volleyball, in the nude. I never got through one of those sessions without one of my classmates trying to grab and fondle my sex organ.

That sort of thing had first happened to me when I was a twelve-year-old Boy Scout in Salinas, California. The scoutmaster had cleverly arranged with my mother to let me spend the night in his care. I felt so helpless and isolated when he molested me. I had no one to turn to for help. That experience bewildered, confused, and angered me. I became even more withdrawn on its account.

As a teenaged boy, I found I was never left in peace if I went to a movie alone. Some creepy man would always spot me, slip into a seat beside me, and try to fondle me. One man, an acquaintance, who I liked and really trusted, who seemed happily married, made the move on me when he got me alone.

Why me? Why always me? What I couldn't have known then was that these pederasts have an uncanny knack for spotting vulnerable boys, boys suffering from a sense of rejection and insecurity, with no one to turn to for advice or emotional support. Such boys have no one to protect them, no one to make trouble for the perpetrator on their behalf.

Being a teenager with no source of good counsel, I had no way of sorting these experiences out. I became convinced that something had to be wrong with me. Otherwise, why did I constantly attract these people? I started carrying a knife.

My mother had remarried several years earlier, when I was six years old. Harry T. Maddox worked as a lineman with the Southern Indiana Gas & Electric Company. This plain-looking man was characteristically quiet, shy, and good-hearted. He totally loved my mother, and she totally dominated him. Even though a good provider and stepfather, he wasn't someone to whom I could really talk.

When he and my mother had gone to Reverend Chapin to ask him to perform their marriage, he flatly refused. He absolutely would not officiate at a marriage for anyone who had been *divorced!* That shocked me. I was six years old and now had a chance to have a daddy. I had been picked on in school because I had none. This was my chance to be like everyone else. Why didn't the church want me to have a daddy?

My mother and Harry Maddox were finally married by a justice of the peace. They had a good marriage, and I believe that the Reverend Addison Chapin regretted his bullheaded refusal to the day he died.

*   *   *

Mr. Fischer's math class was underway. All heads were down, pondering a problem Mr. Fischer had just given the class to solve. All heads but one.

Mr. Fischer's piercing voice jolted the entire class. "AVILEE!"

God, how I longed to change that name. "Yes sir," I answered, startled.

"Now I'm telling you for the last time," he preached, "that you had better stop this looking out the window and daydreaming. I know it's spring and you have spring fever," he added, sarcastically. "But you'd better tend to your work when you're in here with me or you're going to wind up in reform school!"

This pronouncement had followed me to practically every class at Central High, so it wasn't really a novelty anymore. I took a final quick look out the window before tackling the math problem.

Passing by the window in close succession were several trucks with "Tom Packs Circus" lettered on the side. I had found out earlier that the Tom Packs Circus was coming to town for three days at Bosse Field, sponsored by the Police Department.

I could not keep my mind entirely on the math problem. It wandered back to the sounds—the music—of the first circus I had ever seen. That had been one of the happiest moments of my life.

What seemed to be another interminable day in Central High finally ended. I bolted out the door, with a sudden renewal of energy.

Word had already reached my mother about my serious lack of discipline. I was confident of that the moment I opened the door at home.

"AVILEE, come in here to the living room. I want to talk to you." The commanding tone of my mother's voice seemed harsher than usual. "I just got a call from Mr. Harmeyer"—the school principal—"and they want to see you and me in his office next week. As usual, you have disgraced me with your rebelliousness. You're going to wind up in reform school, that's what's going to happen. What did I do to deserve this? Where did I go wrong?

"I've given you a good home . . . and when I married Harry, I did it so you would have a father. I could have married anybody else. I could have married Archie, who has his own airplane. He's handsome, but he didn't want you. And there were a couple of others that would have been good for me. . . . But I settled for Harry because I knew he would be a good father for you . . . and *this* is how you repay me!"

My poor stepfather. My mother lorded it over both of us that she had married beneath her. She had to feel that way, and marry that way, because of her own emotional problems. She tried to push my stepfather into becoming a foreman, which he did not want. She did press him into joining the Masons, then the Shriners, in a desperate bid to be accepted in social circles. She desired a husband with some degree of status but one who she could always control.

She took the position that she was a martyr for marrying him, that he was not quite good enough for her. He was so loving, loyal, and stable that I pondered whether *she* was good enough for *him*. I never felt she treated him nearly as well as he deserved. He was so much in love with her that it made no difference to him.

"Oh, yes," my mother continued, "we are planning to move."

"Where to?" I asked.

"We're not sure yet," she responded, "we need a bigger house. We'll probably get something over near St. Mary's Hospital. It's wise—don't you agree?—to live near the hospital. You never know when something will happen and then we would be right there and. . . ."

I never heard the last part of her sentence. I had already run out the back door.

IV

At exactly 7:00 P.M. a huge firecracker exploded in the air with a resounding boom that echoed throughout the city. This trademark of the Tom Packs Circus gave notice that the big show would begin in exactly one hour. People streamed into Bosse Field from all directions to see the popular annual attraction.

I did not have the money for a ticket. Walking around the wall of the ballpark, I saw a boxcar parked on the railroad tracks that ran alongside it. I climbed up the brakeman's ladder on the side of the car onto the boxcar roof. From there I could see over the wall, and to my good fortune I was able to see the entire performance.

But I wanted to get a closer look at this mysterious, colorful world of the circus. I searched in my pocket and found a quarter. Not nearly enough for an admission ticket, but I had an idea.

The next day I went to the Fisher Novelty Company and bought a can of "clown white," which cost exactly a quarter. When I got to the house my mother wasn't home, so I could do what I wanted to do, unchallenged. I smeared the "clown white" on my face. Next, I got out my mother's make-up kit. With it, I was able to add some lines and create a clown face. Using some clay, I fashioned a clown nose, and using some discarded clothing and rags from the cellar, I made up a clown suit. I looked in the mirror, and then, satisfied with what I saw, headed back to Bosse Field.

A gate led into the ballpark through which the circus performers went to and from their trailers parked outside the boundary wall. Two policemen guarded the gate staunchly. Mustering my courage, I walked up to the gate. With newfound boldness, I said, "Excuse me, please." The two policemen stepped back briskly and opened the gate. I went right on in.

By the time I got inside the big top, the show was under way. I could not believe what I had just pulled off! Then a hand grabbed me firmly by the shoulder. The hand belonged to a stern-faced Jack Leontini, a balding, solidly built man with a rigid, European, bantam rooster posture. As its manager, Jack Leontini ruled the Tom Packs Circus with an iron hand. My heart sank.

Even though these events lasted only a few fleeting seconds, it seemed like an eternity. Then, in his intimidating voice, Leontini demanded, "What are you doing standing around? *Get in there!*" He gave me an unceremonious push toward the center ring, where the clowns were coming in from all directions to perform their number.

Unexpectedly, I became part of the clowns' act. I found myself instinctively reacting to their various bits of clown business. Somehow, I managed to be in the right places at the right times. I even took a pratfall at just the right moment, which brought an extra laugh to the number. Things went so well that I made the next three shows the same way, and nobody knew the difference.

On Sunday night after the last show, while the circus was packing up its prodigious assortment of props and paraphernalia, I showed up, suitcase in hand. Without the clown make-up, I looked my fourteen years. The circus people knew something was wrong. After talking with me, Jack Leontini telephoned my mother.

"I don't know what to do with him, Mr. Leontini. He's been a problem to me from the day he was born. I think I'll just let him go with you to get it out of his system."

"Do you really mean that?" Mr. Leontini asked.

"Yes," my mother replied.

Then as an afterthought, and no doubt with love for me that she simply did not know how to handle, she said, "But—please!—promise that you'll look after him."

*   *   *

The Tom Packs Circus moved on to Ohio. Before the show all of the clowns gathered together in one dressing room. They showed me the proper way to put on my make-up. Happy Kellems watched with interest. One of the all-time great tramp clowns, Happy joked about his buck teeth. "I'm the only guy in the world who can eat an apple through a picket fence," he said. He had bought some costume material for me to use. "One-piece clown suits are strictly party stuff," he explained. "Here's a real character suit for you."

Whitey Harris showed me the fine points of clown make-up. "First smear the 'clown white' everywhere—even on the back of your neck! . . . and behind the ears. No natural skin should show. Good—now pat it down until it's smooth. . . . This takes out any uneven parts. Good. Now here. You'll have to get your own tomorrow but use mine now. It's just a plain white wool sock with white baby powder inside. Give your face a good powdering. This takes the greasy look out of the white and keeps it firm on your face. Now take this camel hair brush and brush away any loose powder."

By now all eleven clowns were gathered, watching the transformation that Whitey was so absorbed in bringing about.

"Now, remember, it is an unwritten law that one *never* copies someone else's clown make-up," he instructed. "And everything in your make-up should tell a story. Now, you made the mistake that everyone else makes at first: putting lines everywhere just for the sake of having something there. That scares kids. Each line should mean something. Let's start with the mouth. Here is a black eyebrow pencil like I use. What kind of mouth should you have?"

"Curved up in a smile," I responded. "A happy mouth."

Whitey showed me how to make a smooth line for the outline of the mouth and then fill it in. I kept it black, like his.

"Let's make the eyebrows curve up in sadness," Whitey suggested. "But it's not really sadness; it's frustration. 'Cause everything a clown tries to do goes wrong. He's always in trouble."

The eyebrows were accentuated and filled in.

"There should be a teardrop line," suggested Chester "Bobo" Barnett. "A clown cries happy tears, because he is doing the work he loves—entertaining children."

"What should we do about your nose?" pondered Whitey.

I grabbed a round bulb nose I had bought. "This one," I said, my excitement growing. "When they were giving out noses I thought they said 'ROSES,' and I said 'gimme a great big red one!' "

"Very good," they chimed in unison.

All the clowns were so engrossed in helping me get ready that they forgot about the show going on outside.

The dwarf clown, Frankie Little (his real name), came running into the dressing room frantically. "C'mon youse guys, we're on. Let's go— let's go!" He looked over at me. He did not know my name. The only thing he knew about me was that the circus had picked me up in Indiana. "And you too, Kokomo, Indiana!" and he ran back out of the dressing room.

I looked in the mirror and made a face at myself. "Kokomo—Kokomo the clown. That's who I am."

*   *   *

Behind the clown make-up I felt ten feet tall. All my shyness and inhibitions vanished. I became a different person. As the Tom Packs Circus criss-crossed the United States, sponsored mainly by the Shriners, I continually found new ways to get a laugh. I would work throughout the entire show, getting involved in everything that was taking place. I learned to juggle and to do magic tricks. Soon I came to approach my clown role more thoughtfully, and began to treat it as an art form. Audiences were taking note of the highly animated Kokomo the Clown. Circus producers began offering me contracts for additional engagements, which now kept me working the year round. The growing acceptance of my clown work along with the new contract offers gave me confidence and a sense of identity I had never known before. These favorable circumstances gave me room to develop as a person.

For the first time in my life, I could converse freely with other people. I enjoyed sharing the many experiences of traveling with my new friends. The circus artists were an education in themselves, and they certainly helped me to broaden my horizons. Several languages were spoken, and most everyone in the circus had some kind of accent. I learned about their countries and picked up bits of their languages. Since the circus had provided me with the first place of emotional security I had ever known—the first place where I ever had a sense of belonging—I would from that first day always be comfortable around people with accents. A strong sense of family prevailed in the circus. What's more, they were positive, energetic, good people in every sense of the word. Not at all like they were always portrayed in the movies.

Only one other clown worked through the entire show as I did, Emmett Kelly. Fate decreed that we wound up on the same Shrine Circus in Buffalo, New York, booked by Al Dobritch. Expecting some kind of artistic flare-up, all of the performers were waiting to see what would happen when our paths crossed.

I started down one end of the track, and Emmett, down the other end, as the show went on all around us. As we neared one another, I simply tipped my plaid cap and tried to continue by him. He stopped me and looked me over carefully, with the greatest of scrutiny. I mimicked an uneasy look. The audience's attention began focusing on us. Then, Emmett took his broom and began "dusting" me over, valet style. When he was finished I tipped my cap in thanks, and started on my way. Tapping my shoulder, Emmett stopped me and stood there with his hand out for a "tip." With a disgusted look, I put my hand in my side pants pocket, going deeper and deeper, finally coming out with a "coin." He studied the "coin" skeptically, bit on it to make sure it was genuine, put it in his pocket, tipped his hat to thank me, and started on his way. Getting a sudden inspiration, I stopped him by tapping him on the shoulder. He looked puzzled as I took his broom from him, "dusted" him all over, turning him around to complete all sides, and then stood majestically with my hand out. Outflanked, Emmett shook his head, dug deep in his pocket, gave me the "coin," and we both went on our separate ways. Not only the audience but all the artists applauded this impromptu piece of business.

During those years, no one even knew that I had any other name. I was simply "Kokomo." Even my performance contracts were made out and signed in that name only. Happily, "Avilee" was gone forever.

V

The opening night performance of the Frank Wirth Circus at the Island Garden in Hempstead, New York, went particularly well. I always marveled at how any circus opening show, with its thousands of details and props, quick set-ups, and last-minute changes, could make it from start to finish. But it always did. This one seemed to run especially smoothly.

I returned to my dressing room and checked my image in the mirror. The tight-fitting three-button tweed character suit, which made me look even lankier than I was, had become a trademark of mine. My white shirt had strands of red yarn through the cuffs, tied in a neat bow for my "cuff links." I had on a plaid cap and big clown shoes.

I removed the suit, slipped into a robe, and sat down at the dressing table. Next came the cap and red wig, revealing my dark hair. I peeled off the red nose that had been attached to my own nose with rubber cement. Opening a can of Abolene cold cream, I smeared it all over my face, making the black and the white areas of my make-up run together into a gob of gray goo. I used a towel to wipe my face clean.

I had outgrown the acne problem I had had at fourteen, when I started. The "clown white" may have helped the condition, since it contained zinc oxide, glycerine, and lard. It was actually good for the complexion. Now, in my twenties, my face had taken on some maturity and character. I liked it better than before, but I still was not really satisfied with it.

While I was putting on my street clothes, someone knocked on the door. "Come in," I said loudly.

A man I had never seen before walked in. "Hi," he said, "are you Kokomo?"

"Well, yes," I replied, rather taken aback at the question. But then, most people never saw me out of my clown make-up.

"My name is Ed DeGroote," he said. "I'm a talent agent. Here's my card."

I rose to shake his hand and take his card. "How do you do, Mr. DeGroote." I had begun to take on an almost European style of formality.

"I've been watching you," he continued. "Your work has taken on a classic mime quality. Where have you studied?"

"Oh, I haven't had any training," I replied. "But thank you for the compliment. It's just something that seemed to happen in the course of my shows."

"Nevertheless," he went on, "I'm casting something I believe you would be just right for. It's a classical mime production to be called 'The Littlest Circus.' There is a loose story line about a small, traveling Italian family circus. They are so poor, they cannot afford animals. So, the family must play the animals as well.

"It looks promising. It will be directed by Nelle Fischer and Wolfgang Roth, who will also design the costumes. Rehearsals start in New York City in two weeks, and you would be paid for the rehearsals. We already have some dates booked in upstate New York, and there is a very good possibility that it may go into an off-Broadway theater. It may be a good thing for you. Interested?"

*　　*　　*

I took a room at the Knickerbocker Hotel on West Forty-fifth Street as rehearsals began in the Eleanor Gould Theatre, on the lower east side of Manhattan. At rehearsal, the performers all wore black leotards. Only the tops were changed, to suggest the costume and evoke the mood for each sketch. This was to be a classical mime presentation in its purest form.

They were going to utilize everything I could do: the magic, the juggling, and the music. I took up Nelle Fischer's offer to attend her ballet classes for free. I felt like a gym shoe at a formal banquet in that first classical ballet session, and was referred to as "cycle foot" more than once. I improved with practice, and with the discipline of ballet I became aware of every part of my body, including the hand and finger movements that subtly enhance a mime performance.

I was to play four roles in the production. I derived the names of each of my characters from my "Kokomo" name: there was Kokolino, the great magician; Captain Koko and his one-man band; Kokolovsky, the great violin virtuoso; and Koke, the juggler. Each of these characters was billed as being played by Kokomo the Clown.

Each character required a different face, walk, and demeanor. A dressing table had to be set up for me in the wings, since there was no time between my entrances for me to get to my dressing room upstairs. With the wonderful direction and coaching of Wolfgang Roth and Nelle Fischer, I had developed each character to a fine level of classical mime.

At last, the time came for dress rehearsal. An all-night photo session was scheduled to begin right afterwards. The theater was darkened, except for the stage lights. What unfolded was indeed a charming, delightful show. At the end of the performance rehearsal, two people applauded enthusiastically from the darkness of the unlit house. A voice in the dark called out, "I want this in my theater."

The house lights came on. It was Alexander H. Cohen, the producer. He wanted us for the Golden Theater, a Broadway theater! Another man approached the stage. He was tall and dark-haired. "Kokomo," he said, "I am Sonny Fox, host of 'Wonderama' on Channel Five. I want to book you to perform on my show this Sunday."

*   *   *

When I woke up that morning—December 9, 1959—I thought I felt normal. After all, today was just another show. "The Littlest Circus" had already given several performances out of town and had received rave reviews. I felt comfortable. I told myself again it was just another show. But I found it more and more difficult to get my breakfast down.

I walked the two blocks from the Knickerbocker Hotel to the Golden Theater. As I approached the theater, it began to dawn on me. This was *Broadway!* Try as I might, I could no longer tell myself that this was just another show. This was *it!*

A warm, receptive audience filled the theater, with several celebrities in the audience, including José Ferrer, Rosemary Clooney, Marge and Gower Champion, and Jack Sterling. I shall never forget the sound of Ferrer's deep, infectious laughter during the show.

I found myself more at ease than I expected. My numbers, including some ad lib mime situations, brought roars of laughter from the audience. The show was a smash.

Scores of visitors and celebrities came backstage with congratulations. There was a big cast party afterwards. But I didn't go. Instead, I was in my room at the Knickerbocker Hotel, throwing up everything I had eaten. Just another show, indeed!

*   *   *

Still a little indisposed, I walked in the Golden Theater stage door the next day. When I got to my dressing room, my heart dropped to the floor. All my things had been removed.

"Dear God," I thought, "I flopped. I didn't make it. I've been fired!"

Behind me, a jovial voice boomed, "Hello, star!" It was Jay Devlin, a tall beanpole of an actor who played the ringmaster and lion tamer, and danced a pas de deux with ballerina Alice Shanahan in the show.

"How cruel," I thought.

"Hey, what's the matter?" he said, studying my face. "Haven't you read the papers today? The reviews?"

I stared at him, puzzled.

"Every paper," he continued, "including the *New York Times* singled you out. They think you're great. The theater even gave you a new dressing room. Congratulations!" Jay Devlin was genuinely delighted for me.

After that, invitations streamed in for me to appear on various radio talk shows. One, "The Bea Kalmus Show," originated live from Jack Silverman's nightclub on Broadway. Joey Bishop was the co-host that night. The first television talk show I did was "The Joe Franklin Show."

Talk shows were difficult for me. I felt ill at ease. Performing was one thing. Then I felt in control. But to be just me, plain me, and just talk was a problem. I always had the nagging feeling that I had "just lucked out," that I had "gotten away with things" during those years. But eventually they would see through me, figure out that I was a fraud, a nobody, and send me back where I came from. Since I had never really accepted myself, how could anybody else accept me, just as I was, with no costume and out of character? I felt overpowered and especially inadequate when established stars were on the program.

I accepted a performance offer, beginning as soon as "The Littlest Circus" completed its engagement on Broadway. It would be a musical play for General Electric, to be performed in Lake Placid, New York, before an audience filled with G.E. executives. It was directed by Don Hershey and featured, among others, Michael Dunn, the dwarf actor who later starred in "The Ballad of the Sad Cafe" on Broadway, co-starred in the movie, "The Ship of Fools," for which he was nominated for an Academy Award as best supporting actor, and played the evil Dr. Loveless in the popular television series, "Wild, Wild West."

At Lake Placid, I was to play the part of a magician, actually performing some magic tricks in the role. We were given our scripts to block and study and told to report to the stage the next morning to begin rehearsals. All went fine until my entrance. The entrance itself, in a puff of smoke, went off properly. But when I opened my mouth to speak my first lines, the awful truth came out. My dreadful, nasal voice could not project past the footlights. I tried pushing my voice from my throat as hard as I could. That made my voice rise an octave and sound strained, making things even worse. The harder I tried, the worse it got.

In exasperation, I fled to the safety of my dressing room. I sat there, with my face buried in my hands. I should have known better. With my voice, how could I possibly have thought I could have pulled this off? I was a mime. A clown. I was good at that, and that was where I belonged.

Nowhere else.

Someone knocked on the door.

"Come in," I said, weakly.

The door opened and Delbert Mann, one of the other actors, came in. "Having trouble projecting, eh?"

"You noticed that," I answered, disconsolately.

"That can be corrected," he declared.

"Oh no," I said, dejectedly, "it's a defect. I've had it all my life. I was born with it."

"I'm telling you, it *can* be corrected," he said confidently. "I teach voice on the side, and I can give you some exercises now that will get you started."

"You would do that for me?"

"Of course," he said. "Now, let's get started."

I followed intently as he instructed me.

"First of all, I want you to *try* and be nasal, and sing, 'ming, ming, ming.' Hit the 'mings' hard, and go up scale with it. Now take the scale up a notch and keep raising it until you can go no higher. Then do it again. Your problem is that you are trying to push the words out of your throat and that is precisely why you have that nasality problem. It *must* come out of the diaphragm. Every time you take a breath, push out the stomach muscles until this becomes natural. You are pulling the air down there instead of just into your chest." He pointed to my stomach. "Now, push out your stomach muscles. Think of the pit of your stomach muscles, and as deep as you can, go, 'mmmmmmmmmmmmmmm.' Come on, pull that down to your diaphragm. Now open up that full tone—full! Now, even if you don't take a breath before you say your lines, push out your stomach muscles, then let the words come out of there." He again pointed to my stomach.

I did the exercises the rest of the afternoon. Back in my hotel room, I worked on them most of the night. The next morning, I was able to project my voice—my new voice—over the footlights, all the way to the back of the house, with little effort. Delbert Mann had changed the whole course of my life!

I was next cast in the role of a surgeon in an episode of the TV series, "The Nurses." At last, I would be doing something out of clown make-up, with my own face, establishing my own identity. With anticipation, I reported to the studio and was given my wardrobe. I learned, to my dismay, that I would be playing the entire part behind a surgical mask.

I worked in many films during the next several years. In Sandy Howard's "Mack & Myer For Hire," I played the part of a master magician who accidently saws his assistant in half, then hires new assistants, played by

Joey Faye and Mickey Deems, for a big show in New York.

Even in my twenties, I looked immature. Gray was added to my hair to age me a little. I also did some nightclub work and shipboard cruises, performing a comedy magic act.

During that forward-moving, positive period in my life, I made the biggest mistake possible. That mistake would complicate my life and the lives of those close to me for many years to come. Considering my lack of formal education and low self-esteem, it was bound to happen. Crushed, heartbroken, and bewildered, I left New York and returned to the one place where I knew I would feel secure, protected, and sheltered.

VI

The sounds of the circus—the roar of lions, the chattering of chimpanzees, musicians warming up, the murmur of the crowd coming in,
the backstage conversations in different languages and accents—were always
comforting to me. To me these sounds said, "family."

"Welcome back, Kokomo." The voice, which I recognized, had a French
accent. I happily turned around to greet Robert Baudy. He and his wife,
Charlotte, did an act with Siberian tigers. The good-looking Baudy performed
in the large steel arena, his bare chest ornamented by a big necklace with
a tiger's tooth. He was so vibrant and charismatic, his presentation so
spectacular, that his act always drew cheers from the audience. I always
wondered how the film talent scouts from Hollywood could have missed
him.

Baudy studied me for a few moments. "Are you O.K.?" he asked,
thoughtfully.

"Yeah," I replied. "It'll take a little time—that's all."

"I was so sorry when I read about it," Baudy said, his concern for
me evident in his voice. He must have been as curious as the next person
about what had happened to me, but he was careful not to pry. There
is such a thing as respect for privacy in the circus.

"How old is your little girl now?" he asked.

"Two and a half," I answered. We walked across the arena as we
talked, glancing occasionally at various props and pieces of equipment here
and there. The vendors were already in the aisles hawking their wares.

"I was surprised, although happy, to hear that you were given custody
of her. It is very unusual for a court to give the custody of a little child
to the father," he went on.

"There were good reasons," I responded. I looked into space for a
moment. "Very good reasons."

Baudy did not press it any further. "Your little girl's name is Lori,
isn't it?"

I nodded my head.

"Where is she now?"

"At my mother's house in Indiana, while I get my life back together."

* * *

That spring tour with the Frank Wirth Circus was just what I needed. The further refinement my craft had undergone during "The Littlest Circus" carried over into my clown work. I was getting excellent advance publicity, and was now billed as "Kokomo, the World's Greatest Clown." But I had set my professional sights on something else.

Frank Wirth, the owner and producer of the circus, had a well-respected circus name. The Wirth family and their circus had come from Australia. Mae Wirth, Frank's wife, was considered the greatest woman bareback rider in the world, and was revered and honored by circus fans everywhere. I approached Frank Wirth with the idea of my becoming a ringmaster. He wasn't very receptive. He knew me only as the tall, lanky, goofy Kokomo the Clown. That role had become so crystallized, and I fit it so well, that people found it hard to imagine me in any other. "We already have Jack Montez," he said, "and he's been with us for years."

"Oh, I know," I answered, "and he's a good man. I wasn't suggesting for this particular show. When you get a second date and need another unit—that's what I mean. Would you give me a try? I think I would be good at it."

"I'll think about it," he said, placating me.

I shared a dressing room with Jack Montez. One day I arrived at the arena an hour early. Checking to be sure nobody else was around, I undressed and slipped into Jack's ringmaster suit. I surveyed my appearance in the mirror. "Yes," I thought, "I could be a very distinguished ringmaster, indeed. . . . Well, back to real life." I slipped off the ringmaster suit, applied my clown make-up, put on my clown clothes, floppy shoes, and made my way out into the arena.

Jack Montez looked the part of a ringmaster, with his handsome face and neat black mustache. In his red tails, white breeches, and black boots, he looked stunning. His commanding voice held everyone's attention. He had expanded his lucrative career with periodic announcing at the Steel Pier in Atlantic City. He was also very adept at announcing sports shows.

This debonair ringmaster, who looked as if he had everything in the world going for him, was actually going through his own private hell. His lovely wife, to whom he had been totally devoted, had died of a heart attack two years earlier. That acute, painful loss had almost destroyed him.

* * *

The Frank Wirth Circus returned to the Island Garden in New York. Running behind time, I rushed through the stage door to my dressing room. Frank

Wirth was standing by my dressing room door.

"You told me you wanted to be a ringmaster," he said in steady tones.

Not sure what to expect, I nodded my head.

"Now's your chance. Jack can't make it. Think you can do it?" he asked.

"Yeah," I said, a bit startled, "Yeah. I can do it."

Wirth looked me over. I always came to work in a three-piece suit. "Just wear the suit you have on," he said. "That'll be O.K."

"No, no," I said, rather evasively. "I—have an idea that—Jack's suit just may—fit me."

Things were happening so fast that I didn't have much of a chance to think. When I got out to the arena, dressed in Jack Montez's outfit, there were still a couple of minutes to spare. I certainly did not want to be seen by the audience before it was time to start the show. I was nervous enough as it was. I looked at my watch again.

This was it. From behind the bleachers, I blew my whistle. The bandleader looked around, and seeing no ringmaster, shrugged his shoulders. I leaned out just far enough so he could see me, gave him an expansive gesture, and blew the whistle again. This time, he hit the downbeat for the overture.

The tune was a lively, "Hey, Look Me Over." Standing at the end of the track behind the bleachers, I quietly counted off the bars of music, figuring out just how much time I would have. Then, I made my entrance. The spotlight swung onto me. As soon as he saw me, the bandleader automatically slowed the music in time to my walk.

The audience began to applaud. I reached the center ring and took the microphone off the stand with a flourish. Just as the music reached its last note, I doffed my top hat and took a sweeping bow. Recalling that first ringmaster I had seen when I was five years old, I exclaimed, "Ladeez and gentlemennnn!—Children of alllll ages! . . ."

We got off to a good start. Frank Wirth and the performers nodded their heads in approval. The show looked entirely different from this vantage point. Before I had only had my own clown numbers to worry about. Now, I had everybody's act on my shoulders.

I wasn't really sure I had the order of the acts correctly in my mind. A prop hand rolled an elephant tub behind me.

"Borjevous' juggling act in ring number one after this," he said out of the corner of his mouth.

I smiled when I saw what they were doing. The prop men unobtrusively cued me throughout the show. The entire performance went like clockwork.

When I made my exit at the end of the show, Frank Wirth was waiting for me. With a satisfied smile on his face, he shook my hand. "I'll have a new contract for you tomorrow," he said.

There were many visitors backstage that opening night. It seemed as if every important circus producer in America had been in the audience, and most of them offered me contracts. I never got back into clown make-up again.

*   *   *

Even when my schedule crowded two and three shows into a day, I never tired of the constant spectacle unfolding all around me. Somehow, the enthusiastic intensity of any wide-eyed youngster seeing his first circus never left me. Several newspaper reviewers noticed that, and reported it. The public and the press were receiving me extremely well.

I carried my flamboyant ringmaster image over into my everyday wardrobe. I wore special Chesterfield suits, a Chesterfield topcoat in winter, a homburg, and I carried a black, gold-knobbed walking stick. I stayed in the best hotels and ate in the finest restaurants. I was recognized wherever I went. Radio and television talk shows were coming easier for me, and I was being asked to do more and more of them. I thoroughly relished life and the success it was bringing me. Even so, at times it was still hard for me to believe that I actually was the official ringmaster for the most prestigious Shrine Circus engagements in the United States and Canada.

Then came that special moment I knew was bound to happen. It was inevitable. A certain major circus had offered to make me its ringmaster and performance director. I had accepted without hesitation. With keen anticipation, I walked in the stage entrance of the Wichita Field House, that eighth day of November 1964 and spotted him right away. The intervening seventeen years had diminished neither his solid good looks nor his rigid, bantam rooster posture. Aware of every movement in the arena, he suddenly looked up when I came in and walked over to me. He had been expecting the new ringmaster, and from my photographs, he recognized me as the one.

"Hello," he said with disarming warmth, "I am Jack Leontini. Welcome to the Tom Packs Circus." He extended his hand. I could not help but grin as I shook his hand. "I've heard nothing but good things about you," he went on, "and I've wanted to get you over here for some time." Then, as an afterthought, he asked, "How did you get started in this business?"

"With you," I replied.

He looked at me, puzzled.

"I'll tell you about it later," I said. "It's a long story."

The Hustle

VII

The opening night of any circus is a hectic affair. We never believe we will make it through the first show without a disaster. It always seems like an ordeal. In the heat of the moment, any other job in the world would be more appealing. There are seemingly thousands of details to sort out and put in sequence. The announcements, lights, music, and prop movements must all blend together.

The ringmaster must commit to memory and thoroughly master the routine of the show, along with the six-syllable European names of not only the artists but oftentimes the animals as well. There are many cues that must be announced during an act, and for a three-ring display, that requires special timing and concentration. The ringmaster must always be ready to stretch the announcements, in case a prop delay or problem with an animal makes it necessary to stall.

I could see that this was going to be a great show, but an extremely demanding one. In exasperation, I said to Bill Pruyn, the bandleader, "I've got an idea. Let's start with the *third* show, and do the *first* one later in the week."

I went to the dressing room to get ready. Dressed in my stage outfit except for the long-tailed, red coat, I sat at the dressing table to brush my hair. I stopped for a moment to study my reflection in the mirror. Even at thirty-one, I still looked immature. I had a full head of mod-styled dark hair, with long, curved sideburns. My nose sloped down, then gently upward. I could never understand how I came to possess such high cheekbones. They did help to offset the squat chin that I never liked. The sideburns also helped to deflect attention from that defect. The bright capped teeth helped to make that region of my face more presentable.

After putting on the red tails, top hat, and white gloves, I took my place at the rear curtain of the arena. When my watch showed the appointed time, I blew my whistle. The house lights went out just as the timpani roll announcing my entrance began. The spotlights trained on the curtain. Then, I walked out to a majestic fanfare.

Although a big challenge, the first half of the show went smoothly.

I had been conscious of one of the artists standing in the shadows, studying me intently. That distraction quickly passed. Satisfied and relieved at the way everything had gone, I announced the intermission.

Closing the dressing room door behind me, I leaned against it for a moment, took a deep breath, removed my top hat, and wiped the perspiration from my forehead. I responded to a gentle knock on the door. Bobby Yerkes, the catcher in the flying trapeze act who had been watching me with such interest, felt that he had something of vital importance to discuss with me. Bob's face reflected his German heritage. He had a rugged look, contrasted by his fair complexion and thinning hair. His face seemed to point straight out with a pious confidence. He had the air of a man who had known life's frustrations and disappointments, but who had managed to find a peace within himself. In his hand he held a Bible.

"I'd like to talk to you when you have a moment," he said.

"What about?" I asked.

"About your salvation," he replied with sincerity.

"Oh, great!" I thought. "Just what I needed. One of *them* right here in the circus!" I seemed to be particularly targeted by Christian "witnesses." They were continually approaching me. One of those planted right here in *my* world would not be so easy to evade as the ones outside. "Look," I replied, "I'd be happy to talk with you. But my 'salvation' lies in my being able to get this second half of the show over with."

During the second half of the circus, I watched Bobby's act, now studying him intently. He was an excellent performer, with the best trapeze act in the business. That commanded my respect.

After the show, Bobby talked to me further, his voice gentle and soothing. "Everything is vanity without Christ," he explained. "Everyone without exception needs Jesus. You have a good career. Money. But how long can it last? You'll find out one day that it is not enough, that there's something lacking. And that emptiness was put there by God himself to make you reach out to Jesus. I'm telling you, pal, Jesus is the *only* answer to real peace and true happiness. And this isn't temporary like your career. This is eternal. Jesus loves you—so much that He died on the cross for you. Died an agonizing death—for *you*—so you could be saved by grace. You owe your life and your success to Him. He wants you to accept Him as your personal savior."

I began to fidget. Bobby quickly noticed it.

"You know," he continued, "you've only scratched the surface of life. You haven't even come close to your full potential, have no idea how complete your life could be, as it is when you have Jesus. Here." He handed me some tracts. "Look these over. You owe it to yourself to at least make some honest inquiries into this. Some Christians are getting together for breakfast tomorrow morning. Come with me. At least meet some of them. I'll treat you to breakfast. It could be the most important breakfast of your life. Will you come with me?"

The trapeze artist radiated warmth toward me. His relaxed face expressed a refreshing kindness. His concern for me, his caring for me as an individual, appeared to be genuine.

"O.K.," I said.

*   *   *

"Good morning. It's 7:30 A.M.," proclaimed the cheerful voice of the hotel switchboard operator after an assaulting ring of the telephone.

"You woke me up to tell me *that?*" I retorted. While getting to my feet, I murmured, "How anybody could ever talk me into getting up at this hour, I'll never know."

All over the dining room, one could hear, "Praise the Lord, it's good to see you, brother." The prayer breakfast of the Wichita chapter of the Full Gospel Business Men's Fellowship International (FGBMFI) was about to begin.

After the call to order, the chairman asked for visitors to make themselves known. Bobby Yerkes stood and introduced himself and me, saying we were both with the Shrine Circus. That made the men visibly restless. They became overly nice to us, trying a little *too* hard to make us welcome. It made me uncomfortable. It doesn't take that much effort when people are *truly* welcome.

The chairman stood up to pray for the Lord's blessing upon the meal and meeting. His voice seemed to quiver nervously when he said, ". . . and we especially ask your blessing upon our two special guests this morning, and that group they represent that is so difficult to reach. . . ."

This display of prejudice made my blood boil. I did not hear the rest of the prayer. "How dare he?" I thought.

By the time the long, droning outpouring to God had ended, my seat was empty. Everyone else had been so absorbed in it that I doubt any of them heard me mutter, "Go to hell," as I left.

Bobby, too, had been upset by the prayer but had stayed through the meeting out of courtesy. Afterwards, he set about trying to convince me that all Christians were not like that. "Besides," he said calmly, "the Bible tells us to keep our eyes on God, not man."

"Such blind judging of people they know nothing about!" I said angrily. "If that's what being a Christian is all about, I don't want anything to do with it."

It was only my high regard for Bobby as a person that induced me to yield and accompany him to another Christian meeting.

"I know the men personally in this chapter," he reassured me. "They're what Christians are supposed to be, I promise you. You will like them, and they will like you." That touched a sensitive spot. I wanted to be liked.

The men of the Christian Business Men's Conference (CBMC) were just what Bobby had promised. I felt a real rapport with them. They were more low key than the FGBMFI, and this put me a little more at ease. Despite the barriers I put up, I enjoyed their fellowship.

Their speaker was a "completed Jew" from New York. When I was introduced as a special guest, his eyes lit up. After his "testimony," he headed straight for me and shook my hand vigorously.

"I feel led by the Lord to pray a special prayer for you," he gushed. Although I tried to resist and back away, he clasped his hands on my head and intoned a long prayer. "Didn't that feel good?" he asked at the end. He wanted me to agree. "Couldn't you just *feel* the presence of the Holy Spirit?" The next thing I knew, he was hitting me up for a big donation for his "vital work" in New York. "God has ordained me to take His message to the Jews and the people of New York. God told me that He had blessed you and was depending on you to help, that He wants to bless you in return." It was a hard sell.

"Dammit!" I said to Bobby Yerkes. "That's all Christianity is, just one big money-making racket." I stormed out of the place.

Bobby was crushed. The next day, bare chested, wearing white tights and clog shoes, he came to my dressing room before the show. "Please don't let what happened turn you off. That would be tragic. That guy was out of line, and had no right to hustle you for money like that. The whole chapter was upset by it, and will never have him back again."

"Bobby, please say no more about it," I said, putting on my red tails. I reached for my top hat. "I like you and all that. You're great to work with. I wish every performer were like you. I enjoy your company. But you're not to ever, I mean *ever*, try to sell me Christianity again."

Bobby stood pensively for a moment, then slowly straightened up, his prominent chin moving slightly forward. His eyes brightened.

"Have you ever stopped to think," Bobby said with renewed authority, "how extraordinary the events have been to keep you away from the truth, the Gospel of Jesus Christ? Did it ever occur to you that God has chosen you and wants to do great things in your life, and the devil knows that and doesn't want it to happen? That the devil is standing in the way, doing everything he can to keep you from coming to Jesus? The Bible says it clearly: 'Satan moves about like a roaring lion seeking whom he may devour.' There's a battle going on for your soul. God wants to save it, the devil wants to destroy it. Please—for your sake—don't let the devil win."

I was taken aback. Bobby Yerkes had touched a raw nerve with this reasoning. It was overwhelming, even frightening. I pondered it for a moment, and then regained my composure.

"Please, Bobby, I don't want to talk about it any more. Let's have an understanding that you will never bring the subject up to me again."

"Sure, pal," he said, unable to keep his face from showing the hurt. "I'll respect your wishes. I'll not bring it up to you again unless you tell me you want to discuss it. We'll still be friends." We shook hands, and prepared to begin the show.

Bobby kept his word and never brought the subject up again. He continued to extend his friendship to me. One night in New Orleans, Bobby, his wife, Dorothy, and I went out to dinner. When the cocktail waitress came to our table to take our order for drinks before dinner, I began to order but suddenly thought better of it, and asked Bobby and Dorothy if it would offend them if I ordered a martini.

"No, pal, go ahead," Bobby answered. When I had ordered, he said to the waitress, "We'll just have a Coke."

I felt abashed. Maybe I was wrong to have a drink. Bobby and Dorothy certainly seemed to have it all together. Maybe they did have something in those "Christ-centered" lives of theirs. I felt ill at ease with my martini, and didn't finish it.

When the tour ended and we were saying our goodbyes, Bobby's eyes were downcast. He felt he had failed me and failed God. He seemed to take it as an affront to his own faith that he had not succeeded in leading me into the "born-again" life. To him, my independent, carefree, successful life represented a challenge.

VIII

S ummer tours were the most enjoyable for me. The performances took place in ballparks, like Forbes Field in Pittsburgh. That innovation in circus presentation had been introduced by Tom Packs. Outdoors in the open air, one felt a great sense of freedom. With some artists performing as high up as 120 feet in the air, it really seemed like the sky was the limit. The spectacular ten-ring outdoor shows always culminated in a resplendent fireworks display.

My joy in that summer was especially meaningful, as I had brought Lori with me for the first time. She was not quite four years old. I had acquired a camper for the summer. In the protective atmosphere of the circus, everyone looked after everyone else's children, so it was easy to find baby-sitters. Helen Wallenda, wife of the renowned Karl, was *Muti* to Lori, who spent many an hour in the Wallenda trailer. There were plenty of other children to play with. Lori loved seeing the circus night after night. She picked up a smattering of the different languages spoken by the circus families.

One morning, we gave a special show for the orphans of the city. Before the show, dressed in my ringmaster's uniform, I said to Lori, "See those children out there? They are all orphans. They have no mommy or daddy. At least you do have a daddy, and one that loves you very much."

"I know, Daddy," she said, squeezing my hand. "I'm very lucky."

Lori had brought a purpose and a new sense of direction into my life. The desire to be a good father eclipsed all other goals and being called "Daddy" was music to my ears. I resolved that the next fifteen years of my life would be devoted to my daughter.

I cancelled all outside activities, including writing my column, "The Tall and the Short of It," which had been a regular feature in *The AGVA News,* the American Guild of Variety Artists' newspaper. I put my pursuit of a television and film career on hold. Except for actual circus performances, I intended to devote myself full time to Lori, and give her that sense of security and acceptance I had missed as a child. We received strong emotional support from the solid families of the circus.

That summer held some strange experiences in store. In the deep south, it was customary to have an "invocation" or prayer at the start of any public gathering. The local Shrine Circus committee met with me before the show in Montgomery, Alabama, to discuss the order of events in the preliminaries for the show. These included the National Anthem, the introduction of the committee members, and the invocation.

One pious-looking Shriner interjected, "Ah jest don't know 'bout thet invocation."

"Whadaya mean?" asked another.

"Well—this bizness of sayin' a prayer an' then puttin' on a circus," he said with disdain. "That would seem to me to be hypocritical."

I glared at him in disbelief. This man was a member of the Shrine committee sponsoring us. He regarded the circus as sinful and Godless, and he let his contempt for it be known loud and clear. But he seemed to have no compunction about bringing us to town to make a profit off of us. Now, *there* was true hypocrisy!

"Excuse me," I said, in a voice more resonant and commanding than usual. "I will spare you the agony of the conflict in your soul. *I* will give the invocation."

I turned around and walked away. I really did not believe in God or in praying. I had been very hurt as a child by the callous behavior of the Presbyterians toward my mother, and the rejection of me that had resulted. The Christian breakfast and lunch Bobby Yerkes had taken me to had turned me off altogether. But—dammit!—I couldn't let this supercilious Christian paint us as inferior, Godless savages. Even at the expense of making myself a hypocrite for a moment, I would not let it happen.

After I made my grand entrance, my voice came booming over the sound system: "Would you now stand and bow your heads for the invocation." The 7,500 spectators in the grandstand popped up obediently. I took off my top hat with a flourish. The crowd grew silent. I shot a glance at that pious Shrine committee member. Haltingly, he removed his fez. I waited another moment, to gain just the right mood.

"Our heavenly father," I intoned with welling authority, "I ask a special blessing on everyone who is here tonight. Each and every one in the audience. All the Shriners who devote their lives to helping others. And all the artists who will perform tonight, from the world of the circus, where family life is sacred, adultery is unheard of, divorce, rare. A world where there is little juvenile delinquency and no drug or alcohol problems. But a world maligned and misunderstood because of ignorance and misinformation.

"I would ask a special annointing of LOVE to flow deep within all of us and to never let us forget that we are ALL God's children, and all God's creatures are special. I thank you for this, in Jesus' name. Amen— and Amen!"

I immediately blew my whistle. Bill Pruyn, the bandleader, picked up on what I was trying to do and had the band ready for the downbeat that same instant. The artists ran to the ten rings, as I proclaimed, "The show—is—ON!"

Two performers in their costumes were standing with Lori, on the side. "Wow!" said one performer to the other, a satisfied grin on his face.

*   *   *

The Tom Packs Circus next traveled to Birmingham to play in front of the grandstand on the State Fairgrounds. We all arrived the day before the show was to open.

A big tent was set up on the fairgrounds. A Baptist revival had been going on there all week. Since we had the evening free, several of us decided to take in the service. In the middle of a fiery sermon, the preacher suddenly exclaimed, "Now, y'all jest don't worry 'bout thet circus a'settin' up over there by the grandstand. We'll be here *long* after thet bunch has left town."

Scattered "amens" wafted up from the seats. I looked over at the artists who were with me, shrugged my shoulders, and shouted, "Amen!" The artists joined in as a renewed, vigorus chorus of "amens" and "hallelujahs" filled the tent.

The next night, thousands of people poured into the fairgrounds to see the Shrine Circus. Bill Pruyn, the bandmaster, stood out in front of the grandstand entrance with me, watching the people come in.

A car plastered with "revival" banners particularly attracted our attention. It drove slowly by the crowd near the ticket booths. In the car was the preacher I had heard the night before, with three of his associates. Their tightly drawn faces exuded menace and hatred. With withering glances, they were trying to intimidate the people coming into our show, hoping to catch anyone from their flock who might have strayed.

That night, one of those events happened that truly *must* have been an "act of God." During the fireworks display, one of the pyrotechnic canisters that had been hurled into the air failed to ignite. It continued its journey to the other side of the fairgrounds and landed right on top of the revival tent where hellfire and damnation were being preached inside. It exploded with a loud "whoosh," burning a big hole in the tent. The "sheep" inside scattered in all directions.

"It's the devil! The devil's fighting us!" the preacher screamed. No one stayed around to listen. The service was over. The tent was ruined.

Driving to our next engagement in Springfield, Massachusetts, the following day, I could not stop chuckling.

"What's so funny, Daddy?" Lori asked.

"Oh, I don't know, Honey. Everything, I guess. That preacher. The fireworks. His tent." Uncontrollably, I chuckled some more.

"That couldn't have been a more direct hit, if we tried. Y'know? That preacher thinks the devil did it. And the devil's supposed to be red. Do *you* know the name of our fireworks man? Our pyrotechnician?"

"Why, yes," Lori said, with a sudden smile. "His name is Red Wisdom!" She began to laugh too.

"We'll have to tell him," I said.

*   *   *

"Daddy, I don't feel good," Lori said, as we pulled into the Eastern States Exposition Grounds, where we were to play the coliseum.

"Do you still feel sick?" I asked Lori later, from my position behind the curtain, as I waited to make my entrance. I put my hands on her face. She had a temperature. "Do you think you'll be O.K. while I do the show? In the meantime, I'll get a Shrine doctor to look at you."

"Yes, Daddy. I can make it."

Trying to cheer her up, I said, "Do you know why ringmasters wear boots?"

Lori shook her head "no."

"Because ringmasters can click their heels and fly. Watch."

The moment they finished announcing me out in the arena, there was a timpani roll and the spotlight trained on the curtain. I clicked my heels smartly, and disappeared through the curtain. A smile came to Lori's face as she got swept up in the fantasy.

"It's German measles," the doctor said in our motel room after the show. Fortunately, the motel was within walking distance of the coliseum.

"German measles," I said to Lori. "Looks like we've too many Germans in the show."

"Keep very little light in the room, to protect her eyes," the doctor advised. "She'll have to stay in bed for a few days."

"We're here for a week," I said, "so that will be no problem, and someone will be with her every minute."

The next day, Lori was feeling the full brunt of the illness. "Oh, Daddy, I'm so sick," she said weakly.

Being a parent can be painful. I would have given anything to be able to take her sickness into my own body, to be able to spare her that ordeal. I ached inside, and had to force myself to do the two shows that day.

The circus women took turns looking after Lori. In full costume, one would stay until it was time to do her act, when another would dash in to take her place. Word spread through the circus that Lori was sick. When I came into the room after the last show, I found the ceiling covered with bright-colored balloons. The concession man had paid a visit.

A few minutes later there was a knock on the door. When I answered, a voice with a French accent said, "Lori, a visitor has come to see you." Robert Baudy had brought a snarling tiger cub.

As sick as she was, Lori gave a delighted smile as she petted her little visitor.

IX

The IBM Country Club in Poughkeepsie, New York, was alive with the spirit of Christmas that sixth day of December 1965. There was a hint of snow in the crisp, clean air. Decorations were up everywhere, transforming the mood from ordinary to festive in every neighborhood, no matter how drab it may have been before.

The annual Christmas party was the highlight of the year for the IBM employees and their families. A one-ring, forty-five-minute circus produced by Nick Falzone had become the traditional featured entertainment. The joy of Christmas, combined with the colorful magic of the circus, was an unbeatable combination.

The circus was set up in the IBM Country Club ballroom. Bleachers had been erected along the sides, leaving room for a huge Christmas tree, a circus ring, and a platform for the musicians. The Joe Basille Circus Band were decked out in red jackets. Brightly colored balloons were everywhere.

We were about halfway through the fifth and last show of the day. In the middle of a dramatic announcement, I suddenly stopped. "That's funny," I exclaimed. "I could have sworn I heard—sleigh bells!" The jingling of sleigh bells came from behind stage. "Wait a minute! December—the IBM Christmas party—sleigh bells—that can mean only one thing! That SANTA CLAUS is here!" The band struck up "Here Comes Santa Claus" as Santa made his entrance amidst the cheers of the audience.

In my dressing room afterwards, I was finishing packing. I had just put my tall black silk hat into its box and was tying the string, when Gunnar Amandis, who together with his family did a teeterboard act, stuck his head in the door.

"Where are you spending Christmas?" he asked.

"At my mother's house in Indiana with Lori," I answered.

"Oh. Tell Lori Happy Christmas from Uncle Gunnar."

"Thanks, Gunnar, I will. You have one too."

As the train from Poughkeepsie rumbled towards Manhattan, I watched the flickering of the Christmas lights decorating countless homes as we passed by. I wondered what the families in those homes were doing. Probably nestled together by the fireplace. How wonderful that must be. Despite the stimulating career I was enjoying, with such fascinating people, my life just did not seem complete.

There is no place on earth like New York City at Christmas. The lights, the elaborate window displays, the Rockefeller Center tree, Fifth Avenue. New York had become a wonderland. I took in as much as possible as the taxi negotiated the traffic on the way to East Side Airline Terminal.

With a suitcase in each hand, and that awkward hatbox held against one suitcase with my right thumb over the string, I lumbered through the doors of the terminal. It was packed with holiday travelers. The Christmas music playing over the loudspeakers had a calming effect on the knots of people, pushing on toward their myriad destinations in an atmosphere of near chaos.

I spotted the TWA counter, with several lines of people checking in. I chose the line being served by a tall, attractive brunette. I was deep in thought as the line inched forward. As the traveler ahead of me moved away, the brunette turned to put his suitcase on the conveyor belt. In spite of myself, I found myself appraising her. She was big-boned, yet delightfully feminine. Her long, straight legs were properly punctuated by attractive, trim ankles. The overall figure on her tall frame was perfectly proportioned. She turned around briskly to greet me, her short, straight dark hair flowing outward for a moment and then resettling around her face when the turn was completed

The music on the loudspeakers suddenly changed to Bach's "Let the Sheep Safely Graze." It seemed to get louder as we held each other's gaze for a few lingering seconds. What natural loveliness. She wore no make-up at all. Her hair, parted in the middle, dropped down to caress the sides of her face and then turned up slightly at the ends. That aristocratic face, with the full, sloping Roman nose, intimated strong character. Her eyes sparkled. Her expressive mouth was firmly set but friendly. Even before a word had been spoken, the elegant charm of this pretty young woman stood out.

"Are you traveling alone?" she finally asked.

"Yes," I responded.

She looked at the hatbox I was carrying. "Do you have a vife?"

I detected an accent, and that served to put me at ease.

"No, I don't have a wife," I said almost triumphantly.

"Then why vould a man like you be carrying a hatbox like dat?"

"Oh that! I'm a professional circus ringmaster, and this is the top hat I wear in my work. I've just come off a tour." My explanation seemed to delight her.

"Oh," she said with interest, "ven I vas a little girl in Switzerland,

I used to go to the Circus Knie. I loved the horses. They were so beautiful. Do you have horses in your circus?"

As we continued, absorbed in our conversation, the people in the line behind me shook their heads in exasperation. One by one, they moved to another line.

"Are you going to be spending the holidays with relatives?" she asked.

"Yes, that's where I'm going now. In fact, I need a ticket to Youngstown tonight. Tomorrow, I will go to Evansville. I'm going to my mother's house to spend Christmas with my little girl, Lori. She's almost four. I was granted complete custody of her. My mother has been helping me with her."

She looked up from the flight schedule book she was consulting. She seemed particularly attentive to that last piece of information. "I always wanted to meet a man with a little girl," she exclaimed, making no effort to conceal her interest. "Here's your flight schedule," she said, handing me a piece of paper, "and the cost of your ticket to Youngstown is thirty-three dollars and eighteen cents."

"What is your first name, Miss Müller?" Her name tag had come to my aid.

"Rose Marie." She took the check I handed her.

"And you are"—she read my name off the check—"Mr. Maddox. Al Maddox."

"I plan to return to New York right after New Year's. May I call you? Perhaps we could have dinner together."

"Yes," she responded instantly, "dot vould be nice. Here, I give you my address and phone number. Now, don't lose my number. It's unlisted. But if you do, you can always reach me here."

"Don't worry," I said with growing enthusiasm, "I won't lose it, and my address is on the check. I'll see you soon."

The bus took me to Kennedy Airport. I walked through the departure terminal in a semi-daze and presented my ticket to the clerk at the gate. As she checked it, she arched her eyebrows.

"And where are you going this evening?" she asked.

"To Youngstown, then to Evansville."

"Then why are you trying to board a plane for Mexico City?" she asked, dryly. In the meantime, Rose Marie had dispatched my luggage to Los Angeles.

Later that night, the phone at the home of Peter Marcellos would ring. Peter, who was from Greece, and his German wife, Gisela, had been close friends of Rose Marie for many years.

"Peter—Gisela," Rose Marie said excitedly, "I've just fallen in love with a man I have met for the first time!"

*   *   *

"I hope you don't plan on uprooting Lori anymore." My mother sounded concerned as we sat by the Christmas tree in her living room. "She gets all settled. Then you come and take her out on a tour, and that's not good for her, dragging her all over the place like that. Besides, she'll be starting school soon. She's better off staying here with us."

My mother was aging well. Her hair, now gray, was perfectly coiffured. Her comely face was still beset by tense lines. One could find her impeccably dressed at any hour of the day. She had become a real estate agent, and was active in several civic clubs. She and my stepfather regularly attended social functions at the Hadi Shrine Temple, where he was an active member. My mother had felt fiercely driven to upgrade her social standing, and to her those affiliations signified a substantial measure of progress toward her goal.

My mother was ambivalent about my life with the circus. While she enjoyed being in the limelight far more than she would admit when a story of one of my exploits found its way into the Evansville newspapers, she also felt that the circus was a coarse way of life, less worthy of respect than other forms of show business.

My mother and stepfather now lived in the best section of town in a big home. It had been owned by a doctor. They were accepted by the local upper crust, and were well liked.

"She is my daughter, Mom, and I want to have as much time as possible with her. She's my whole life. One day soon I want to make an official home of my own for her."

"Well," my mother replied, "you'll never do that traveling around with the circus. The only way you'll be able to do that is to get out of show business and settle down."

"That could very well be," I answered, yielding to the force of her logic.

Lori and I had a delightful holiday season together, going on long walks together, taking in the Christmas decorations, visiting Santa Claus. While Lori was talking to Santa Claus, I thought about the lovely Swiss girl in New York, and could almost hear the strains of "Let the Sheep Safely Graze."

Just before Christmas, a wildcat bus and subway strike hit New York City. It came just in time to wreak havoc on the holiday shoppers and gain national publicity for the city's flamboyant new mayor, John Lindsay. That settled one decision for the time being. New York was all but unmanageable without public transportation. I scribbled a note on the Christmas card I bought for Rose Marie. "See you shortly after the subway strike is over. Al."

I settled into the relaxing, untroubled atmosphere of Indiana. During the first week of January, the newspapers were full of Mayor Lindsay, who was taking his bows for settling the strike. The doorbell rang in my mother's house, and a telegram was handed to me. It read, simply, "How long is shortly? Rose Marie."

*　　*　　*

After making great preparations for my arrival, Rose Marie took a day off from work to welcome me.

I took the airport bus to mid-town Manhattan and checked into the Hotel President on West Forty-eighth Street across from Mama Leone's. Without unpacking, I dug out my list of directions and set out for Forest Hills. First the IND E or F train to Queens, transfer at Roosevelt Jackson to the GG local, get off at Sixty-seventh Avenue, take the stairs to the street, left on Sixty-seventh Avenue where the drug store is, to the end. I studied the twin buildings of Forest Hills plaza. l found the entrance corresponding to the street address, went up to Apartment 5-N, and rang the bell.

Rose Marie, in a long multicolored house dress with a generous slit up the side, opened the door. Her bare legs were shaplier than I had remembered. She was manicured and pedicured with clear nail polish. The little one-room apartment reflected a European flair, with understated elegance. Immaculate like its inhabitant, it was romantically lit by candles. There were two cats: an independent Siamese named *Musch-Musch* ("Cat-cat") and an affectionate Persian named Sinbad. A convertible couch was already opened to a bed.

Rose Marie opened the door and I went inside. The door closed behind me, and we just stood, gazing deeply into one another's eyes. From some unseen source came Bach's music. Without saying a word, we slowly reached out, joined hands, and pulled one another close. Our lips touched, lightly at first, then greedily and hungrily. We eased ourselves down to the edge of the bed as my hand found its way through the slit in her dress. Her legs were smooth and warm.

We both let out a slight gasp as my hand found what it sought. Clothing was being discarded piece by piece, as we gently explored each others' bodies. When all the clothing was out of the way, I paused a moment to gaze upon her exquisite loveliness before me. If an artist could have captured on canvas what I saw at that moment, he would undoubtedly have titled it, "Perfection."

Her magnificent naked body glistened in the soft candlelight. Her perfectly formed, round, full breasts were firm, the nipples, small and now erect. Yet as incredibly firm as they were, they yielded to the slightest touch or caress.

With growing excitement, our lips joined in the exploration from head to toe of our pulsating bodies. We each delighted in discovering the other's deepest secret responses until our bodies, worked up to a feverish frenzy, were locked together in rhythmical motion.

The candles burned down to the wick and then flickered out, as we lay in each others' arms, pleasantly exhausted. Then Rose Marie paid me a compliment that stirred conflicting emotions in me: "You're the best I ever had."

The next day I returned to the Hotel President to pick up my things. Rose Marie asked why I had bothered to check in there at all. She moved things around to make room for me in her closet and to clear drawer space for me.

"This is all new to me," said Rose Marie. "I've never lived with a man before."

X

The following days were filled with museums, theatres, concerts, and meeting friends, as Rose Marie and I continued to discover each other. She taught me to appreciate art and history for the first time. While I had always enjoyed classical music, now I was learning to understand what I was hearing. She awakened me to literature, architecture, antiques, period furniture. Such things had been outside my awareness before.

Rose Marie had opened up culture to me—the whole dimension of savoring life rather than gulping it down. New York took on an agreeably different character in my eyes. I began to feel a new vitality.

I was fascinated by the breadth of Rose Marie's knowledge. She spoke German, Swiss German, French, Italian, and English flawlessly. During a long walk through Forest Hills, I learned that before coming to America to work for TWA, she had been the governess of the children of the Italian ambassador in London, and a stewardess for Swissair.

"What does your father do?" I asked.

"He's an artist. A painter. He's semi-retired now, but he was considered the best restorer of cathedral frescoes in all of Europe. He has restored much of Michelangelo's work in the domes and on the ceilings of the churches. He had to hang parallel to the ceiling just like Michelangelo to do this."

Beneath Rose Marie's obvious admiration for her father's artistic skills, there was something matter-of-fact and distant about her assessment of him. The warmth or love of a daughter for a father was not in it.

"And your mother?"

"She died when I was two."

I could see in Rose Marie's eyes that I had touched on a painful matter. She had seemed guarded and uncomfortable in any discussion of her family, so it seemed best to let the subject drop. It wasn't important anyway. Her family was across the ocean. I had met Rose Marie as an independent, working European girl, and I would accept her as just that.

Every minute of those days, I looked forward to the candlelight nights in the tiny apartment that had become my first real home. There was a sense of stability about Rose Marie, which gave me a happy, secure feeling.

Her aristocratic bearing and dignity elicited respect in any situation. Yet, behind that facade she was deeply romantic. She would put a stack of Edith Piaf records on the Sears and Roebuck stereo, and then come over, snuggle in my arms, and begin to translate the words.

"She's saying, 'Love is forever. Ven you give your heart, you give your soul and you can never be the same again. A uniting of the hearts can nefer die or grow old.' " Rose Marie lifted her head slightly, reflections of the candlelight dancing across her face. "Do you know, the swan mates for life. Dey are nefer unfaceful." (The word, "faithful" always came out, "faceful.") "Even if dey are separated they nefer go to another swan. If one dies the other knows it even if they are separated, and the other dies a short time later. Dey are totally devoted to each other for life."

One day I met Rose Marie for lunch at Howard Johnson's on Forty-second Street, not far from the East Side Airlines Terminal where she worked. She seemed uptight, even tense, as I tried to carry on a conversation with her. Finally, she sat up arrow-straight and blurted out exasperatedly, "I vould nefer have considered marrying *any* man. My friends tink dot no man has vat it takes to make me his vife!" (When Rose Marie was excited or angry, her accent became thicker.) "I really tink—I really tink dot you vould be the von man dot would be MAN ENOUGH to make me marry him—and you don't even discuss the matter."

She had hit the nail right on the head. During the almost two months we had been together I avoided the subject of marriage. Maybe I just wanted to leave well enough alone. Things were going so well. How could our relationship possibly be improved?

I was still nursing my wounds from a disastrous past union. But then again, I shouldn't let that disappointment rule the rest of my life. Maybe the trouble had been American girls. They were never very responsible; they played games with men. European girls were obviously different. I could see it reflected in the solid marriages in the circus. And also, all of Rose Marie's married friends showed great loyalty and respect for their marriages. It was crystal clear that Rose Marie would never enter into such a union lightly.

*   *   *

On that cold night, March 1, 1966, a special mood could be felt at the East Side Airlines Terminal. Rose Marie had finished her shift, changed out of her uniform, and taken a seat in the center of the waiting area with a small bouquet of flowers in her hand. The ticket agents from all the airlines watched approvingly as I walked into the terminal with my flight bag and went to her. Rose Marie was respected and well liked by everyone who knew her. They waved and smiled as we went out to board the airport bus.

When the TWA plane landed in Boston, snow was piled high around the runways. The air was cold and crisp. Peter and Gisela met us and took us to their home in Auburn. We had already had our blood tests in New York, and the results had been sent on ahead.

The next morning we filled out our "Intention of Marriage" form at the Town Hall in Reading, Massachusetts. I looked over Rose Marie's shoulder as she wrote out the information, and then exclaimed, "I didn't know you were born in Casablanca."

On the clear, beautiful morning of March 5, in the book-lined office of Boyd Stewart, Justice of the Peace and Town Clerk of Reading, Rose Marie and I, respectively thirty-three and thirty-two years of age, gave our marriage vows with Peter and Gisela as our witnesses.

Always elegant, Rose Marie looked stunning in her white dress cut just below the knee, with an understated ruffle around the hem and sprinkled with lace. She wore white stockings and low-heeled black pumps. I wore a charcoal Chesterfield three-piece suit with a velvet collar.

As we walked out the front door of the quaint steepled town hall, Peter and Gisela, laughing joyously, tossed rice at us. I looked around at the typical, New England scene. A white frame Methodist church with a tall steeple stood across the street, and patches of snow lay here and there. Rose Marie and I embraced and kissed. This was the happiest moment of our lives, and the beginning of the most meaningful experience life has held for me.

*   *   *

"I don't know how Uncle Fritz is going to take this," Rose Marie said worriedly when we returned to Forest Hills.

"Uncle Fritz?" I inquired.

"Uncle Fritz raised me. It's a long story. I did write him that there was a nice young man that I had been going to the museums and concerts with. I vas trying to prepare him, but I know it vill be a difficult situation. Uncle Fritz had already picked out someone he thought vould be a suitable husband for me."

"An arranged marriage?" I responded incredulously. "Do they still do these things in Europe?"

"It's very practical among wealthy families. It keeps the wealth intact, and to combine the wealth gives added strength and power."

Her reasons for being so mysterious about her family were beginning to be clear. Her apprehensions about family reaction to our marriage would soon be resolved. News of the wedding had reached Switzerland, and Uncle Fritz flew to America in a rage. Rose Marie and I were sitting on the couch talking when someone shouting in German began to bang on the door.

"Oh my God!" exclaimed Rose Marie, jumping to her feet. "It's my Uncle Fritz!"

"Mr. Maddox," he shouted in broken English, "I am coming in!"

Rose Marie, a grown woman long independent, was rigid with fright. It made no sense. We were honorably married. Why should we worry about the disapproval of her uncle or anyone else? Uncle Fritz had backed up as far as he could, lowered his shoulder, and made a lunging charge at the door—just as I opened it. He hurtled across the room and landed awkwardly on the couch, still clutching his briefcase.

"*Wie gehts, Herr Fritz?* (How are you, Mr. Fritz?)" I said in the few German words I knew. It was a proper greeting.

Uncle Fritz Stitzel, sturdily built, balding, with a full nose, carried himself sternly, with the same sort of bantam rooster rigidity as Jack Leontini. Uncle Fritz ruled Rose Marie's family with much the same unyielding iron hand as Leontini ruled the circus. I felt surrounded.

Uncle Fritz scarcely acknowledged my presence. He did not offer to shake hands. He would glance at me only fleetingly, and then turn his eyes to Rose Marie. They had an animated conversation in German. He took out several important looking papers and handed them to Rose Marie.

"What's happening?" I asked Rose Marie. "Is he disowning you?"

Rose Marie shushed me. I went to the other side of the room and sat down in a chair. The tense conversation was finally concluded and Uncle Fritz left.

"What's going on?" I asked.

"My uncle is a retired banker. He's very wealthy and I am supposed to inherit from him. He wants to be certain that you did not marry me for the money. He wants to meet with us tomorrow at the home of a Swiss friend of his, who is head of a pharmaceutical company in New Jersey. The friend speaks fluent English and Uncle Fritz feels we can have a better conversation there."

The meeting took place the next day. The gist of Herr Stitzel's grievance seemed to be that I had married Rose Marie without proper clearance and permission from him. As his friend looked on, he handed me a piece of paper.

"He wants you to fill this out," the friend said to me. "He wants to have you investigated." The form called for a variety of information: parents' names, place of birth, amount of income tax paid, what illnesses I had had, and a lot of other highly detailed personal data. I looked at the paper in disgust.

"I'm not asking you for a bank loan! I'm not asking you for anything! This is an insult!"

"Then I have come here for nothing," he thundered. "I know nothing about you."

"Let's get something straight," I said firmly. "I married Rose Marie for love. I had no idea her family had money. I thought she was just a European girl who works for a living. But I see the picture quite clearly. Take her." Rose Marie gasped. "That's right. Take her home with you. You pay for the divorce. I don't want family problems like this. It's not worth it."

Uncle Fritz was taken aback. "I just want it agreed," he said, assessing me, "that the Swiss francs remain in Switzerland."

That was the final straw. "Sir," I said with mounting hostility, "you can take your Swiss francs and stuff them up that part of your anatomy that is outermost!"

I stormed outside to the backyard, slamming the door. Rose Marie came out behind me. She was in tears. Suddenly Uncle Fritz's friend yelled out the window, "Come quick! Fritz is sick!"

We rushed in. Uncle Fritz lay on the floor, clutching his chest and gasping. No one had ever talked back to Fritz Stitzel. Once he slapped a nephew by marriage in the face. The nephew took it without complaint. Everyone inside the family and out had great respect for his money. It seems I, alone, did not.

Rose Marie sat on the steps, staring down at her uncle on the floor. "Good," she said icily. "Maybe he will die and leave everyone alone." I looked at her askance. No matter how miserable a person he might have been, he was still the uncle who had raised her.

The ambulance had been called. Uncle Fritz began to turn blue. I could no longer stand idly by. I went to him, felt his pulse, and found it dangerously faint. Ripping his shirt open, I began to massage and pound his chest until the ambulance, its siren wailing, at last arrived.

"All dis excitement," Rose Marie exclaimed.

"How long have you been doing this?" one of the attendants asked as he took over.

"About twenty minutes," I answered.

"You probably saved his life," the attendant said. They gave Uncle Fritz oxygen. When the color had returned to his face, he motioned for the oxygen mask to be taken away. For the first time, he looked me in the eye.

"You do dis?" He made the motion of rubbing his chest. I shook my head "yes."

"It feel *gut. Danke* (thank you)." He extended his hand to me. Then he turned to his friend. "I'm going back to Switzerland tomorrow."

"You can't do that," the friend protested. "You've got to stay in the hospital."

"I insist!" replied Uncle Fritz sternly, emphasizing the point by thrusting his forefinger dramatically in the air.

"Oh," responded the friend, "he *insists.*" This was deferently taken as the last word on the matter.

The ambulance sped off for the hospital with Uncle Fritz.

"This was really something to see," said the friend, shaking his head. "You two are about to kill each other, then you wind up saving his life."

The next day, true to his word, Uncle Fritz checked himself out of the hospital and returned to Switzerland.

Rose Marie was moody for the next several days. At last, she said to me, "I thought that you vould fight for me, that you vould stand up to him and say, 'Dis is my vife, and dere is nothing you can do.' Instead, you vould have just let him end it. You were supposed to fight for me."

XI

My career had taken a noticeable upswing. Besides my regular engagements with the Tom Packs Circus, there were new contract offers to consider. I was constantly flying into and out of New York City.

Rose Marie would fly out on weekends to visit. The circus artists liked her immediately. Her ability to talk to many of the European performers in their own languages made her an instant success with them. She started a scrapbook of clips about me and the circus. She also made several trips to Europe and brought me back the latest in men's fashions from Paris, including Pierre Cardin suits and jackets.

"Dose velvet collar suits are O.K. for here," she said, "but dey vill nefer work in Europe. You'll see vat I mean ven ve go there. You haf nefer seen true elegance until you've been to Europe."

My new everyday wardrobe got more attention than I bargained for. "Rose Marie," I exclaimed during a phone call, "a TV show I was just on wants to have me back tomorrow, to talk about men's fashions. I really don't know anything about fashions and clothing. Tell me what to say."

Rose Marie's European way of life delighted me. Under her influence I began making adjustments in my thinking and behavior. It was a refining process. The European lifestyle suited me, and made me feel fulfilled for the first time in my life.

A certain formality that I had not known before became manifest in everything. Rose Marie displayed poise in any situation. Once, a very ill-bred man yelled at her, accusing her of taking his place in line. "Oh, I *beg* your pardon," she said graciously, yielding to him on a deftly struck note of condescension. The matter had ended almost before it began. "An aristocrat is an aristocrat, no matter what conditions exist, or whom he is with," she had once commented to me.

In New York City, we had a rich cultural life, and regularly "made the scene." One Broadway play we attended, "The Royal Hunt of the Sun," struck a particularly responsive chord in Rose Marie. David Carradine played a "savage" Inca king. The Catholic missionaries who came to convert the Incas rapidly destroyed the race and its priceless art treasures, which they greedily melted down for the gold. The play is based on historical fact. Over a late meal and wine in a French restaurant after the play, we discussed what we had seen.

"Dose Christian missionaries haf done nothing but harm. Dey haf destroyed entire cultures and art that could never be duplicated," Rose Marie pointed out. Clearly, she had strong feelings on the subject. Having been brought up in Europe, touring the torture chambers of the Inquisition—the place where, for denying the Trinity, Michael Servetus was burned at the stake at John Calvin's behest—and the battlefields of the Wars of Religion—much as we visit Gettysburg or Mount Vernon—Rose Marie had a dim view of Christianity in general.

*   *   *

Bobby Yerkes subtly continued to try and "win" me "to Christ." His mere presence reminded me of his quest to "save" me. I did like him, though. He seemed to lack the annoying temperament of most artists, who—myself included—need to blow off steam from time to time. In the most heated situation, he kept his cool. It was reassuring to know that there was at least one person I could approach without having to worry whether he was in a good mood or a bad one.

After our closing show in Nashville, he appeared in my dressing room. "Hey, pal, I brought you something," he said, handing me a paperback book. It looked like one of the contemporary affairs books the *New York Times* publishes. It was *Good News for Modern Man*.

"What's it about?" I asked naïvely.

"It's the New Testament in modern English." I glanced up, arching an eyebrow. "Jesus loves you, pal," Bobby continued, "and one day He is going to reach you even if He has to *perform a miracle* to do it."

Later in my motel room, I thumbed through the book, tossed it onto the dresser, and picked up the phone to call Rose Marie.

"Guess what, Sveetyheart?" she said, excitedly. "A bigger apartment, two bedrooms, opened up in the other wing of the building. It's on the twelfth floor, Apartment 12-P. It's got a big living room, foyer, dining area, walk-through kitchen, one and a half baths, cross ventilation—and a view!"

"I'll take a look when I come home," I answered, indifferently.

"You don't haf to. I've already signed the lease."

"What? Shouldn't you have waited and talked to me about it first?"

"Oof, dere's no time for dot. You've got to do something ven it's dere. You vait around and you lose it."

"How much is it?"

"Two hundred twenty dollars a month. I signed a two-year lease."

"Two hundred and twenty dollars? I'm not sure I can afford that much."

"Nefer mind. Ve need a bigger place. Ve don't have enough room as it is. Besides, Lori will be coming to live with us."

On my way back to New York, I took a side trip to visit my parents and Lori. In the living room, my mother sat stiffly, with an expression on her face as if she alone possessed some weighty piece of knowledge.

"How are you, Mother?" I asked.

"Not so good," she answered glumly. "There's no question that there is something seriously wrong with me. I went to the hospital and they took every kind of test and they still cannot find out what it is. Even the doctors don't know." My mother had become a classic hypochondriac, and was constantly developing the symptoms of all the latest diseases.

She studied me for a few moments. "Is there anything you have to tell me?"

"What do you mean?" I asked, evasively.

"I mean, isn't there anything you want to tell me?" As I sat motionless she reached into her purse and pulled out a newspaper clipping. "You couldn't even bother to let your mother know you got married?"

"Oh, that. I was going to tell you, but I've been so busy. Her name is Rose Marie. She's from Switzerland. We met in New York. She works for TWA. She's different. She's very nice. You'll like her. I really think she is sincere."

My mother shook her head skeptically. "Sometimes, I just don't understand you."

When I got back to Forest Hills, Rose Marie had already moved into the new apartment.

"Who moved our things over here?" I asked.

"I did," she said, standing extra tall. "Claire came and helped me. Ve borrowed a hand truck from the doorman, and ve moved everything."

"Even the big convertible couch?"

"Everything. Dere's nothing I cannot do. I'll bet I could even build a house if I put my mind to it," she said proudly.

The new apartment proved to be just right for us. The two bedrooms had a view of the New York skyline in the distance. Looking out the living room window to the left we could see the famed Forest Hills Tennis Stadium. Piece by piece, we began to acquire new furniture. From an ad in *The Selling Post*, Rose Marie located a big Spanish-style desk in dark oak. She had to go to Brooklyn to get it. The desk itself cost fifteen dollars. Moving it to our apartment cost twenty-five. Rose Marie laboriously re-finished the top, making a real showpiece of it. Then she bought a five-hundred-dollar red leather executive chair to go with it.

I used an electric drill to put up bookshelves on the wall. Our library consisted of about forty books. I had brought with me a set of law books, some "how to" books, and a few biographies. She had brought the Horizon art books and some historical novels.

"It's time for you to bring Lori here," said Rose Marie. "Dis is where she belongs. I have already changed my work schedule to days so I can be here to take care of her in the mornings and be here in the late afternoon and evenings."

I made several trips back and forth to Evansville to prepare everyone for the transition. In Evansville, I handed Lori a package.

"Here, honey, Rose Marie brought you a present from Switzerland."

"From Ros'eree?" Lori asked.

She opened the package. There was a little red skirt, sweater, and tam inside. They were a little large for Lori.

"Humph!" my mother snorted. "She doesn't even know Lori's size."

"She doesn't even know my size!" Lori parroted.

"Now, come on you two," I responded, "don't be so negative. First of all, Rose Marie has never seen Lori. I think it's great that she had Lori in mind when she went overseas."

"I guess you plan on taking her back to New York," my mother said, sadly. My mother and stepfather had become attached to Lori and it wasn't easy for any of us. But it was important for me to have my own home at last and my family intact.

A delighted Rose Marie greeted Lori and me on our arrival in New York. Now she could fulfill her pent-up maternal instinct. She had tastefully furnished Lori's room, put up special wallpaper, and had handpainted a cabinet with Lori's name on it. A big Emmett Kelly clown doll propped up in a corner waited for her. It was a charming little girl's room, distinctively Lori's alone.

When we got in the apartment, Lori, with a dramatic sweep of her hand, said, "I have a headache. I need an aspirin."

"I tink ve got her away from Indiana just in time," said Rose Marie.

XII

I had looked forward to meeting Gil Gray. The circus he owned played the western United States under Shriner auspices. Though not one of the larger circuses, it had a particular reputation for excellence and elegance, and justifiedly billed itself as "The Show Beautiful." I had agreed to do a string of shows, beginning at the Mid-South Fair in Memphis. There, the show would be a no-extra-cost attraction for the fair-goers, under the big top.

As I drove my white '65 Plymouth Valiant onto the fairgrounds, workmen were scurrying about putting up the food and concession stands. I made my way to the circus tent, where more workmen were setting up seats and a teeterboard group was running through its act.

Gil Gray watched all the activity with a supervisory eye, his white hair blown in all directions. His face, gently lined with wrinkles, was friendly but full of authority. He wore a diamond stickpin in his tie and a big diamond ring. The omnipresent cigarette in his hand was like a sixth finger. When he saw me, this master showman rose and greeted me warmly.

The circus tent was brightly colored, with purple velvet drapes over the performers' entrance. Above the entrance sat the bandstand, decorated with lamps. The white ropes were spotless, and everything was freshly painted. It looked more like a Hollywood movie set than a working circus.

I set about gathering information on the acts in preparation for opening night. This engagement would be a particular milestone for me. Even though I had ringmastered for several years now, this would be my first time under a big top. The idea appealed to me very much.

The show opened to a capacity audience. For a while everything went smoothly. Suddenly, some spectators in the bleachers began yelling out to me to get my attention. During this era, political demonstrations of all kinds were occurring. "Oh, God," I thought, "don't tell me we're going to have a demonstration here." More people joined in the shouting.

It is extremely unusual to let anything interrupt a circus performance. It had never happened in a performance I ringmastered. But this disruption could not be ignored. For the first time in my career, I signaled the band to stop playing and brought the performance to a halt.

"What is it?" I asked over the microphone.

"Heart attack. Get a doctor!" someone shouted.

It seemed prudent to get the audience to remain seated. "Please stay in your seats. We need every entrance and exit way cleared. Every second could make a difference in this man's life." I looked over at one of the prop hands. "Go out to the front, to the tower—quickly—have them radio for an ambulance." I then addressed the crowd: "Is there a doctor or a nurse in the audience?"

A nurse emerged from the audience and rushed over to the stricken man. She felt his pulse, then put her head to his chest. She began to massage his chest, then pounded on it. She put her head on his chest and listened again. She looked up and shook her head. Some men came over. In a united effort, they pounded his chest desperately. The nurse listened at his chest again. They all began shaking their heads.

The audience grew restless. Sounds of the fair going on outside filtered into the great, still circus tent. I began to worry that, with so many attractions beckoning, people might begin to leave. Even if only one person got up to go it would start a mass exodus. I would lose my audience!

With a stroke of pure showmanship, to keep the audience in their seats, I made a sudden, expansive gesture and intoned, "I'm going to ask now—that everyone here who has the faith—please bow your heads—and in your own words, and in your own way—pray earnestly for this man."

The atmosphere in the circus tent turned into an eerie, intense silence. A strange, tingling sensation went through my body like a mild electric shock. It unsettled me for a moment. Out of the corner of my eye I saw the ambulance attendants arrive, put the man on a stretcher, and take him out the back exit. Into the microphone, I said, "Amen."

I immediately got the performance going again. Veno Berosini, the wire walker, was the next act. I could see from his expression that he was shaken by what had happened. Circus people are superstitious, and to him this had to be a bad omen. Visions of my first performance under the big top being ruined by an accident on the high wire passed through my mind. I signaled to him that I was cutting his act, and called Ruby Landrus the dwarf clown over. The two of us ad-libbed a clown number, getting some much-needed laughs from the audience, which helped to break the tension. Finally, we got the show back on track and brought it to a rousing finale, with the band playing "There's No Business Like Show Business." The property superintendent Max Craig and I exchanged nods while the song was playing. Wasn't *that* the truth!

The next afternoon, as I walked onto the fairgrounds, everyone seemed especially friendly. The people in the radio and television broadcasting booth greeted me with a wave. As I neared the big top, I encountered a crowd of people standing around and talking earnestly. This group of people seemed different than the usual crowd coming to take in a matinee circus performance.

As I got closer, little Ruby Landrus came running up to me.

"Where 'ave ya been? We've been lookin' all over for you!" she said.

With what must have been a puzzled expression on my face, I answered, "This is the time I usually arrive for a matinee."

"Oh," she said, in her thick, Cockney accent, "Boy, that was really somethin' last night, wasn' it?"

"Oh, yes, so it was. By the way, how is the man? Does anybody know?"

"Whadya mean, 'ow is the man?"

"Just what I said. How *is* the man?"

Ruby looked askance at me. "D'ya mean to say you don' know what 'appened last night?"

"I know that a man had a heart attack during the show."

"Wait a minute, ya really don' know what 'appened?"

"Would you please tell me what happened!" I said, impatiently.

"Well," she said breathlessly, "we were in the middle of the show and this chap 'ad a heart attack—"

"I know, I know. Just tell me what *happened.*"

"His heart stopped beatin'. He was *dead,* ya know! Things were very serious indeed," she went on dramatically.

"Yes, yes, I know—just get on with the story!"

"Then you did a marvelous thing. You 'ad everybody bow their 'eads and pray. I was standin' right next to the chap, and I bowed me 'ead too, but I kep' one eye on 'im at all times!" She paused, still catching her breath, and mimicked that moment, with one eye tightly closed and the other open.

"Go on," I prodded.

"Well, things got tremendously quiet. Then, I felt a power go through the tent. I felt it go through me whole body! And—the chap started breathin' again."

"What?" I reacted with amazement. "And, today?"

"Oh, the chap completely recovered and they sent 'im 'ome from the 'ospital. The whole fairgrounds is talkin' about it. In fact, the 'ead of the fairgrounds, Mr. Young, was just here wantin' to talk to you. I can tell ya one thing: I'm gonna be in church Sunday mornin'."

It seemed as if every person who had been in that circus tent the night before had come back, just wanting to talk. They all agreed that at that precise moment they had felt a strange tingling sensation.

Usually after the last performance of the day, I would be famished and would head for the nearest restaurant. But this night I went straight back to my motel. I closed my room door and leaned up against it, my mind whirling. What had happened? Did a miracle really take place? I could almost hear Bobby Yerkes saying, "Jesus loves you, pal, and one day He is going to reach you even if He has to *perform a miracle* to do it."

I sat down in a chair by the desk, rested my chin in my hand, then rubbed my eyes. When I looked up, my eyes settled on a Gideon Bible on the dresser. I had seen those in almost every hotel and motel room I had been in across the country, and I always pushed them aside to make room for my things. Haltingly, I picked it up and flipped it open. My fingers came to rest on James 5:15: "And a prayer of faith shall save the sick, and the Lord shall raise him up. . . ."

My eyes were transfixed by that verse. I read it over and over. There seemed to be an inescapable reality behind that passage at that moment. I stared into space. I could almost hear Bobby Yerkes' voice saying, ". . . perform a miracle—a miracle—a miracle. . . ." I flipped some more pages, as if trying to bury the scripture I had just read and never see it again. When I looked down, I saw that my fingers had come to rest on Matthew 18:20: "For where two or three are gathered together in my name, there I am in the midst of them."

I pondered that verse for a moment. We were in Tennessee, deep in the so-called "Bible Belt." Obviously, there had been far more than two or three people in that tent who believed in Jesus. Possibly, I could have been the only person there who did not. But others did, and seemingly they had prayed a man back to life.

I set the Bible down on the desk gently and paced the floor. Was Jesus really real, like so many people had been trying to tell me? Had God actually honored a prayer I had instigated with a miracle? Was Bobby Yerkes telling me the truth when he said that there was a God who wanted me in His service, and that the devil had tried to stop me from learning the truth?

Had the man actually been dead, or had he only appeared so? Did the emotion of the moment that swept the crowd create a false impression of the situation, magnifying what had actually happened out of proportion? A steady stream of believers were proclaiming to me that God had performed a miracle. Even if one rejected that view, it had still been an extraordinary experience. I thought again of what Bobby Yerkes had said to me. Confusion and conflict filled my mind.

I needed to talk about all this, to get help in sorting it out. I dialed the phone. "Hello?" answered the voice at the other end, almost with a question.

"Hi, Rose Marie, it's me. I need to talk to you."

"Oh, Sveetyheart, I'm glad you called. I've got some news!"

"But—"

"Never mind," she said, "you can tell me later. Dis is *important*. Uncle Fritz has invited us to Switzerland so he can present you to the family."

XIII

Zurich, Switzerland, spread out panoramically below us. Rose Marie pointed out the plane window.

"Look, Sveetyheart, we are flying directly between the lakes for our approach. Isn't it beautiful?" The alpine Swiss-German architecture, framed by the snow-capped Alps, presented us with an unforgettable picture.

Walter Slezak was on our flight. Lori had started talking to him and I had become involved in their conversation. The distinguished actor lived in Lucerne, and commuted back and forth to his film work and Broadway plays.

While the plane made its final approach, Rose Marie grew pensive and asked, "What am I going to tell the family you do for a living?"

"Tell them that I'm a circus ringmaster," I said. Her question had caught me by surprise.

"Then how am I going to explain the fact that you're not with Ringling Brothers? At least they know about the Ringling Brothers circus, and it is considered the best."

"Well, the Shrine circuses are very big in the United States, too, and respected. Besides, I make more money and have more freedom in my work with the Tom Packs Circus than I ever would with Ringling."

"I know—we'll tell them that you are the *director* of the circus," she said, arriving at the solution she thought would go over best with her family.

"No—hang it!" I said, impatiently. "I am *not* a director. I am a ring-master—one of the best in America. I am proud of my profession and my reputation."

We said our goodbyes to Walter Slezak as he went to his waiting white Mercedes-Benz limousine, while we joined Uncle Fritz, who had come to the airport to meet us in his brown one. I was enchanted by the scenery and by the quaint houses and buildings we passed as we made our way from the airport to Zurich, and then on to Uncle Fritz's apartment in Zolikon on the outskirts of the city.

Then, it was a non-stop series of visits. When I saw the homes of the various family members, I realized that the word "wealthy" was inadequate to describe their affluence. Only Uncle Fritz's apartment was modest. Most of the others had palatial homes, filled with statuary and tapestries. One even had its own aviary. In the home of one aunt I noticed a familiar-looking pencil drawing inconspicuously hung on a wall in a little windowed alcove. I went up to it and looked at the signature.

"Rose Marie," I asked, "is this an original Rembrandt?"

"Yes," she answered, quite matter-of-factly.

"Why, that must be worth a fortune. And it's hanging here?"

"Ya, it's dere because it fits. Dots the trouble with Americans. Dey put a price tag on everything and want to display value with neon lights. In Europe, we put things where they fit best."

Conversations would often switch abruptly, from High German to Swiss German, to French or Italian. English had all but ceased to be spoken from the moment we arrived.

"Switzerland is four countries in one," Rose Marie told me. "The peasants know only the local dialect of their region, but the better families know all of the languages."

The language barrier got on my nerves, and was particularly frightening and confusing for Lori. This was a strange world to her. To ease the tension, the two of us took walks together along the Lake of Zurich and composed songs about the swans and ducks we saw there. These were special moments.

*   *   *

Seventeen of the most prominent members of the family prepared a reception for us in a swank banquet hall in the center of Zurich. I stood at the door with Uncle Fritz, his wife Rosilee, Rose Marie, and Lori. We formed a receiving line, and each relative was introduced to me on the way in. A regal version of "The Schwabing Polka" played in the background. Tante Rosilee kept looking over at Lori with what seemed to me disapproval. It bothered me. I decided to use some of my showman's skill to knock them all on their aristocratic behinds.

When everyone was seated, Uncle Fritz rose and, speaking in High German, introduced me. According to custom I was to acknowledge the wedding gift the family had given us.

"Herr Stitzel," I said, recognizing the head of the dynasty with proper decorum and a bow, "and members of the family. Thank you so much for your hospitality in greeting and welcoming us. The Swiss clock you gave us will always be a cherished possession in our home.

"As I meet the members of Rose Marie's family, seeing her background, I can understand how she developed into the exceptional person she is, and I do love her very much." Rose Marie began to cry.

"However," I continued, "one thing puzzles me, and that is *Gogolee.*" The mood quickly changed and everyone began to laugh. *Gogolee* was a nickname given to Rose Marie when she was a little girl. "Everyone calls Rose Marie *Gogolee.* I found out that name means 'bird legs.' I suppose I will never understand that description."

Now that the atmosphere had been changed, I could build up to my finale.

"My parents in America extend to each of you their warmest greetings," I said, with an expansive gesture. The clan all nodded their heads.

"In fact," I continued, "if they were here, they would say, '*Wie gehts,* Herr Fritz Stitzel—Frau Rosilee Stitzel—Herr Doctor Deesay. . . .' "

To their mounting astonishment, I pointed to each member of the family in turn, calling them by their correct names and titles. I had used the same methods I used as a ringmaster to memorize the names and titles of each performer in the circus.

That broke the ice. I had disarmed them. They responded with a resounding burst of applause. I accepted it with a gracious bow and then sat down. The music resumed.

During dinner, Fritz's brother, Albert, who looked like a double for Mussolini, leaned over to compliment me on my blue double-breasted suit. "You would nefer find that quality in a suit made in Switzerland," he commented, feeling my lapel. I couldn't help grinning. I had bought the Swiss-made suit that very afternoon in a store on *Bahnhofstrasse.*

I said "*danke,*" and let the matter drop.

After dinner, Uncle Fritz pulled his chair closer to me. He handed me a small gift-wrapped package. "Dis is for you," he said.

My present was a solid gold Türler watch. When I opened it, Rose Marie, astonished, said to Uncle Fritz, "You're crazy!" Later, Rose Marie told me this was the most elaborate gift Uncle Fritz had ever given a new member of the family. "I think he was ashamed of what happened in New Jersey, and he saw that you did not care about the money."

*   *   *

I saw other sides to the family as we traveled across Switzerland. One cousin was obviously of very modest means. He worked in a factory. I found a refreshing sweetness about him and his wife. He wanted to give us a wedding gift, and presented us with an engraved silver plated cup he had won in a bowling contest. That gift touched me more than any other.

As we neared Fribourg, in the Italian section of Switzerland, I could see the gathering tension in Rose Marie's face. She had not seen her father, Franz Joseph Müller, for a number of years.

Herr Müller was a tall man with big hands. His long, handsome face somehow lacked the resoluteness so prominent in the faces of all the other family members I had met. Rose Marie's stepmother, a stocky, stern German woman, would have been perfectly cast as a concentration camp guard. I could not understand how these two ever got together. They lived in a very poor apartment.

When I shook hands with Herr Müller, it was strictly a formality on his part. The pressure of his hand immediately guided me to the right, away from him. Clearly, he had no desire to form any kind of relationship with me.

I retreated to a chair to watch. The visit was cold and brief. He did give us a magnificent eagle he had made out of metal, set on a marble base. Rose Marie asked for a small mosaic he had made, of three white ducks on a black background, for Lori's room. He gave it to her. "I want you to remember," Rose Marie told her father, "that one day I want those Chinese statues." The four valuable ivory statues she wanted had been brought over from China by her grandparents. The visit over, I was glad to leave.

We went back to Uncle Fritz's apartment in Zurich, and were repacking for a trip to Vervey, in the French section, to visit Aunt Claire and Uncle Coe. Tante Rosilee kept looking over at Lori, as she had at the family banquet, and talking in German to Rose Marie.

"Tante Rosilee was saying that she was noticing Lori's crooked feet," Rose Marie explained. "She is making an appointment with a foot doctor here when we come back next month. He is the best foot doctor in all of Europe, and he will be able to correct the problem."

A little while later, Tante Rosilee stood up on a small stool to fetch something from a top kitchen cabinet. The stool slipped out from under her and she fell heavily to the floor, breaking her wrist. She grimaced only slightly at the pain. Uncle Fritz, in a very business-like way, felt the wrist, set it, and bandaged it.

A few minutes later, Aunt Claire telephoned. Tante Rosilee took the call. "Yes, we are leaving within ten minutes," she said. She did not even mention that she had just broken her wrist.

When we arrived at Vervey, Aunt Claire noticed Tante Rosilee's bandaged wrist. "What happened to your wrist?" she asked.

"Oh, I fell off a stool this morning and broke it," she said, matter-of-factly. That was the end of the subject. They went on to other topics they thought more important. This impressed me. Had this happened anywhere in Indiana, the event would have been proclaimed far and near in graphic detail to everyone who would listen, with some added suffering thrown in to advance the drama of the situation.

Rose Marie's cousin, Günther, another artist in the family, had seen Charlie Chaplin that day, who lived down the hill. Chaplin had been driving his little Peugeot.

'How is he liked here?" I asked Günter.

"Well the people have become quite upset with him," he answered, "He was buying property, then dividing it up to build and sell more houses. The people here do not want houses crowded together."

"What about him as a movie star?"

"Oh, in the cinema, he is the best."

"Come on, Sveetyheart," Rose Marie said, leading me out of the living room. "Let me show you the house. Down here is Tante Claire's room. Now, over here is Uncle Coe's room."

"Rose Marie, what is this business of everybody having separate bedrooms?"

"Dot's the vay it's done in the better families."

"But don't they like to snuggle—have sex?"

"Of course!" answered Rose Marie. "For instance, Uncle Coe makes an appointment with Tante Claire when he wants to have sex."

"How far ahead does he have to make his appointment?"

"He might make an appointment for, say, a week from Wednesday."

"Good lord!" One could be out of the mood by that time. Then, again—maybe it takes some people that long to get ready."

"Oof—dot's all you think about, is sex! If you want to be a peasant, den be a peasant. Dey alvays sleep together in the same room."

"There's a lot to be said for the peasants," I said wearily.

*   *   *

Back in Zurich, Rose Marie and I were walking by the Lake of Zurich, watching the swans and the ducks. The cold air was refreshing. She had on a wool tam and I had on a new cossack cap, also made of wool.

"You have quite a complex family," I said. "I don't really know where I stand with any of them. I am curious about one thing. They are all so wealthy, except for your father, who appears to be poor."

"My father is quite irresponsible in many ways," she explained. "When the head of the family died years ago, he left a business. Each member of the family was to inherit the equivalent of fifty thousand dollars. They had a family meeting and proposed that everyone should take their share of the inheritance and put it back into the business, to keep it together. Everyone agreed except my father. With everyone together, the business succeeded and they became rich. All but my father, who took his fifty thousand and squandered it on his lusts. But what can you expect from an artist's temperament?"

"You don't like him, do you?"

"I hate him! My mother died when I was two years old. I was alone with her when it happened. I put a stool up to the door in order to be able to undo the latch. Then I ran down the hall, knocked on the door of a neighbor, and said, 'Please, come quick! Something is the matter with my mother.' "

Tears began to well up, as Rose Marie relived the experience. Her mother, Lili Wirz, had been a soft, gracious, beautiful woman filled with love, who had made Rose Marie's clothes by hand.

"And I think she died of something she caught from my father," Rose Marie recalled angrily. "He had many girlfriends and I know that he brought something home that killed my mother. He immediately married my stepmother. She hated me and was cruel to me. She would beat me and lock me in the cellar for hours at a time. It was damp and dark. Fortunately, there were many books there, and I read to keep from going crazy. Because the light was so bad, I ruined my eyes, which is why I must wear glasses, and my lungs are very weak because of the dampness I had to endure.

"Once when I was seven, my stepmother stripped me naked and threw me out in the front yard and locked the door. Den—dey put me in an orphanage.

"Uncle Fritz married my father's sister, Rosilee. Ven he found out I was in the orphanage, he said, 'Vat is dis?' and he took me out of the orphanage to his home and raised me. During that time I learned to love books. In fact, I read all of *War and Peace* when I was twelve years old. Uncle Fritz sent me to the best schools and then on to finishing school in London."

Uncle Fritz had instilled his hard-nosed business sense in Rose Marie. Her sense of independence likely came from him too, but it had backfired. It had taken her to America and her job with TWA. She would show the world that she would survive, with or without an inheritance. Marrying me, someone not picked by the family, was another statement of her independence.

It began to snow. The breeze was sharp and cold as it rose from the lake.

"You would nefer be unfaceful to me, vould you?"

I reached for her, pulled her to me gently, and held her. "Are you kidding?" I responded. "I love you, Rose Marie, with all my heart—with a love that will never die or grow old."

Her arms tightened around me. Rose Marie was capable of intense love. Still, she was afraid to allow herself to depend totally on anyone, even though deep down she wanted to. We both glanced up at the same time, to notice two swans on the shore nestled together.

Hand in hand, we walked back to Uncle Fritz's apartment building. "You go on upstairs," I said, "I just want to walk for a few more minutes."

I continued to walk until I came to a church. I went inside and sat down, deep in thought. Something else had been very much on my mind—that experience in the circus tent in Tennessee.

XIV

This time, before departing for my next engagement, I packed a Bible with my ringmaster's uniform. The Bible had been given to me by my mother as a Christmas gift when I was a boy.

I went to see Bobby Yerkes in his dressing room before the performance. "Where do I start reading this?" I asked, displaying the Bible in my outstretched hand.

Bobby's face lit up. "From the beginning would be the best place." He studied me for a moment, and the look on his face became pensive and questioning.

"Something happened recently," I told him. "I'm not exactly sure what. Maybe this will give me the answer."

"Start with the Book of Acts in the New Testament," he suggested, "then the Book of John, the Epistles of John, and then start with the beginning of the New Testament and go straight through."

"Time to get ready for the show," I said. "Talk to you later."

As I walked down the hall toward my own dressing room, I saw Jack Leontini coming toward me. Discreetly I moved my hand with the Bible in it out of sight behind me. Bobby Yerkes watched this with interest.

When the show was over, Bobby came to my dressing room.

"Why did you hide your Bible behind you when you saw Jack Leontini?" he asked.

"Well—I don't know—I guess because this is personal—and—"

"Jesus didn't deny you when He died for you on the cross."

"I'm not ready for this yet," I sputtered, "I just want to study the Bible for a while first."

* * *

I found a worried and distressed Rose Marie when I got back to Forest Hills.

"There's been some strange things happening," she said, "and I've learned that the FBI is investigating you. What have you done?"

For a moment, I just looked at her. "Let's go for a walk," I suggested after an awkward silence.

We walked for some distance before I finally spoke. "Rose, I didn't want this to come out. I didn't want you to become involved in it. I kept thinking this was going to stop, that it would blow over. But it looks like it is just something I will have to live with. I'll tell you briefly. And then, promise me that we will not talk about it any more."

Rose Marie looked at me intently, her silence bidding me to continue.

"Lori's mother—I don't even want to speak her name—it's a name I never want to hear again—was a dancer. She went to work for a modeling agency. I didn't know until she left me that the modeling agency was involved in—certain other activities. Those activities involved the highest office of the United States, and—the murder of a movie star. Because I know about all of this through my past connection with Lori's mother, the U.S. Government considers me a threat."

"And you have proof of all dis?"

"Yes. Documented."

"I don't know about dis," Rose Marie exclaimed, shaking her head. "I come from a good family. Ve know nothing of this kind of thing. If I had known all of dis—I vould nefer have married you!"

For Lori's protection, we put her in a private Catholic school in Forest Hills. The head priest agreed to keep her enrollment a secret from any inquiring officials.

Perhaps it was the combination of the stress I was experiencing from being dogged by the FBI and my genuine truth-seeking that led me to spend more and more time reading and searching the Scriptures.

One day, while walking down Broadway in New York City, I met Johnny Woods, who did master of ceremonies work and fancied himself a ringmaster. He appeared overjoyed to inform me that at a recent Shriners' convention he attended the FBI was there asking questions about me, and that the Shrine committee was having second thoughts about booking me for its circuses.

Lori's birth mother had found out about my marriage to Rose Marie and had begun a vindictive scheme to get custody of Lori. That touched a raw nerve in Rose Marie, who became hysterical at the thought of being separated from Lori. Even though a reversal of the original custody decision would have been impossible, Lori's birth mother could force a hearing, and then I would have no choice but to present the same lurid evidence again that had won me Lori's custody the first time. That prospect caused panic in government offices. This time it might not be possible to hush up the matter so easily. The FBI increased its pressure on me, interfering in every area of my life.

"Your stepfather's not well," my mother informed me, "and this FBI agent, Richard Eisgruber, keeps intruding into our home."

The FBI waged a very skillful harassment campaign. Had there been any kind of legitimate charge against me, any real grounds for suspecting I had committed any federal crime, they could simply have come and arrested me. My work made me one of the easiest of people to find, what with all the circus publicity pinpointing where I could be found and when. Instead, they kept their distance from me, but succeeded in wreaking havoc in every aspect of my life behind my back.

A newspaper called *The Hollywood Free Press* came in the mail. Bobby Yerkes had taken up with Duane Pederson, who spearheaded a new "Jesus" movement and whose ministry published the newspaper. I opened it up and saw the bold words of Romans 8:31, "If God be for us, who can be against us?" The article told about God's protection in our lives.

That scripture affected me powerfully, and seemed to point the way to something I very much wanted and needed in my life. Maybe God was there and wanted to look after me. Bobby had often said to me, "God always looks after His own." Maybe I had all these problems because I had not accepted Jesus, had not allowed Him into my life. How could I expect God to help me if I didn't let Him in my life? Yes, yes, I was at the mercy of the devil out there by myself. Why had I been so bullheaded? What could have been a plainer statement that God was real than that miracle under the big top in Memphis? Yes, coming to God through Jesus Christ was the only way to have a better life, a life with love—and protection.

Bobby met me at the airport in Los Angeles. We went directly to a Christian Businessmen's luncheon. This time, I was totally open and saw only positive things. During a worship time, I prayed "the sinners prayer" with Bobby and became a "born-again" Christian then and there. My life would never be the same.

"Behold, all things
are become new"

XV

The Thanksgiving week I spent in New Orleans that year stands out in my memory. The Tom Packs Circus played there at the same time each year. As was the tradition, some of us from the circus staff sat down for Thanksgiving dinner with the Shrine executive committee between the day's two performances.

I felt particularly joyful that Thanksgiving. My new Christian birth had given me a whole new demeanor. My new name—Austin Miles—added to my sense of being a new man. The interference of the FBI had become so intolerable that I felt myself being driven to take some drastic measure to stop it. It had been the only time in my life when I seriously thought of committing murder. Rose Marie and I devised a way to have my name legally changed and leave no paper trail behind us. Somehow, we thought that would ensure our privacy.

Before the second performance, the backstage area of Municipal Auditorium was abuzz with the activity of the performers, musicians, and Shriners.

"Now, I want to see you carry your Bible openly and *proudly,*" Bobby Yerkes admonished me.

"Oh, I don't know Bob," I said, resisting.

"Jesus said in the Bible that if you deny Him on earth, He'll deny you in heaven. Do you want that?" Bobby warned.

The words of the Bible had begun to take hold of me. I felt a love for humanity I had never felt before. I was excited about my new Christian faith, but felt that this personal relationship between me and Jesus was private.

"Jesus hates a lukewarm Christian," Bobby continued. "In fact, He says in His Word that He will spew the lukewarm Christian from His mouth, or vomit him from his mouth." I cringed at that statement. "Actually, you're worse than the unsaved, being a lukewarm Christian, because you're doing nothing for the Kingdom when you know the truth. Mark 16:15 commands us, 'Go ye into all the world, and preach the gospel to every creature.' That is the *duty* of every Christian."

"Bobby, I'm not ready yet," I protested.

"You're ready from the moment you accept the Lord Jesus Christ as your savior and become a born-again Christian. You have to start immediately to proclaim your faith and stand up for it. Now, you have to make a *total* commitment to Christ if you want victory. Remember, pal, Jesus loved *you,* Austin Miles, so much, even when you were in sin, that He died a painful, agonizing death *for you* on the cross. Shouldn't that mean something to you? The devil would like nothing better than to inhibit you to keep you from serving Jesus, to rob you of the joy— the victory! Now, you're either a Christian, or you're not. James 1:8 says, 'A double minded man is unstable in all his ways.' "

The force of his argument overcame me. "One should never do anything halfway," I thought. And God had seen fit to show *me* His power when the man was healed in the circus tent.

I looked at Bobby and smiled. I straightened up taller than usual, pushed my chin out piously, and walked toward the dressing room with my Bible in full view. Maybe *this* would prove that I had never been unsure of myself. The performers noticed, and glanced over at Bobby. He had a satisfied expression on his face. This represented a double victory for him. As I walked past Jack Leontini, he was clearly very much aware of the Bible I was carrying. I suddenly began to *feel* pious. I pushed my chin out a little farther. It was a defensive but strong posture.

After that, it got easier. I did feel a strange new confidence and strength. I shouldn't have worried about what the nonbelievers thought of me anyway. If anything, they were to be pitied. Hopefully, one day they too would realize the truth and be saved.

With encouragement from Bobby to "share my testimony," I called the public relations firm handling the New Orleans engagement with the circus. "If there is any Christian station in the area," I told Ike Chapman, our publicist, "I would like to go on as a guest. I'm asking this as a personal favor. I will not be plugging the circus." Sam Ford, of WYOG Christian Radio, scheduled me immediately.

"Where and when is the Shrine Circus, and how much are the tickets?" Ford asked, after introducing me to his listening audience.

"That's not important," I replied. "I didn't come here to talk about the circus; I came here to talk about Jesus."

"Praise the Lord! We must be in the last days when a *ringmaster* from a *circus* comes on the air and doesn't want to talk about circus tickets but about Jesus. I never thought I would see this day," he gushed.

Feeling great love for Christ and having an open, vulnerable heart, I took this as a nice bit of levity. It never occurred to me to bristle at the cheap shot at circus people.

"Mr. Ford, something extraordinary happened to me in Memphis that changed my life. . . ."

A man in another studio noticed us through a glass window. "Can you pipe that sound in here? I want to hear what's going on," he said to the engineer, who nodded. The man propped his elbow up on the console, listening and watching intently.

The interview concluded with my giving credit to the Lord for the transformation in my life. Approving listeners immediately began telephoning the station.

As Ford and I were leaving, the man in the neighboring, smaller studio hurriedly got to his feet and came out to speak with me. He reached out to shake my hand.

"Praise the Lord!" he said exuberantly. "I was here making a tape and had them switch on the sound in my studio so I could hear your interview. My name's Coleman McDuff. I'm an evangelist, and I'm having a crusade at the Westwego Assembly of God Church. Would it be possible for you to come Sunday morning and give your testimony? I think it could sure bless a lot of people."

A sturdily built Texan of medium height, Coleman McDuff had dark hair and long sideburns that curved at the ends, accenting his handsome, gentle countenance. I admired the air of peace and joy he conveyed. I wanted more of what Coleman McDuff had.

"Yes," I answered, "I would be happy to come. What time's the service?" I was thinking about my matinee at 1:45 P.M.

"Service starts at eleven," the evangelist said. "Only one thing: it usually gets over about 12:30, and it's so far to the Municipal Auditorium, you probably won't have a chance to get lunch before the show."

With a waxing Christian spirit stirring within me, I said without hesitation, "I'll skip a meal for the Lord anytime." Reverend McDuff shook my hand again, his mouth turning up in a warm grin. I felt very good about myself for having said that.

On Sunday morning, a young man named Glenn picked me up at the Hotel Jung to drive me to the Westwego Assembly of God. Glenn was a nice looking teenager, if a bit subdued for his age. His "Sunday best," a sport coat and slacks, was inexpensive at best, and put together the best way he knew how. He seemed to be a very sheltered and respectful young man, almost overawed by my position in the circus, a world he had only heard about. His only surroundings had been the "born-again" church. He had never known anything else.

"Here we are, Brother Miles," he said, as we pulled up to the church. I could hear the sounds of the worship service coming out of the building. As we entered, loud, fervent prayer filled the air. The pastor's voice over the loudspeakers rose above all the others. People were praying independently, some of them intelligibly, others in "tongues." Many had their hands and faces lifted upward. This was a far cry from my staid, Presbyterian background and, when I think of it, an altogether unlikely place to find me.

Even though it seemed a little much at the moment, I thought to myself, "This is it." I had studied 1 Corinthians 3:19: "For the wisdom of this world is foolishness with God. . . ." Preachers use that scripture constantly to remind their flocks that everything of the "world" is folly, pretense, "vanity." I had also heard the radio and TV preachers quoting Acts 10:34, ". . . God is no respecter of persons." No matter what position one has, or how much money, we are all one in the eyes of God, and can only come to Him in one way—openly and without reservation. We must give *all* to God, holding nothing back. There is no other way to victory.

Even though I did not completely understand everything that was taking place, the events beginning with the man being prayed back to life in the circus tent had set me on a path of no return—leading here. The praying made way for the congregational hymn, "Clap Your Hands All Ye People."

Reverend McDuff spotted me standing in the back and motioned for me to come up to the platform. He then gestured for me to be seated next to the pastor, Paul Radke. Pastor Radke, another husky Texan, had his head bowed in prayer as I sat down. Keeping his head bowed, he opened his eyes and tilted his head toward me. A smile flashed across his face, and he squeezed my arm in welcome. Although somewhat ill at ease, I felt a wonderful sense of acceptance. Reverend McDuff sensed my nervousness and said, "Now, don't worry about what you're going to say. Just let the Holy Spirit guide your words and keep your mind on Christ." Those words served to relax me completely, and I thought only of Jesus.

Using the Bible my mother had given me, I gave my first "testimony" in a church. A glow and inner peace seemed to engulf my body. I had never felt this way before. It was an ecstatic happiness, and I wanted more of it.

After the service, the feedback was all favorable. Everyone wanted to meet me and shake my hand. Some said, "What a blessing you were this morning, Brother Miles. God bless you!"

Others seemed to gain more from the service. One said, "Brother Miles, I had a terrible pain in my back this morning. I didn't even think I would be able to come to church. But praise God, while you were speaking Jesus took away the pain and I feel wonderful!"

"Our meeting in the radio studio was no accident or coincidence, Brother Austin," Reverend McDuff said. "God arranged that. I'm going to be calling you in a few days. Will you be back in New York?" He invited me back to speak again the next Sunday. I accepted immediately.

I invited Pastor Radke and Glenn, along with their families, to come to the circus as my guests. Glenn was overwhelmed. He had never seen any kind of public performance before, and his eyes were filled with wonderment. My guests took photos of their families with me. The one with Glenn's family is a study in contrasts: I was in an expensive three-piece wool suit from England, carrying a homburg and a gold-knobbed walking stick. Glenn was poorly dressed, as was his mother, who was overweight besides. His father wore a hearing aid in each ear. His brother was slightly deformed. I thought nothing about it. We were all brothers and sisters in Christ.

Pastor Radke gave me a booklet *Power Through Prayer,* by E. M. Bounds, an illuminating study of the power of prayer in the committed Christian life. I basked in the tremendous outpouring of love and acceptance by the Pentecostal Christians all week, which served to draw me closer to the Assemblies of God church.

After the service the following Sunday, there were again profuse compliments about my talk. Many spoke of my "anointing."

"Everyone can see that God has His hand in your life," one man said.

"Brother Miles," said a woman with great sincerity in her face, "I saw an aura around your head as you spoke, like a halo. Has anyone ever told you that before? I could actually see it!" I was so caught up in it all that I was ready to believe it—and, indeed, did believe it.

I turned, and came face to face with an older man in a black suit. He had a pointed face and stood stiffly. His face was tight, though he was trying to smile at me. "Brother Miles," he said, "some time ago I had a brother that came and told me that one day when the devil comes he'll be wearing three-hundred-dollar suits. I've never forgotten that." He was looking my suit over as we spoke.

Only for a moment was I confused and taken aback. Then I reached out, felt the lapel of his suit, and said, "May I compliment you on your wardrobe, sir." I turned and walked away from him.

I stopped and reflected on this for a moment. What was it that he was trying to say to me? And why? It was obvious that I was being called by God. The positive response of God's people confirmed it. One of them even saw God's aura around me! I shrugged off the reproach and ignored the underlying message that all these people might not be so loving as they seemed. Instead, the all-purpose rationalization that the devil had put the man there to deceive and discourage me came to mind. How clumsy of the devil!

"What are your plans?" Pastor Radke asked me as he drove me to Municipal Auditorium.

"I—I feel God has called me to the ministry," I said.

He did not seem surprised. He nodded his head thoughtfully, in affirmation. "I have some books I want to give you to begin your studies. When do you leave to go back to New York?"

"My plane leaves tonight after the last show. I have a show in New York tomorrow night."

"I can't get them for you until tomorrow," Pastor Radke said. "Is there any way you can stay over?"

I inquired at the airport and was told every plane was booked solid. Yet, I felt strongly that God wanted me to have those books without delay. Taking a big chance, I asked to be put on standby for one of the fully booked flights.

The next day, I was in my room packing when Pastor Radke came to drive me to the airport. The books he brought me included *The Spirit Himself* by Ralph M. Riggs and *Bible Doctrines* by P. C. Nelson, which contained mostly Assemblies of God theology.

"Have you had 'the Baptism' yet?" He was referring to the Baptism of the Holy Spirit, where the Spirit of God takes over one's body and one speaks in "other tongues."

"No," I said, "but I'm open for it."

"Yes," he continued, "this is very necessary for an effective ministry. What about your wife? Is she saved?"

I had spoken affectionately of Rose Marie and Lori in my talk that Sunday. The question was put so blandly that I did not realize how a wedge was subtly being driven between Rose Marie and me, as I answered, "No, she is not. Hopefully that will change."

"We'll pray for her," he answered. The presumption that Rose Marie needed to be prayed for drove the wedge deeper. It implied that she was now our spiritual inferior.

"Brother Miles, I want you to pray for *me*," he said, breaking the mood at just the right moment. "I've started a local television ministry. As you can see, New Orleans is steeped in sin. There are so many in this city who are lost. Their only chance is to be reached by the Gospel of Jesus Christ. We can do that through television. But the devil has fought us every step of the way. That's the last thing the devil wants—is for this area to be reached for Jesus. And the devil could win if someone doesn't help us financially. Air time is so expensive. We may have to go off the air if God doesn't give us a financial miracle. Please pray with us on this."

"How much does it cost for the TV time?" I asked.

Pastor Radke had the facts and figures ready. He gave me the cost breakdown for each broadcast, as well as the monthly and yearly projections.

Before we left for the airport, I went into the bathroom, wrote out a check, and put it in my inside coat pocket in an envelope.

When I was about to get out of Pastor Radke's car in front of the airport, I took the envelope out. "As you know, Pastor Radke, I can't be in church next Sunday. So, will you put this in the offering plate for me?"

Pastor Radke could not contain the happiness in his face as he took it. "Brother Miles, you have a unique calling of God upon your life. He will open the way for you to have a ministry of miracles, of special gifts. Oh, you'll be hated by the devil for it, but God will bless you in return. Remember, the devil will do everything he can to discourage you and keep you out of the ministry because he knows God plans to use you mightily. And I want you to consider yourself as a member of our church in good standing." He took me by the hand, offered a special prayer for me, and asked that God would touch Rose Marie.

I would have been in deep trouble professionally had I not made the performance in New York that evening. Yet, I sat in the waiting room unconcernedly reading *Bible Doctrines* while waiting to find out if a seat would become available. During the final boarding of the plane at the last minute, the announcement was made that there was one seat for me. I arrived in New York in plenty of time to do the show.

XVI

Attacks of homesickness out on the road were particularly acute as the Christmas season neared.

"Dear Lori," I wrote to my daughter. "Everybody in the circus asks how you are. Our baby elephant is sick. It's hard to find an elephant doctor in Canada, where many people have never even seen an elephant. Say a prayer for the little elephant. I'll let you know how she is. Looking forward to being home for Christmas. Love, Dad." Trying to make up for being away so much, I did everything I could to make Lori feel involved in what I was doing and to let her know that she had a father who loved her.

I had been involved in making a children's film in Italy. Something had gone wrong with the soundtrack, and I got a transatlantic phone call summoning me back to Rome immediately to reshoot. I had no other choice but to go. Rose Marie was in Switzerland, visiting her family.

"Daddy!" Lori exclaimed, when she saw I had come to pick her up at school. When I told her we were going to Rome, she received the news with precious nonchalance. Even as a first-grader, Lori had been back and forth to Europe several times.

When the plane was airborne, a concerned expression suddenly came over Lori's face. "Daddy, this is Halloween, and you promised me that I could go trick-or-treating!"

"Has Daddy ever failed to keep a promise to you?"

"Well, no, but—"

"Do you feel that I have forgotten my promise?" I said, keeping a straight face.

Lori struggled to get off the hook. "Well—no—but—"

"Take a look in your flight bag." She opened it and found a Halloween costume. Thirty-five thousand feet in the air, Lori, dressed in a monster costume, walked up and down the aisle trick-or-treating, to the delight of the passengers and flight attendants who loaded her down with goodies.

Those were the moments I worked and lived for. I spent as much time with Lori as I could. I made a special effort to have times when I gave her my undivided attention. An important part of those years was our "big chair" discussions. When Lori had something important to talk to me about, we would both sit in my big, red leather chair and talk earnestly about it. No distractions were allowed at those times. If a radio or TV was on, it would be turned off.

But on the road, any spare time was spent studying my Bible and the books Pastor Radke had given me. I continually found new joy and meaning in the words. I developed an extraordinary hunger to read all the Christian books and pamphlets I could get my hands on. I went to church on Sunday mornings and visited Christian bookstores during the week. During the long hours in the car, I would search the radio dial, hoping to pick up a Christian preacher or teacher. The more Christian teaching I took in, the more stricken I felt about the "self-centered" life I had led. I felt more and more guilty about the success I had worked for, so long and hard. How selfish I had been!

In Ohio, a chambermaid spoke to me as I was leaving my motel room. "You're Austin Miles the circus man, aren't you?" When I affirmed that I was, she said, "One of the girls told me that the circus man was staying in Room 214." Something about the way she said "circus man" put me off. Then, in a curious defense of me, she continued, " 'But you see that Bible he has there,' I said." To that chambermaid, the mere presence of that personal leather-bound Bible among my things signified that I was better than anyone else in the circus. Her reacton made me feel all the more superior and pious. I found it agreeable to be thought of as above others. It was the perfect antidote to my lingering childhood sense of rejection that had left me feeling unsure of myself despite my successes. It was the ultimate acceptance. It would induce me to display my Christianity more and more, and to give larger and larger cash gifts.

The last performance for the season completed, I was enjoying my drive home up Highway 81. Al Hirt's rendition of "Sleigh Ride" was playing on the radio. I arrived home to a wonderful Christmas celebration. The tree was decorated European-style, with real candles. Uncle Fritz had sent eighteen new one-hundred-dollar bills in an envelope by registered mail to buy a piano for Lori. Rose Marie had purchased a Steinway upright, and had arranged for Mrs. Anna Beck to come and give Lori a private lesson once a week.

An elaborate table was set for a Christmas party, with the finest linen, china, and silver. Friends who had been invited came to celebrate with us, all dressed in their best clothing.

Rose Marie said to me, "Lori's present to you is a song she has practiced just for you." By the light of the Christmas tree candles, Lori sang "Angels

We Have Heard On High." The way she carefully moved her mouth to form the full tones showed that she had practiced quite hard and seriously. As the notes went up, she reached up slightly with her whole body, as if it helped her reach a higher note. Deeply and thoroughly enchanted, I reached out to give her a big hug. It was the best Christmas present I had ever had.

The relaxation of pressure from outside allowed our family life to become closer. We had been free of FBI interference since I had changed my name. In a telephone conversation, Bobby Yerkes interpreted it this way: "Give God credit for that. God said in Psalms 105:15, '. . . Touch not mine anointed, and do my prophets no harm.' *You* are God's anointed, and God protects His own." I felt grateful to God's people, and was allowing myself to become dependent upon them as well. Somehow the real satisfactions in my life seemed too pale and I yearned for something more substantial beyond them. The experienced "born-again" Christians seemed to possess that more substantial something, and the right answers as well. I trusted them totally. How could Christians be anything other than honorable?

*   *   *

Rose Marie, Lori, and I stood at the Lincoln Center fountain after a concert. Lori had been coming along impressively in her piano lessons. I said, "You know, Lori, you're very fortunate. One day you will be a great pianist, and you'll be able to play beautiful places like this. Daddy's with the circus. Now, the circus has been very good to us, but you will be able to perform in elegant places like this." No sooner had the words left my mouth, when the thought "Why shouldn't I be able to play places like this?" streaked across my mind.

We rushed home and I began jotting down ideas for a "circus fantasy," using acts that could play a proscenium stage. The next day, I contacted Leonard Green, the manager of Emmett Kelly, Jr. A partnership was formed, and the Emmett Kelly, Jr. Circus was born. One week before our tour was to begin, the office was a madhouse of activity. Six conversations were going on at once. A telephone rang.

"Hello, Brother Austin," said the friendly voice with an unmistakable Texas accent at the other end. "This is Coleman McDuff. I am holding an evangelistic crusade at Calvary Temple Assembly of God Church here in Springfield, Missouri. You've been on my heart for several weeks. I really feel you would be a blessing out here. There are a lot of young people attending the crusade who need direction. Could you possibly fly out and give your testimony tomorrow night? The church will pay your plane fare and expenses, and give you an honorarium." I was so naïve about church talk that I thought an "honorarium" was a mention in the newspaper.

To the consternation of the entire production staff, I made preparations to fly out the next afternoon. Before leaving for the airport, Marvin Kaye, an author and freelance writer, stopped by to interview me about my new circus concept. During the interview, I talked about my "born-again" Christianity. That became a major focus of Kaye's story, published in the newspaper, *Grit*. It also became the main thrust of practically every story that would be published about me for many years to come.

My coming to Springfield had been publicized on a day's notice in the local papers. Even the local TV newscasts gave it a mention. A converted circus ringmaster was quite a curiosity. Some circus people lived in the area, and I recognized many of them in the congregation.

One cannot help but be stirred by a Pentecostal song service. It is audience participation all the way, and everybody *must* get into the act. Peppy songs like "Clap Your Hands All Ye People" animate the singers, their hands popping up and down at each "Hosanna" and clapping for the other parts of the song. The atmosphere is charged, kinetic, exhilarating. When a slower moving, more melodic song like "Seek Ye First the Kingdom of God" changes the pace, a worshipful, even hypnotic mood comes over the crowd. The emotional intensity of Pentecostal worship is startling to anyone not familiar with it.

Pastor Stewart Robinson, a good looking, richly dressed man with graying hair, rose to introduce me. After telling the congregation something about my background, Pastor Robinson said, "This man has come all the way from New York to minister to you. Now, it costs money for his plane fare and expenses, and his time is valuable. So we want you to be really generous. Those of you who wish may write checks." I winced as he continued his hard-sell appeal for a big offering. The circus people in the audience exchanged knowing glances. To them it was all a con game anyway.

As the collection plates were passed along the pews, I could see that the people were responding generously. After all, their pastor had told them to. The "sheep" were obeying the voice of their "shepherd," as they had been programmed to do. They gave even though they had never heard me speak, and my "ministry" had not yet been "proved."

"Dear God," I thought, "if one soul should be turned off tonight because of this, the whole trip will have been made in vain. It would be far better had I not come at all."

The pastor presented me to the gathering. I hesitated, and then spoke: "First of all, I want to sincerely thank you for the generous way you wanted to support me. That was really an exercise in faith. However, I am still working in the circus. I am employed, and through that, the Lord is providing for me. So—I want to take the collection just taken up for me—and turn it back over to this church."

Pastor Robinson's mouth dropped open in total surprise. This was a first in Pentecostal Christian evangelical circles. The people in the congregation, particularly the circus people, sat up with new interest.

Then, very quietly and simply, I testified about how God had reached me through the miracle of the healing under the big top, and how my new "birth" had changed my life. To my own surprise, I found myself explaining how, even with all my worldly successes, something had seemed to be lacking in my life. I had been sold on the idea that my previous life, before I was "born again," had not been an entirely happy one.

At the close of the service, the altar was filled with people kneeling and weeping. A man with cancer asked me to pray with him for healing. Many dedicated themselves to serving Jesus. One, a high school teacher with tears in his eyes, said to me, "I must admit, I was skeptical about you at first, but that really did it for me when you turned back the collection to the church." The teacher accepted Jesus into his life. I thought to myself that if I had not taken the action I did, he may not have opened his life up to the Lord.

In the pastor's study, Coleman was telling me about his ministry, and about his brothers who were also in the ministry. "You know, Brother Austin, Colonel Sanders got saved through our ministry. Here, I want you to have some of my record albums, and here is one with Colonel Sanders' testimony." Proudly, Coleman handed me a record album with pictures of himself and Colonel Sanders on the cover.

Pastor Robinson looked up from his desk. "Austin, I know you meant well out there about the money. But here, let me give you this." It was a check he had just finished writing, payable to me for two hundred dollars.

"Pastor," I responded, "I can't do one thing out there and another back here. Let me borrow your pen. I'm going to endorse this check back to the church. Use it to buy New Testaments for all the teenagers." Pastor Robinson shook his head, but with a glint of approval in his eye.

The Emmett Kelly, Jr. Circus opened its tour and from the beginning received critical acclaim. The highlight of the "fantasy circus" was a sequence where Merlin the Magician appeared in a puff of smoke and produced a Raggedy Ann doll that magically became a real live Raggedy Ann who danced a charming ballet number with Emmett.

I received an urgent message from Rose Marie to call Coleman McDuff. I dialed his number.

"Hi, Coleman. It's Austin."

"Brother Austin," he said, "I've got some news for you. Do you remember the man who came to the altar after the service in Springfield, who had cancer and asked you to pray with him?"

"Yes," I said, "his name was Clark, I believe. I remember that it was overwhelming to me to be asked to pray for a healing like that, that someone would put that much trust in my relationship with God."

"Brother Austin, he was completely healed after your prayer. His doctor has confirmed it and is astonished. He said that Mr. Clark had the worst case of prostate cancer he had ever seen in a fifty-year-old man, in his twenty-five years of practice."

"Is this true? Who is the man?" I asked.

"His name is A. J. Clark. He is vice-president of a bank in Springfield— well known. He doesn't even attend that church. He came because he had read the publicity about you and was curious."

"And it is confirmed that he was healed in that service?" I asked.

"Totally healed, Brother Austin," he answered. "I knew the first time I met you that God was going to use you in a special way."

XVII

The international headquarters of the Assemblies of God is a spacious, modern building at 1445 Boonville Avenue in Springfield, Missouri. Word spread quickly throughout the building about my Calvary Temple appearance. Several key members of the head office team had been there.

One of the more effective ways of raising money for the Assemblies of God was through the offer of "witnessing booklets" containing the stories of "born-again" celebrities. These tiny but attention-getting booklets were sent to contributors to "Revivaltime," the Assemblies of God radio program, heard over six hundred and fifty stations.

Mine was a double-barreled story: A man healed of a heart attack—in a circus tent of all places—resulting in the conversion of a ringmaster. Reverend Lee Shultz, Director of Communications, contacted Pastor Stewart Robinson, then Coleman McDuff.

"Brother Austin," Coleman's warm voice said on the telephone, "I very much encourage you to let them do a booklet on you. This will help many people come to Jesus, and I know that's what you want. Also, this will open the way for your ministry throughout the Assemblies of God churches."

I agreed to return to Springfield during a two-week break in the midst of a hectic schedule. The Assemblies flew me in from New York. I was given the red-carpet treatment. From the moment I arrived, it was a nonstop itinerary of events.

An imposing mural of a warlike rider on a white horse waving a big, menacing sword against a background of puffy white clouds and blue sky dominated the lobby of the Assemblies of God world headquarters. A sound and light show told the story the mural portrayed several times a day.

"Praise the Lord, Brother Miles!" the pretty receptionist said, welcoming me. "We've been looking forward to your coming. Reverend Zimmerman is anxious to meet you." She turned to an aide. "Take him there first."

Reverend Thomas F. Zimmerman ruled as General Superintendent of the entire Assemblies of God denomination and President of the World Pentecostal Conference. There was scarcely a more central or respected figure in Pentecostalism. I was escorted up to the third-floor executive suites, then into his ultra-plush office. The Reverend Zimmerman was impeccably dressed and manicured, his white hair perfectly barbered. One could *feel* this man's presence as well as see it. An obvious leader, he positively radiated strength. He rose from his desk, made his way gracefully around it, took my hand, then gave me a warm, "Pentecostal" hug. He glowed with smooth, spellbinding charm. I found myself in awe of this man of God.

"What a pleasure to meet you, Brother Miles. I've heard so much about you," he said, smiling. "They tell me we are going to feature your story in our new miniature booklet. The stories of several great Americans have been featured in these booklets, and we're certainly honored to have you be a part of this. I just know that your story will be a special blessing. Now, if there is *ever* anything I can personally do for you, don't hesitate to call me."

Next, Lee Shultz conducted me to the recording studio to meet Dr. C. M. Ward, the speaker of the radio show "Revivaltime." Dr. Ward cut an imposing figure. His deep, booming voice could intimidate easily, putting him in command of any situation. In contrast to his voice, his unique face made him look like a caricature of an outsized chicken. While pondering something or seeking an answer to a question, he had a habit of leaving his mouth open slightly, his head forward. A bit of jowl gathered loosely under his chin. A rooster's comb on his head would have completed the illusion.

Dr. Ward was the greatest Pentecostal preacher of all time. He knew his Bible inside and out, and used his knowledge to create superb sermons that are considered classics. His books include what are regarded as the definitive works on biblical prophecy in Assemblies of God circles. He was also something of a rebel, and was called on the carpet more than once to explain some outrageous comment or put-down uttered over the air. The latest "C. M. Ward stories" were continually being circulated. Once he got called upstairs to account for his use of a vulgar word in one of his sermons. "It's really amazing, what can come out when you're under the 'anointing,' " he boomed at his inquisitor.

"That entire third floor of the Assemblies of God headquarters must be on the pill," Dr. Ward once mused in a sermon. "They haven't come up with a fertile idea in years." Another time, while hammering home a point, he blurted out, "That place is dryer than the Central Assembly baptistry!" Dr. C. M. Ward had become a legend in his own time.

He taped a long interview with me, getting my testimony. This was edited and printed in a booklet they decided to title, "The Ringmaster Meets Jesus."

Next, we posed for pictures. I could not help but notice Dr. Ward's poise. It all seemed—too professional. This bothered me for a moment, but the impression quickly faded. Despite his antics, here was a man totally "sold out" to God. I could not resist his gruff friendliness, his good humor, and his unpredictable candor. I liked him instantly, and my good feelings toward him would never change.

Reverend Lee Shultz, who also served as the announcer for "Revivaltime," was another Assemblies of God insider with whom I felt a special rapport. He and Dr. Ward took me on a tour of the building after lunch. This vast operation had its own printing plant. "We print and send out more Christian literature than any other organization on earth. We ship more than fourteen tons of literature every working day," he said proudly. "And this," he said, taking me into another section, "is where we print and ship out books and study material to the missionaries and future ministers. We have a program for training, equipping, and ordaining ministers in their own countries. Assemblies of God churches are rising up in every country of the world."

I was given several samples, including bound copies of C. M. Ward's sermons, record albums, teaching tapes, and a handful of the miniature booklets. Reverend Shultz also enrolled me for a complimentary subscription to *The Pentecostal Evangel*, the weekly Assemblies of God magazine.

Before departing, I was taken back to say goodbye to Reverend Zimmerman.

"Thank you for coming, Brother Miles," said the world leader of the Assemblies of God, graciously. "I trust your visit was meaningful to you."

"I enjoyed myself thoroughly, Reverend Zimmerman," I responded. "I am particularly impressed with your missionary program."

"We have the greatest missionary outreach of any denomination in the world," said Reverend Zimmerman loftily. "The Assemblies of God places great emphasis on raising up and supporting ministers and missionaries in their own countries. That is precisely why God is blessing the Assemblies of God so mightily, and why we have become the fastest growing denomination in the world!"

"And all this is financed by the church?" I asked.

"By the *people*. They give generously to our missionary programs."

That evening, I had dinner at Pastor Robinson's. "I have a burden on my heart," he revealed to me after dessert. "I'm getting ready to make a move. I was over in Africa recently, visiting a missionary, and while there I saw thousands of people come from the most remote areas to hear the Word of Jesus. One pregnant woman carried a child, walking seven miles each way to hear a service. After the service, that woman, with tears in her eyes, said, 'Please tell me more about your Jesus.' The people are so hungry for the Word that I feel a call to go there."

I glanced around the opulently furnished parsonage in which we were sitting. Reverend Robinson drove a big luxury car, dressed in expensive clothing, and had the finest food on his table. He pastored an affluent church and made a large salary. "What about all this?" I asked, making an encompassing gesture.

"It means nothing to me," he answered. "God just loaned all this to me for the time I was here. I must go where I feel the Lord wants me."

Pastor Robinson drove me to the airport. It touched me deeply that this man would give up his secure, comfortable lifestyle to go live in some simple hut in a foreign country in order to preach the Gospel to hungry hearts. I had met some of the world's most famous people. "But now," I figured, "for the first time I have met truly great men. Unselfish, giving, great men." I said goodbye to Reverend Robinson and boarded my plane.

During the flight back to New York, my mind busy reflecting on all the new impressions I had taken in during the visit, I dug out some of the miniature booklets from my briefcase. While I was thumbing through them, I suddenly sat bolt upright in my seat. I stared at the booklet in my hand. It was entitled, "J. Edgar Hoover Testifies. . . ."

J. Edgar Hoover? Christian testimony? I knew a thing or two about J. Edgar Hoover, the late head of the FBI. He was the most ruthless, despicable, power-mad individual who ever inhabited Washington, D.C. Suspicions about his bizarre sexual perversions were confirmed by the revolting pornography collection found in his home after his death. The great personifier of truth, justice, and the American way had been an unbridled homosexual! He had wrought so much havoc in my life that I had been driven to change my name to get away from him. And my stepfather's death four years earlier had most likely been hastened by the stress caused by Agent Richard Eisgruber's constant harassment of my family in Evansville—done under the direct orders of J. Edgar Hoover.

At one time, I had flown to Washington, D.C., in a rage to confront Hoover and his FBI. I did get in to see Thomas B. Coll, whose role as Hoover's intimate and hatchet man was clarified after Hoover's death. I had compiled a list of the FBI agents who had gone to my parents, to the Tom Packs Circus staff, and to various people connected with me through my work. These names had been copied from the credentials the agents had presented and from the calling cards they had given to people who they had questioned about me. Coll denied categorically that any of the men on my list had ever worked for or were even known to the FBI.

"Why, somebody is playing a joke on you, Mr. Miles," he said dismissively. "I must ask you—have you ever been hospitalized for exhaustion or nerves?"

"No, I have not and you know it," I said, my anger growing.

"Well, Mr. Miles, I did a cross-check of both names on you—"

"Aha," I interrupted, "so you know about my name change. That explains a few things."

"As I was trying to say," he continued in a tone of irritation, "I checked our files and you are not and have *never* been under *any* kind of investigation by the FBI."

That was what I was waiting for. "You're a goddamned liar, Mr. Coll," I thundered. "Some time ago I applied for USO papers as an entertainer, and I voluntarily submitted to an FBI investigation of ten years of my life in order to be cleared for those papers. Good day, Mr. Coll!"

All those years, I had wondered why Hoover was so interested in me and whatever information I had on a certain president. Was it that he was genuinely trying to protect the president, or was it due to Hoover's obsession to learn the personal secrets of U.S. leaders in order to have power over them? Whatever the reasons, Hoover was the same unregenerately wretched man he had always been up to the day he died. There was never a time when he was even a decent man, much less one who would reach out and embrace the principles of the Christian faith. And the Assemblies of God was endorsing *this* man as a *model* Christian?

Surely, the Assemblies of God would never intentionally perpetrate a fraud. The men with whom I had just been meeting were not capable of that. Yet, a booklet detailing the "Christian conversion" of an American icon, the infamous Mr. Hoover, would certainly stir up a lot of interest and raise a lot of money for the Assemblies. With difficulty, I squelched my negative thoughts for the time being.

I returned to the Springfield headquarters several times while the miniature booklet about me was being put together. Each time, Reverend Zimmerman made a special point to greet me. I saw him as the most humble, loving, Godly man on earth.

*   *   *

The touring schedule of the Emmett Kelly, Jr. Circus permitted a few brief breaks. Rose Marie and I made several quick trips to various countries in Europe. Within the space of a few months, several letters with black borders arrived, each announcing the death of a member of Rose Marie's family. These letters diminished the happy times Rose and I had together. Each of the departed family members had disinherited her. "It's because I married you," she blurted out in exasperation.

I tried to reason with her. "Rose Marie, you disassociated yourself from them by moving to America. You never really spent any time with them or wrote to them. Naturally, they would leave everything to family members who are there and have been there." Rose Marie was not to be consoled that easily.

"Hang those inheritances anyway!" I said angrily. "The best thing that could happen is that all of them would disinherit you completely so that you would depend on me for support." I was sick of the way that everything in life seemed to hinge on money. What about just plain human relationships? Rose Marie's determination to be independent had become a trial for me.

During a ski trip in the French Alps, Rose Marie was having a bad morning and almost had an accident. Frightened and frustrated, she sat down in the snow and started to cry. At that moment, all of her willful independence was gone, and she looked uncharacteristically soft and delicate. I went to her, took her gently in my arms, and held her. That wonderful, tender moment seemed to relieve the tension between us.

One more black-bordered letter arrived. At first she read it with interest. Then she broke down, weeping angrily. "That no-good bastard!" she screamed, in one of the very few times I ever heard her use such a word. She dropped the letter and ran to the bathroom. I picked it up, and deciphered the High German in which it was written. Her father had died and left everything he had to an eighteen-year-old mistress. Rose Marie went to Switzerland immediately and sued her father's estate. She was awarded the four Chinese statues he had promised her.

Lori grew quickly. Mrs. Beck came twice a week to give her piano lessons. The sound of Lori playing Chopin, Bach, Schubert, and Mozart filled the apartment. She practiced several hours a day after school, in preparation to enter musical competitions. She won medals in most of them. During the summers, she attended finishing schools in the French part of Switzerland.

Computers had come to the airline and travel industry. Rose Marie had to go back to school to learn the new system.

Women's rights were making new strides forward. "Aha!" exclaimed Rose Marie, one day as she came in from work. "So, you don't like 'vomen's lib'! Vell, listen to dis: The family of a voman employee is now covered on her hospitalization; so, dis means you now haf hospitalization." She began to laugh. "So dere. The vomen have won!" I groaned silently.

Coleman McDuff had gone to South Bend, Indiana, to hold a crusade at a very large Assemblies of God church. Coincidentally, it was called "Calvary Temple," the name of the church where we had first appeared together in Springfield. He asked me to come and give my testimony, and I agreed. There was plenty of lead time for publicity about the converted ringmaster coming to speak, to assure a big crowd.

Pastor Jack West asked that I close the service in prayer. As the service was breaking up, a young, mod-looking couple got up and came down the aisle at a brisk clip. The man was stylishly dressed and had razor-cut hair. The young woman was a willowy beauty with long blond hair. I assumed they knew the pastor and were hurrying down to say hello to him before he disappeared into the crowd. But instead, they came straight to the front of the church and knelt at the altar. Others followed them and did the same.

The young man looked up at me misty-eyed and said, "We just saw the movie 'Marjoe' about an evangelist fraud, and decided on the spur of the moment to come to your meeting for a few laughs. But we saw something real here tonight, and want to give our hearts to Jesus!"

How ironic! Marjoe Gortner's grandparents helped found the Assemblies of God in 1914. They had the money-making potential of such a movement figured out well in advance. The family made Marjoe into a child evangelist with "special gifts." They put glitter in his hair, sewed extra-deep pockets in his clothing to hold the money, and pushed him mercilessly as they merchandised God. Marjoe grew up to be sick of the fraud and got out of the Assemblies of God altogether. But not before making the scathing documentary "Marjoe" exposing the movement's more tawdry aspects. The documentary won an award, and Marjoe later had a degree of success as a movie actor.

By the time I saw "Marjoe" I had been so totally swept up in Pentecostalism that the message of the film escaped me. I had accepted the stock explanation for such things: It was just one more attack by the devil to try to stop the Word of God.

After the gathering had broken up, Coleman McDuff and I went with Pastor West to his study. Pastor West sat in a big leather executive chair behind his desk, studying me intently. Coleman had a grin on his face. There were still sounds of excitement from some people who lingered in the sanctuary to pray or to "fellowship" with their fellow believers.

"Some people were healed tonight," said Pastor West. "I know the ones who were touched, and there is no way you could have known their condition in advance, to pray about them from the pulpit like you did. God was here with us tonight."

*   *   *

When I got back to New York, I tried to share my experiences with Rose Marie. She had been hearing about the healings that were being claimed as the result of my ministry, and took a totally dim view of them. "Please, Al," she said, "I'm asking you not to get too involved in the Bible and religion. I won't be able to take it."

"Rose Marie, you don't understand what's happening!"

"Yes, I do know what's happening and I don't like it. There has been nothing good about religion. Christian missionaries have destroyed entire cultures. As for dose healings, dey are either hypochondriacs or dey nefer had the disease to start with. Dose people get caught up in the hysteria of dose meetings, and will say anything for attention."

Rose Marie went off to bed. I could not accept what she had said. She was *wrong!* I had the power of God in me. God was using me—*me*—to heal people! God had chosen *me* to release His power. That was why people saw the aura of God around me. What's more, I, too, felt something when people were healed at my services. The devil knew this and wanted to stop me. That explained why I had experienced so many difficulties in life. I sat in the living room praying, busily turning these ruminations over and over in my mind, until the sky showed the pink glow of morning.

Within a few weeks, Lee Shultz notified me that my miniature booklet was stitched, bound, and ready to ship. It would be introduced on the "Revivaltime" broadcast the following Saturday night.

"The time you have been waiting for is here!" Reverend Shultz announced on the broadcast. "The new miniature booklet is ready. Austin Miles, the world's greatest circus ringmaster, met Jesus Christ in a circus tent when a man was raised from the dead. This dynamic, powerful witnessing tool is called, 'The Ringmaster Meets Jesus.' Here is Dr. C. M. Ward."

Dr. Ward, with his usual showmanship, hyped the story to the hilt. He emphasized again and again the point that "a man was raised from the dead when Austin prayed." I had never thought of the events in the circus tent in exactly that way. I had never drawn a connection between my experience and Jesus' raising of Lazarus from the dead. Nevertheless, Dr. Ward had built his whole talk around that idea, and he was a minister I particularly respected. Whenever I told the story from then on, it was Dr. Ward's version of it that I told, and not my own.

Dr. Ward boomed on about how my life had not been really happy and had been full of frustration until I allowed Jesus into my life. "As Austin says," he proclaimed to all the world, "the supreme satisfaction in life is to be locked in with Jesus. So, when you send your donation to 'Revivaltime,' ask for the free booklet, 'The Ringmaster Meets Jesus,' the story of Austin Miles, the greatest Christian witness of all times."

I sensed someone behind me and turned around. Rose Marie had been quietly standing there, listening to the broadcast. "What did they say the name of the booklet was?" she asked, with a look of disapproval on her face.

"The Ringmaster—Meets—Jesus." I was not comfortable saying it.

"Al, I must ask you a favor," she said solemnly. "Some time ago during a weak moment, I told you some personal things about my youth. Please forget that I told you those things."

Rose Marie was distancing herself from me. Still worse, I did nothing about it. Being a man called of God, I was to keep my eyes on Jesus only. Besides, the acclaim I was receiving *proved* that God's blessing was upon me. I wanted more of it. My true purpose in life had been defined. Nothing else mattered.

XVIII

"All we like sheep . . ."
—Isaiah 53:6

C ritics heralded the Emmett Kelly, Jr. Circus as an "artistic triumph!"
We gave two performances at the White House and were featured
in a national television commercial for Kodak. I had proved a point with
my concert hall stage circus concept, and was ready to move on. The show
reverted to the traditional circus format and continued without me.

I accepted a new contract as narrator for the famed Royal Lipizzan
Stallion Show. This would be a more refined style of announcing than
in my flamboyant circus ringmaster role. At age thirty-nine, I had added
a new dimension to my show business career.

Within a week after starting with the Lipizzan show, on Friday, August
17, 1973, I flew from Edmonton, Alberta, to Miami for the General Council
meeting of the Assemblies of God Fellowship. There, my miniature booklet
would be introduced and ten thousand copies would be distributed. I was
also listed as a guest speaker. John Finley, the director of the Lipizzan
show, took my place while I fulfilled this previously scheduled appearance.

When I got to the Miami Beach Convention Center, I was taken immediately to see Reverend Thomas F. Zimmerman. On the way to him,
we passed dozens of booths and displays. It was like a typical commercial
trade show, with the latest in church supplies, from choir robes to communion
sets, Bibles, Christian books, and gifts of every description, on display.
There were elaborate displays of the latest in audio and recording equipment.
The new high-speed audiocassette duplicating machines were attracting
particular attention, as "taping ministries" had come of age and a new
revenue generator had been born. "New, effective witnessing tools" were
exhibited in great profusion. Some were imaginative and clever; others,
crass and gimmicky. All were attention-getters.

Scattered everywhere were booths manned by evangelists who were
giving out brochures and showing film clips about themselves in the hope
of getting bookings. Gospel singers and music groups occupied other booths,

with the same end in view. The musicians performed constantly, before big posters telling who they were. The gospel singers watched for approaching ministers. When one came along, they would switch on an accompaniment tape and begin singing at the tops of their lungs while they clutched their brochures in their hands. To the unenlightened, this would have seemed like a spiritual supermarket.

When I eventually managed to work my way to the huge meeting room, Reverend Zimmerman welcomed me effusively and conducted me to the platform. Along with 17,000 ministers and their wives I sang "Clap Your Hands All Ye People," clapping to the beat, and popping up and down at the right times. After a flowery introduction from Reverend Zimmerman, I spoke.

After my brief talk, a flood of ministers approached me and invited me to speak in their churches. "My name is David Norris," said one of them, offering his hand. "I pastor a church in Sarasota, the circus capitol. I *must* have you in my church. This will reach a lot of people I've been trying to reach in that town."

"When your Lipizzan show comes to Milwaukee," another said, thrusting his calling card at me, "please let me know and I'll book you in my church, or, if you have some open time, I'll fly you there."

"Brother Miles," said a voice that stood out because it had neither a southern nor a Texas accent, "my name is Leon Cooke." I turned to see a scrawny man with a long, almost delicate face and penetrating cow-like eyes. His dark cropped hair lay flat on top of a head that seemed too big for his body. His mouth was large and his lips were full. He had rounded shoulders and slim hands with long fingers. I attributed his swollen wrist to arthritis. That intense, searching face on top of his slim frame gave Reverend Cooke a sort of artistic look. He would have looked perfectly at home in the middle of a symphony orchestra.

"I'm close to where you live in New York," he said. "I have a church in Bay Shore, Long Island, and I'd like to arrange a date with you." He gave me his card. "I'm also the Presbyter for the Long Island section," he continued, without missing a beat. "I'll book you in all the Long Island churches. We have something in common. I was a professional violinist before entering the ministry, so I know something about the field of show business."

"I knew it," I said to myself. There is an unmistakable look about someone who has been involved in the arts. I was especially happy to make his acquaintance. He would understand me and where I was coming from. "I'll call you as soon as I get back to New York," I told him.

Reverend Zimmerman had arranged for me to speak at Trinity Assembly, pastored by Ernie Eskelin. The Eskelins' son, Neil, was also in the ministry. That was the first of the bookings I got at the General Council meeting. An overflow crowd attended for each of the services. From that time forward, I would not have a free moment. The Lipizzan show usually played Friday, Saturday, and Sunday afternoon engagements in the same city, leaving me Sunday morning and evening to speak in an Assemblies of God church. Assemblies of God insiders saw to it that I had invitations everywhere I went.

I talked with Lee Shultz a few weeks later about how the booklet was advancing my ministry. "People are funny," he observed. "A woman sent back your booklet and said that 2 Corinthians 6:17 plainly states, 'Wherefore come out from among them, and be ye separate. . . .' She went on to say that there is no way you can call yourself a Christian when you are still in that sinful circus world. If you were truly born again, you would 'come out' of the circus and serve God. That was a letter that I took great pleasure in answering myself. I told her that you had a ministry right there, and if we took you out of the circus, who would witness to those people?"

Reverend Shultz had obviously seen a lot of blind, ignorant judging by God's people. I dismissed it as an isolated "nut" case, and did not reflect on how representative and symptomatic it might be.

Gradually, I stopped reasoning things out and stopped looking beneath the surface of events. Passively, I let my thoughts be programmed into that unquestioning, blind faith that the pastors carefully instill in the faithful as the only way to know God. That narrowing of my view, that closing of my mind, had become a vise that choked off free will and intelligent action. Instead, I let them fill my mind with stereotyped thoughts and falsified feelings. The displacement of my true thoughts and feelings produced a euphoric state and a sense of release from the evils, cares, and responsibilities of this world. It was like sweeping all those things under the rug. There was no room to question or challenge: such thoughts were simply enemies of faith. The pastor to whom one should submit would always be there to assist, to guide, and to have the last word.

Like most believers, I never bothered to think through the significance of likening the pastor unto a "shepherd" and his congregation to "sheep." Had I considered the matter with any degree of intelligence, it would have occurred to me that a sheep is one of the dumbest animals on four legs. Sheep don't even know enough to come in out of the rain. If one runs off a cliff, the others will blindly follow, to their deaths. The shepherd controls them completely, and however kind he may be in the meantime, his purpose is to shear them or, worse, lead them to the slaughter.

When I became "born again," when I lifted up my hands in "surrender to Christ," I became one of the "sheep." Why had I accepted such a brazen insult?

Ordained—PTL!

"For many are called, but few are chosen." – Matthew, 22:14

XIX

Everyone agreed that Austin Miles was good for the Assemblies of God church. I presented a positive image for the denomination, and my services were bringing in people who normally eschewed Pentecostal churches.

Once inside, the open friendliness extended to the visitor in such a church is so impressive that many return and eventually join the movement. That is, of course, the prime objective—church growth resulting in increased strength. I was an attraction who could get the new people in for that crucial first contact.

As with many Christian groups, the Pentecostals are constantly "encouraged" to "tithe" ten percent of their income to the church faithfully. They are also expected to give generously for "missions" and various "special offerings" over and above the tithe. There is much talk of giving "sacrificially."

I, too, was "moved" to give large cash gifts with, as one minister so delicately put it, "some of the money God has entrusted you with." I learned to equate giving money to "touching God." My existence was being justified by the benefits the church was reaping through me. Here, like nowhere else, it seemed I was totally loved, needed, and wanted. "God has made you an instrument of His blessing," pastors often said to me.

It was only a matter of time before I was encouraged to write to the New York District of the Assemblies of God in Syracuse to apply for ministerial credentials. Reverends Radke, McDuff, Cooke, and almost everyone else I talked to thought I should. "The Assemblies of God is the *only* church that preaches the full power of God for today, for this day and age. You are speaking in those churches. Miracles of healing have been taking place in the ministry God has given you. You should be officially recognized as a minister of the Assemblies. This would authenticate your ministry, since it would signify that you had submitted yourself to the discipline of a body of Godly men to oversee your work." I heard these words everywhere. Everyone seemed to be telling me the same thing.

It made sense. The world would have to take heed of me and respect me as a full-fledged ordained minister. The title "Reverend" would set me apart as a man of distinction, a man worthy of respect. I *liked* the sound of it.

The Lipizzan show was to play Binghamton, where the District Secretary for New York and an Executive Presbyter, Reverend R. D. E. Smith, lived. I wrote to the Presbytery and was instructed to contact Smith when I arrived. "Praise the Lord!" I shouted when that letter arrived. "God has worked this all out in advance."

Reverend Smith and Pastor Ernest Steffensen of the First Assembly of God in Binghamton met me for breakfast at the Treadway Inn. A tall man, Reverend Steffensen possessed a movie star's good looks. The pretty, blond hostess of the restaurant flashed him what appeared to be a very familiar smile. "That was a wonderful sermon you preached Sunday morning," she chirped. Surely, I did not detect a flirtation here.

Later Reverend Steffensen questioned me for six straight hours regarding my suitability for Assemblies' ordination. After all, it was essential to be sure that only men of the highest quality, men who lived lives of uncompromised holiness, be allowed in the ranks of these virtuous men of God. I welcomed and appreciated the strict procedure. I was approved to take the examination and assigned sixty-five short essays in the two weeks before the next district presbyters' meeting. "Use and quote Scripture as much as possible to back up your answers," Reverend Smith advised me. I spent every spare minute on the road in a library or some other quiet place working on the essays. God's hand seemed to be manifest in the booking of the Lipizzan show in Hershey, Pennsylvania, where the public library served all my resource needs for the joyfully undertaken homework.

On the day of the meeting, October 15, 1973, I drove from Utica to Rochester for an early morning television interview, and then rushed to Syracuse for the 9:30 A.M. meeting. I completed the last essay in the car during a gas stop on the New York Thruway. First, my essays had to be approved. I passed! Next, a written examination under supervision. Passed!

I was then taken in to be presented before the Presbytery—seventeen dour looking men seated around a long table. Reverend Joseph Flower, the Superintendent for the New York District, sat at the head of the table. As I walked in the door, they turned around in unison with obvious curiosity.

"Brother Miles," Reverend Flower asked, "why have you come to the Assemblies to apply for ordination?"

"I've been speaking only in Assemblies of God churches," I answered. "I agree with the theology of the Assemblies, and here is where I feel God wants me to be."

The Presbytery put me through a rigorous verbal examination about the Bible. "Brother Miles," asked one of them gravely, "how would you interpret Matthew 8 where it tells about how Jesus cast the demons out of the insane man? The demons pleaded with Jesus to let them go into a warm body, so Jesus cast them into a herd of swine and the swine ran violently over a cliff and were killed."

I pondered this incredible story for a moment. "Well," I reasoned, "wasn't it against the law for a Jew to eat pork? So, if it was a Jew who owned the swine, he would have been defying the law. If a Gentile owned them, he would have been guilty of tempting his Jewish neighbor. That was a double problem. So, Jesus cast the demons out of the man, thereby healing him, the demons went into the swine, the swine jumped over the cliff and were killed, and Jesus had solved all the problems with one whack!"

The presbyters sat bolt upright over that one and exchanged poker-faced glances. One discreetly moved his legal pad in front of him and jotted down some notes.

"Brother Miles," said another presbyter, anxiously, "what do you think of the story in 2 Kings 2:23, where the children mocked Elisha, calling him 'thou bald head,' and Elisha cursed them in the name of the Lord, and then two she-bears came out of the woods and tore the children up? Would you feel that was unreasonably harsh judgment upon children?"

"It does seem unusually harsh from a merciful God. I think the word 'children' is where the problem is. I read once where Abraham was referred to as 'the child Abraham.' I did some checking of biblical time frames and figured that the 'child' Abraham, as he was called, had to be about thirty-one years of age. So the 'children' involved in that story could very well have been adults. 'Thou bald head' was the height of insults, meaning no truth or substance in the head. Elisha was a man next to God, so that could have been considered a blasphemous statement by rebellious adults who should have known better—and an insult to God Himself, due to Elisha's standing with him. It was a very primitive time, and God handled it in a very primitive way."

"What about the Song of Solomon?" asked still another.

"It's an expression of the intense passion Solomon had for the Shulamite girl. It's quite clear."

The Presbytery unanimously disagreed. "It is an allegory of the love Christ has for the church. Would you consider enrolling in the Berean Bible School if we ordain you?"

This astonished me. Even in my compliant frame of mind at that time, I knew that the Song of Solomon had been written 1014 years before the birth of Christ. It took an overactive imagination to find a parallel. The idea of comparing the steaming sexual lust of Solomon to the love of Christ offended me. Couldn't Christians just accept that God's Word contained a candid acknowledgment that one of the Bible's "stars" was turned on by a woman? I stood my ground, and suspecting that there would be other such differences, I agreed to take the Berean Bible course by correspondence.

After a long period of what I considered stimulating questions, I was asked, "Brother Miles, you've been active in a life in public. What would you advise someone wanting success in public life?"

"Here's my advice," I responded without hesitation. "There are two steps. First, heed Matthew 6:33: 'But seek ye first the kingdom of God, and His righteousness; and all these things will be added unto you.' Secondly, when success comes, don't believe your own publicity."

"I'd like to remind some of our ministers of point two," Reverend Flower quipped.

They excused me from the room to deliberate. It took less than a minute. They came out all smiles and welcomed me into the family. I was licensed immediately and told I would be ordained at the District Council meeting the following May. They were making an exception in my case to the usual two-year waiting period between licensing and ordination. I looked at my watch. It was 9:00 P.M. Twelve and a half hours of questions and examinations!

"Join us for something to eat," suggested Reverend Smith, "we're all going to a Chinese restaurant."

"Where did you receive 'the Baptism'?" asked Reverend Almon Bartholomew at dinner. He was referring to the Baptism of the Holy Spirit. Special emphasis on this "second blessing," based on Acts 2:3-4, is a hallmark of Pentecostalism.

"At a Full Gospel Businessmen's meeting in New York," I replied. I had gone through this ritual several times. Finally, I let out a string of unintelligible syllables. I had not felt anything earthshattering within or outside my body at the time, but the evangelist, Robert Thom, declared that I had received it. That had fulfilled a requirement for my being recognized as a Pentecostal Christian.

"What about your water baptism?" Reverend Bartholomew continued.

"As I mentioned earlier," I replied, "I was baptized as a baby in the Presbyterian church."

"You'll have to be officially baptized into the Assemblies of God by immersion. This should have been done before licensing you. But we can take care of that in my church. Let's check your schedule to see when you'll be near Webster, and I'll also book you as a speaker at the same time."

When the appointed time for my ordination came seven months later, on May 20, 1974, the scheduling had again been "worked out by God." I had a day off from the Lipizzan show between cities and was able to get an early morning flight to New York.

*   *   *

"Rose Marie, please come with me to Utica for my ordination ceremony. This is the most important moment of my life and I want you to share it with me."

She flatly refused. "I did not marry a minister, I will not be married to a minister, and, what's more, I vould nefer haf married a minister!"

I couldn't understand it. Everyone who knew us could see that as I drew closer to God, my attitude toward life and toward others had improved remarkably. Gone were the hostilities and the impatience. "I must admit," Rose Marie agreed, "that you have become a better person since you got involved in all dis, but dis just isn't for me."

The District Council meeting that night was well covered by the press. Before I went in, a reporter asked me, "Isn't any of your family here?"

I choked back the emotion welling up within me. Taking some comfort in the large crowd going in the doors of the church, I gestured toward them saying, "Take a look. I'd say my family is very well represented here." This recognition by my new "family" of God, extolling the favor I had supposedly found with Him, was rapidly becoming more important to me than Rose Marie. Her needs had become secondary. Ministers had begun telling me that every man entrusted with a great ministry had to pay a great price. "P. C. Nelson once said, 'I've paid that price everyday,' " Reverend Smith entoned solemnly. A distinct "martyr" quality was evident in many Assemblies of God ministers, and I was beginning to take on the same mentality.

I became resigned to the prospect that Rose Marie would be part of the price I would have to pay. It was something I would just have to accept in good spirit, without complaining. The counsel I was receiving from various ministers led up to this, but I still had difficulty accepting it. I loved Rose Marie and the home we had together very much.

Lively hymns rang out in the church. "Clap Your Hands All Ye People" seemed especially joyous. More than four hundred ministers were present. Even though there were only a few minutes before the ceremony, I was ushered into an anteroom. One of the ministers asked me to pray for his healing. He said he had a brain tumor, and there was a noticeable swelling on the upper right side of his head. His eyes winced from the pain that could no longer be controlled by medication.

Together with the other ministers who had gathered I laid hands on him and prayed. Everyone present gasped as the swelling appeared to go down. The pain left him, and his eyes relaxed. Everyone in the room shouted and clapped. One jumped up and down. Out in the sanctuary, the gathering was singing "Power In The Blood." It was, to me, a most auspicious beginning to my life as an ordained Assemblies of God minister.

We went out. The ceremony began. There was a hush as my name was called. Superintendent Flower asked my intentions.

"To serve God and the body of Christ as His minister," I responded.

The ministerial charge was given me by Reverend R. D. E. Smith. Standing directly in front of me as I knelt at the altar, he read the charge from 2 Timothy 4:1-5:

> I charge thee therefore before God, and the Lord Jesus Christ, who shall judge the quick and the dead at his appearing and his kingdom. Preach the word: be instant in season, out of season; reprove, rebuke, exhort with all longsuffering and doctrine. For the time will come when they will not endure sound doctrine; but after their own lusts shall they heap to themselves teachers, having itching ears. And they shall turn away their ears from the truth, and shall be turned unto fables. But watch thou in all things, endure afflictions, do the work of an evangelist, make full proof of thy ministry.

"Brother Miles," said Joseph Flower, standing on the platform, "with the authority vested in me as Superintendent of the New York District of the Assemblies of God, I ordain you to the Christian ministry." He then asked the Presbytery to come forward, lay hands on me, and offer prayer. "The laying on of hands signifies that you have been 'set apart,' " Reverend Flower concluded. He then asked me to speak.

The crowd in the sanctuary seemed especially attentive to my words. They had never met a ringmaster before, and I was a curiosity to them. I felt grateful to them for accepting me, when mine was such a strange background to them.

Concluding my talk, I said, ". . . there have been many adventures and events in my life, and many rewards. I've had the opportunity to mingle with people in every walk of life. I've known the worst of life, and the best of life. But of all the events, nothing has ever been—or could be—more significant to me than this night, to be ordained into this great fellowship. This is truly the happiest night of my life."

I really felt that way. But it surprised me that I had been, quite frankly, damned nervous giving that talk.

Many of the ministers came to offer me the "right hand of fellowship." "I had to be here tonight," Reverend Joseph Sutera said to me with tears in his eyes, "to believe God for special miracles to come through your ministry."

"A lot of men are upset by what happened here tonight," said another.

I turned in surprise. The voice belonged to Reverend Frank Becker. Despite the rebuking words, he had a sweet smile on his face. "Most of us have to try three or four times before we get our license," Reverend Becker continued. "Then there's the two-year wait to be ordained. It means nothing to be a licensed minister to a community. You're a second class citizen. But we have to spend two years that way. Yet you come along and they rush you right on through. This doesn't seem right to a lot of people. Oh, but don't misunderstand. I'm happy for you that God is blessing you. In fact, I would like for you to come and speak in my church in Troy."

R. D. E. Smith overheard the conversation. "With the way God has been using you and the way you have become a chaplain to show business, we couldn't give you less than full ordination." Reverend Smith took that opportunity to inform me that I would be expected to support the New York District financially, along with an offering to headquarters each month.

"Does tithing my money mean ten percent of the gross—before any deductions?"

"Yes," answered Brother Smith.

"Reverend Smith," I said, looking around, "I've seen everyone from the Presbytery here except Reverend Ernest Steffensen." Since he had been the one to make the initial determination of my worthiness for the ministry, and had gone about it so thoroughly, I would have thought that he of all people would be present.

"Ernest Steffensen is no longer with us," said Reverend Smith slowly. "He was caught in an improper relationship with a church organist, and has been dismissed. It had been going on for some time. In fact, he had the church put in a special direct line to her from the church office. He said he had to be able to reach her at a moment's notice. Her husband overheard one of the phone calls, discovered some love letters from Brother [the title, 'Brother,' was automatic] Steffensen, notified Brother Steffensen's wife, and everything came out."

I was stunned. At the very moment that Steffensen was passing judgment on me to determine my "fitness" for the ministry, he had been engaged in an unusually sordid adultery.

XX

I think it's wonderful, Daddy," Lori replied when I told her about my ordination to the ministry. "I'm so proud of you."

"If you vere going to go into the ministry, you should haf gone into the Episcopal church," Rose Marie grumbled while I was repacking for another trip. "That's where the better people, the *wealthy* people go."

Rose Marie's manner was colder than usual. That increasing coldness had carried over into the bedroom, causing me much frustration. How I longed for her to be a Godly, loving, Christian wife, sharing the "joy of Jesus" with me. I found myself making invidious comparisons between my situation and the Christian homes and pacific families of the ministers. Such an intense sense of peace filled their homes. The wives were loving, softspoken, unshakably supportive of their husbands, and I was quite certain, sexually responsive to them. I saw a quality displayed in their family lives that I decidedly lacked in my own. Because of their example, I became more and more dissatisfied with Rose Marie and my life generally.

When the Lipizzan show returned to Miami Beach, I was booked for the second time at the Trinity Assembly of God. The service that morning seemed unusually charged, and many testified to having been healed during the closing prayer.

"Brother Miles," said the elder Reverend Eskelin, "this is Lyn McMann. You have something in common with her. She was an actress and model in New York before giving her life to Jesus."

Lyn was dressed in a sailor-style dress. Her dark brown hair hung in pigtails. The mock juvenile look set off her ripe beauty irresistibly and conveyed a disarming air of naïveté and accessibility. The paradox caused an impression of warm sensuality to come across to me. A closer look made me take notice that her face and figure were superb.

"Hello," she said, in her beautiful speaking voice. "I must tell you that I have never been so moved in any service as I was in this one. The presence of the Holy Spirit was overwhelming. I was also healed this morning. I'll never forget this service."

Over lunch, Pastor Eskelin told me, "Lyn McMann is married to quite a wealthy man. He owns some race horses."

"Is he a Christian?" I asked.

"No. There are some serious problems in that marriage."

Later, I thought, "How ironic. Why couldn't God have put someone like her in my life instead of Rose Marie? We would have been perfect for each other. We have similar backgrounds and we're both 'born-again' Christians."

*   *   *

The cast of the Royal Lipizzan Stallion Show were not only supportive of my ordination to the ministry, but almost immediately started coming to me for counseling. It seemed to come as no surprise to most of the people who had known me in show business that I had entered the ministry. I gave out gift-wrapped Bibles to everyone in the company, and established chapel services backstage every Sunday morning before the performance.

My Sunday mornings would begin with a service in a local church. In some churches, two successive morning services were held. From there I would dash to the arena for chapel service. I held these in a large dressing room if one were available, or where the portable stalls for the horses were set up, with a hay bale as a pulpit. That left me just enough time to get ready for the afternoon performance. After the performance, some minister who had been in the audience as my guest would take me to his church for the evening service. It was a demanding schedule, with little time to eat, sleep, or reflect. My all-consuming love for God was imbuing me with power, and I felt I had a real purpose in my life for the first time. Show business had become just a means to the end of spreading the Word of God.

Dramatic manifestations of healing were becoming more and more commonplace in the Sunday public services. Occasionally, one of those healings would be discussed on the radio or in the local news media. Members of the show would hear about them on their car or truck radios as we traveled to the next engagement. This increased their interest in the backstage chapel services, and prompted requests for prayer.

One morning when we were in South Carolina, someone knocked on my motel room door. A tall thin woman with ash blonde hair waited for me to open the door. She held in her hands a package and a cake.

"Brother Miles?"

"Yes?"

"It was difficult for me to find out where you were staying, but I had to meet you. When I saw your name in the papers, I said to myself, 'This man has something to do with my father.' I called him, and he told me the whole story."

"Who is your father?"

"A. J. Clark. He was seriously ill with cancer. He told me that you prayed for him in Springfield, and he was completely healed." I invited her inside. "I brought you a couple of things in appreciation. I made you this nut cake. And," she continued, "I brought you this church communion set to use in your chapel services."

"And your father is—still healed—totally?"

"Totally, Brother! Praise God!"

I all but shut the world out of my life entirely, spending every spare moment studying the Bible, particularly the scriptures concerning healing. I also read every book I could find on that subject. I began calling Assembly of God ministers in every city where the Lipizzan show played and inviting them and their families to the show as my guests. "The only catch," I said to one pastor, "is that you and your family join me afterwards for coffee and refreshments. I need your fellowship."

The Lipizzan show was booked in the Coliseum in Charlotte, North Carolina. Coleman McDuff had put me in touch with Hubert Morris, pastor of the Trinity Assembly of God Church on Scaleybark Road. I was scheduled to speak in his church at both the morning and evening services on Sunday, November 3, 1974. I made an advance publicity trip to Charlotte two weeks before the performance and visited Reverend Morris.

"Do you have any free time next week?" the pastor asked.

"Yes. Next Wednesday."

"Could you possibly come back here then? I can get you booked as a guest on a Christian television program here in Charlotte which will help publicize our meeting. And it would also help your show. It's called 'The PTL Club.' It's very popular. Ever hear of it?"

"No, I don't think so."

"It's getting big," Pastor Morris said with enthusiasm.

"What does 'PTL' mean?" I asked.

"Praise the Lord!" he answered, with an exuberance that made his words seem more like a sudden exclamation than an answer to my question.

"Oh. Who's the host?"

"The host is a young Assemblies minister I know you would like. His name is Jim Bakker."

* * *

I had appeared on several local Christian radio and TV talk shows around the country with a variety of ministers and hosts. But Jim Bakker radiated a magnetism, a "charisma," that distinguished him from anyone I had ever met in that field. His natural broadcasting ability added to his distinctive, unforgettable personality.

Perhaps his contrasts made Jim such a fascinating presence. His looks and build were certainly not what one would expect in a "star." Short and overweight, he had a round face and thick, long, dark hair in the style of that era. He looked like a pudgy, overgrown kid. He had nothing of the usual confident star attitude. On the contrary, he seemed unsure of himself. People felt compelled to help him. It was mainly volunteer labor that had transformed the former furniture store at 6500 East Independence Boulevard into a remarkably elegant television studio. Jim's message was sincere and without pretense. His audience was growing rapidly. The PTL Network had grown from three to nine stations in the short time since the studio opened.

Jim's humility put me at ease. Obviously, he loved Jesus and loved people in general. It was very important to him to be loved back. He sought approval constantly, insatiably. He was so anxious not to offend that whenever a controversial issue came up, or he felt obligated to take a position he felt might not be popular, he would raise the pitch of his voice, almost to a falsetto, so as to appear as unaggressive as possible while explaining his point.

Jim introduced me to Tammy Faye. If ever there was a marriage made in heaven, this had to be it. They were built so much alike it looked as if they had been eating from the same plate. Both were short. Even their respective excess pounds had the same proportion and the same distribution. Tammy was more outgoing than Jim, and more loquacious. She had a natural, cute, appealing look. She wore very little make-up then, just enough to keep her face from washing out in the harsh television lights.

The harmony of this place impressed me most. Everyone connected with the PTL ministry was extremely gracious, and they all appeared to have great peace in their hearts. Jim was the perfect television host. He asked just the right questions at just the right times. There seemed to be nothing contrived or stilted about it. Everything came from the heart. The expert camera work and direction made me look better on television than I ever had before. The audience response to my appearance was positive. All the phones lit up. "The PTL Club" presented a first-class production right from the start.

After the telecast, dinner was served in the studio dining room. Jim and Tammy were eager to get to know me. Perhaps they felt freer to draw close to me than to many of the religious leaders who were their guests, because of my own very active public life in show business. "I always loved show business," Jim said to me. "I would probably have been in it myself, had God not called me to the ministry."

"I've never seen a more effective television ministry," I said to Jim.

"God has really blessed us," Jim replied, "but it hasn't been easy. The devil has fought us every step of the way."

"You're not kidding!" Tammy interjected. "When we lost that television station in California, that really did it. We thought the world had ended."

"We'd worked so hard getting that station started," said Jim, picking up where Tammy had left off. "We put our very souls into it. Then it was literally stolen out from under us. We were discouraged. We've had to start all over again—from scratch. We found ourselves in a position where we *had* to *totally* rely on God. There was nothing else we could do. But we can see God's hand in all of it now. Our faith is stronger than it's ever been. There's no doubt in our minds that God wants us here in Charlotte. One thing's for sure. I'm going to do things differently this time. Nobody will *ever* take a television ministry away from us again."

"AAAMEN!" Tammy responded.

Jim and Tammy were sensitive to the point of being fragile. They had built the Trinity Broadcasting Network (TBN) up from nothing. Then their employers, Paul and Jan Crouch, dumped them. That betrayal had hurt Jim and Tammy deeply. Still, they were open, trusting, and vulnerable. "Dear God," I prayed to myself silently, "protect them."

"Have you always been a Christian, Tammy?" I asked, returning from my momentary reverie.

"Since I was a little girl," she answered. "I love Jesus so much. I could never repay Him for what He's done for me." Tears began to well up in her eyes. "My life was hard. My family was very poor. When I was little I had—epilepsy. Jesus completely healed me, and for that I'll serve Him for the rest of my life."

"I have such a positive feeling about your ministry," I said to Jim. "I'm so glad to be able to be a part of the beginning of it. You know, I have a powerful feeling that 'The PTL Club' will grow beyond all expectations and have the most profound impact on the world of any ministry in history."

This was not a prophetic utterance. It was just a sincere gut reaction.

*   *   *

Before I left Charlotte, Judy Stubbs, Jim's producer, booked me for another appearance on PTL. I would be coming back through Charlotte in two weeks, on my way to another city with the Lipizzan show. Since PTL could not yet afford to pay guests' travel expenses, they had to get people on the program as they were coming through.

My friendship with Jim and Tammy grew closer during those early visits, and we always looked forward to having dinner together after the telecasts.

"Jim is always tired after the telecast," Tammy told me, "and he likes to take a nap afterwards." Two solid hours on television does take its toll. The biggest secular television personalities spend a fraction of that amount of time on camera. In Jim's case, the administrative responsibility rested on his shoulders as well. Even though the response was growing and was all favorable, there was always the nagging feeling that the audience might not like you tomorrow, and it could all go down the drain.

I looked at Jim, Tammy, and their little girl, Tammy Sue. There was a sweet innocence about this closely knit little family. "Look Tammy Sue," Jim said after opening a package. "Here's the new 'Tammy Sue DOLL'." This was one of the first PTL promotional items.

I had been functioning in a harsh world of slick show business, where it seemed that everyone was trying to outsmart everyone else. I found the Bakker family and PTL very refreshing, indeed a refuge, and I always looked forward to returning.

My appearances on PTL were growing more popular. It showed in my increasing ability to draw worshipers to my church appearances. During one of my PTL appearances a note was handed to me. Gary Lashinsky, the producer of the Royal Lipizzan Stallion Show, had been watching the telecast. He had called to say that he was impressed and touched by the telecast, and to encourage everyone to keep up the good work. Coming from a Jewish person who was also my boss, this call had particular significance. Yes, this represented still another powerful confirmation that God had His hand on me and that I was absolutely right in putting my ministry above anything else.

XXI

Back in New York during a schedule break, I went to see Reverend Leon Cooke. As he skillfully sank the five ball in the side pocket of the pool table in the recreation room of his parsonage, he confided, "We've got a problem with a minister out here, and we're not sure what to do about him." He looked pleased with his shot, and walked around the pool table to plan his next one. "His name is Eugene Profeta. He's got the Massapequa Tabernacle Assembly of God."

"What's wrong with him?" I asked.

"He's—extravagant. He tips his hairdresser twenty dollars."

"What about his ministry?" I stopped in the middle of my shot and looked up at Cooke.

"I don't know. There's a lot of things I don't like."

This seemed odd. Tipping too generously hardly seemed serious enough to warrant hindering a pastor in his work. It seemed to me that a discreet reprimand about prudent stewardship of the Lord's funds would have been sufficient. I couldn't see that it was a weighty matter, requiring lengthy deliberations.

Profeta's church was practically on the doorstep of Reverend Cooke's. Massapequa Temple had attracted so large a following that it overflowed the building. Some of Reverend Profeta's distinctive devotional practices were a bit much, to say the least.

Once a week, he would wear a long, seamless robe—nothing else—and encourage his congregation to touch the hem of his garment, emulating the Gospel accounts in Matthew 9:20-22 and Mark 5:25-34 of a woman with chronic menstrual bleeding who touched the hem of Jesus' garment and was healed. Ardent followers of Reverend Profeta "testified" enthusiastically that they had, indeed, been healed by taking part in these strange proceedings.

Another odd ritual that taxed credulity even further involved a corpulent woman evangelist Reverend Profeta brought in frequently. She would "fall out in the Spirit" in the middle of her preaching. Worshipers would come and touch her quivering body and then claim divine healing of all manner of ailments. These theatricals, along with the "testimonies" of the healing power manifested through them, brought throngs of the gullible and the curious to Massapequa Tabernacle, and made the name of Eugene Profeta famous on Long Island. My reaction was simply that God works in mysterious ways. To me, the authenticity of the many "testimonies" of miraculous healings seemed clear. Who was I, after all, to question God's infinite wisdom in selecting His servants and determining how He would work through them?

Reverend Cooke continued to inflame the matter until he finally persuaded the denomination to dismiss Profeta, charging him with "desecrating the pulpit." I heard two versions of the events upon which the charge was based. One had it that Profeta, during an energetic, emotional sermon, had jumped up on top of the pulpit. In the other version, he is supposed to have given a pulpit mounted on casters a vigorous shove, sending it rolling across the stage. I could find no provision in the Assemblies' Bylaws—much less the Bible—warranting putting a minister out of his pulpit for either of those actions, or anything resembling them. Why had the Presbyters chosen trumped-up grounds like that? And even if the stories of Profeta's extravagance were true, would a dismissal based on them have been legitimate?

Reverend Profeta's influence over his flock proved so powerful that his entire congregation rallied behind him when the Assemblies tried to put him out of his pulpit. The Assemblies resorted to a court case, and lost.

Profeta gained more support than ever. At Christmas, he rented the huge Nassau Coliseum and held a televised "gift service" for the people of New York. He used the occasion to publicly thumb his nose at the Assemblies. No offering was taken at the service, but the stratagem brought hundreds more into his church, where offerings *were* taken.

Reverend Profeta's pulpit manner continued to be flamboyant and was the subject of much discussion. One night in the middle of a sermon he suddenly stopped, reached in his pocket, took out some money, and gave it to a man in the front row, asking him to go to the McDonald's across the street and bring back two hamburgers. Profeta resumed preaching until the man returned with the hamburgers and handed them up.

Profeta took the bag, walked down the aisle, and gave the hamburgers to a gaunt looking man. "You haven't eaten anything for two weeks, because you have cancer in your stomach," he said to the emaciated man. "God told me He has healed you. Now take these hamburgers and eat them."

Shouts of "Glory," "Amen," and "Praise the Lord" went up, as the man, who reportedly had not been able to keep any food down for a very long time, ate and digested the hamburgers. Reverend Profeta had never met the man or been told of his serious condition.

I did not know what to make of Eugene Profeta, or even Leon Cooke at that moment.

*   *   *

Going through the usual accumulation of mail at the apartment, I thumbed through some issues of *Advance* magazine, a monthly for Assemblies of God ministers. In each issue, themes were laid out for the coming month. One Sunday would be "men's day"; another, "walk in victory day." There were tear-out posters to put up in advance of the service oriented to the corresponding theme. My surprise grew when I found, along with the themes, complete sermon outlines for each week, right down to the Scripture references to be used to drive each point home.

The preachers and evangelists had always given me the impression that God, Himself, had given them the message for the hour. Gradually, I began to notice how, once you became an ordained minister, everything was thought out for you. That took away a lot of the pressure.

Rose Marie watched as I was stuffing some eight-by-ten envelopes with photos and written materials. "Vat are you doing?" she asked.

"Sending out publicity materials to the churches where I'll be speaking."

"Oof, dis is all too planned out."

"The pastors need this information for the newspapers and radio so they will know my background and what the services are all about. They wouldn't know anything about me at the meetings otherwise."

"It's too much like a big business to me," she said.

Rose Marie and I were drifting apart. I paid little attention to her needs. I took her for granted. Wrapped up in myself, in the fascinating world of my ministry and in the acclaim that came with it, I simply tuned her out. I did absolutely nothing to nourish our marriage. I was no longer interested in going out with her friends or listening to what she had to say. I may have been chasing a star, but I certainly was not one of the wise men.

One morning she asked me if I would walk her to the subway. She left for work at 7:00 A.M., and, as I had been keeping late hours on the road, I did not want to get up at such an early hour. I wanted to sleep late and then leisurely read the newspapers. She was crestfallen that I wouldn't make even that small effort to be with her a few more minutes before the long work day separated us. My every action telegraphed that she was least among my priorities.

The large cash gifts that I felt obliged to give as a "born-again" Christian pushed Rose Marie over the line that separates opposition from hostility. "Not only dat," she said, during another heated discussion about Christianity, "it turns out that Mrs. Beck is vun of dose religious fanatics and she talks to Lori about Jesus. I vould fire her and get another piano teacher for Lori if she wasn't such a good teacher."

I smiled a mincing, pious smile. Yes, God, in His infinite wisdom, had taken care of this matter too! He had put a good, Christian witness right in my home to be with Lori in my absence. I felt smug and self-righteous.

*   *   *

The pressure of maintaining a proper public image—avoiding any "appearance of evil"—began to gnaw at me. I was becoming self-conscious about where I went and who I was seen with in public. During the Christmas season—seven months after my ordination—Rose Marie informed me that a good friend of hers, Ken Woodward, a co-worker at TWA, would be joining us for dinner in Manhattan. Afterwards, we were to go to a concert of the Vienna Choir Boys at the Metropolitan Museum. I had just returned from another grueling tour schedule and did not feel up to going anywhere.

"Ken Woodward is a good friend," Rose Marie explained. "Ven I first came to dis country, I got a case of pneumonia. My lungs are weak, and dis could have been fatal to me. He and his roommate, Barclay, took me in their apartment and took care of me for over a month until I got well."

Ken Woodward turned out to be overtly homosexual. He had a schoolmaster's face with granny glasses perched on the end of his nose, and a piercing voice that carried across a room. I felt uncomfortable in his company. At dinner, Ken ordered drinks and wine for himself. Since I had given up alcohol when I joined the Assemblies, the presence of wine at the table added to my discomfort. It irritated me further that I would be picking up his tab.

In the museum, just after the concert began, my "churchy" attitude and fatigue collided. "That's it," I said to Rose Marie, getting out of my seat, "I can't take any more. I'm leaving. You go ahead and stay."

Woodward looked bewildered and hurt. "Well, I was having a good time—up until now," he said.

Rose Marie and Lori left with me. Outside on the sidewalk, Rose Marie broke down, crying hysterically. "I don't know what's happened to you. I've done nothing wrong. Ken is a good friend who *saved my life*. You should like him! I am blameless."

Thoroughly upset, Rose Marie began to hyperventilate, then to gasp for air. Her lungs were dangerously weak. The potential seriousness of the situation failed to register with me. I cared only that the entire episode was an affront to me as a minister of the Assemblies of God church.

*   *   *

The new year, 1975, began with an appearance in the Madison Square Garden Felt Forum with the Lipizzaner Stallions. At the same time, I was also to be officially installed as a missionary of Glad Tidings Tabernacle on West Thirty-third Street, just half a block from the Garden. On January 5, between performances, still wearing stage make-up, I dashed down the street to Glad Tidings and knelt at the altar before a packed church. Then, after the ceremony, I ran back to the Felt Forum, just in time for the next show.

The same week I officiated at a wedding between two members of the Lipizzan company. It took place between shows, with the bride, the groom, me, and the entire company on horseback. I invited Reverend Stanley Berg, pastor of Glad Tidings and Presbyter for the area, to witness the event so that he could make a proper report on how I handled such an unusual wedding. The news media, including all the major wire services and Religious News Service, covered the wedding. Darrell Turner of Religious News Service's editorial staff interviewed Rose Marie.

"My husband is sincere," the article quoted Rose Marie as saying. "But I am not comfortable with the exuberance of the Pentecostal religion. I come from a different background in Europe, of the quieter, more traditional church."

Reverend Berg made it a special point to talk to Rose Marie and to try to put her at ease. "Just know," he said to her, "that you are a part of our church family, and your needs are part of our concern also. We will assist you in any way possible. Please come to services any time you can. In the meantime, we will send you a regular *Monthly Bulletin* to keep you informed of the events and happenings at the Tabernacle."

Tears formed in Rose Marie's eyes. Reverend Berg's warmth and concern deeply touched her. "You see?" she said to me later, "Reverend Berg is a *real* minister. He's been a minister all his life. You can't just suddenly pop up and be a minister like you did. This takes years and years of study."

I told myself that if Rose Marie ever accepted Christ and became "born again," she would understand. During the final Sunday with the show in New York, Rose Marie agreed to attend a service with me at Glad Tidings. It was one of those days when it would have been better to have stayed at home. First, there was a strange, disturbed looking woman in a beehive-type bonnet, who set up her marimba and was attempting to play a hymn for the congregation on it. She said she felt "anointed" to do so. Others got carried away and began twitching, trembling, and moaning as they shouted out their praises to the Lord. Then, after the scripture reading by Pastor Berg, a tall, older woman standing straight as an arrow came up to me, looked me in the eye, and said, "Kabal-loop-teesakay!"

Hesitantly, I turned to look at Rose Marie. "She's speaking to you," Rose Marie said, with a gesture of her hand and a perfectly straight face. Surely, the unenlightened would think this place a lunatic asylum.

While saying good night to Reverend Berg, a woman came up to Rose Marie with a friendly smile, offered her her hand, and said, "I'm going to keep you in my prayers, Sister Miles. I know it's difficult for you when your husband is away. He *is* very good looking, and you never know exactly what he's doing when he's away from you." Rose Marie pulled her hand away and stared at the woman for a moment.

When we were back in our apartment in Forest Hills, Rose Marie said, "Don't *ever* ask me to go to one of dose places with you again."

"Rose, this day was completely out of left field. This is not the way it usually is. This was just one of those wacko days, and for the life of me I cannot understand why it had to happen today of all days when you were there."

Rose Marie stared at me, looking doubtful. The thoughtless, if not downright vicious, comment by the woman at Glad Tidings, volunteering to "uphold" Rose Marie "in prayer," had touched a sore nerve. "Maybe— that woman knows things about you that I don't," said Rose Marie.

XXII

G wen Weeden, the wardrobe mistress of the Royal Lipizzan Stallion Show, looked up in surprise when she saw me walk in the stage door of the arena in Shreveport, Louisiana. "We didn't think we would see you today," she said solemnly.

"Oh yes," I replied, "I wouldn't miss doing the show. Not only that, today is Sunday, and I expect everyone to be at the chapel service."

Later, while conducting the service in a large dressing room, I said, "One of the wonderful things about being a Christian is the assurance that life on earth is merely a preparation for the glorious time when we will all be with Jesus, and that death is not final, but a transition to eternal life. I guess all of you knew before I did that my mother made that transition last night."

The local sheriff had knocked at my motel room door to give me the news after contacting the show's manager to find out where I was staying. Right after the performance, I was taken to the airport for my flight to Evansville. As the next performance was not until Wednesday night, I arranged for my mother's funeral to be held Wednesday morning, so that I could fly back just in time for the show.

"How can you possibly preach at you own mother's funeral?" asked Margaret McCormick, my mother's best friend, astonished at the announcement.

"With great love and belief in Jesus Christ and His Word," I answered. My stepfather had died seven and a half years earlier. I had been out of the country when that happened, and had not been able to go to his funeral. My mother and stepfather had been well liked by the community, and my mother's funeral was well-attended.

I could think of no one more appropriate to officiate at this funeral than myself. Rose Marie and Lori came. The mourners did not know what to expect as I took my place behind the pulpit. I placed my hands firmly on the Bible. "Nehemiah 8:10 says, 'For the joy of the Lord is my strength,' " I said, in a strong voice, paraphrasing the verse. "I feel that strength in my heart this morning, because my mother went in great victory to be with the Lord. I am so glad my mother and I drew so close during these last few years, and that she made an even deeper commitment to Christ. I am also grateful that she hung onto God during those early, difficult years, and tried to instill in me a love for God at an early age. In fact, this Bible I have preached from since I entered the ministry is the one she gave me for a Christmas present when I was a boy."

After the service, I asked Lori, "Honey, did it make it easier for you to have Daddy preach Grandmommy's funeral?"

"Yes, Daddy," she said bravely. "Thank you. I'm so glad we're Christians. Otherwise I would fall apart."

Rose Marie and Lori got on a plane back to New York. When their plane was airborne, Rose Marie broke down and cried.

When my own plane took off, I looked out the window and saw the Masonic cemetery on a gentle rise at the end of the runway. I could pick out my mother's grave by the fresh flowers.

I arrived in New Orleans with enough time to get to Municipal Auditorium and make the evening performance. Reverend Radke and his family met me after the show and took me home with them to spend the night.

*   *   *

The Lipizzan show worked its way to California.

"The weekend you are in San Francisco," Reverend Zimmerman instructed me over the telephone, "I want you to speak at the People's Temple. Brother Jones would be greatly blessed by your ministry."

I knew nothing about Reverend Jim Jones or the People's Temple. Yet I had such a strange gut reaction that I made some excuse to Brother Zimmerman, and took a church in Oakland for that weekend instead.

I made a point of having the ministers and their families who came to the shows as my guests come backstage and meet the company afterwards. "They're all such nice people!" the show staff would often say to me. Among my visitors were an armed forces chaplain and his wife. The Assemblies of God church had been gradually achieving mainstream respectability. By recruiting people like me, with high public profiles, they hoped to gain favorable publicity and upgrade the denomination's image. The term "holy roller" was almost entirely forgotten. Having an Assemblies' minister accepted as a military chaplain had been a major breakthrough.

The chaplain and his wife invited me to their home for dinner. I watched the chaplain's wife as she prepared and served the food. There was a striking, peaceful radiance in her face, which to me seemed very loving. She was a little overweight, but the comfortable Christian glow about her somehow counteracted any unattractiveness in my mind. "They're all so soft-spoken," I thought to myself.

Why couldn't Rose Marie be like that? Why did she have to be such a shrew? Why did there always have to be such stress and turmoil around her? Here, even the dog and the cat seemed imbued with Christian tranquility.

After dinner, a couple with two small children dropped by unexpectedly. The children got rambunctious and knocked over a treasured porcelain vase, breaking it to pieces. With extraordinary control—without even flinching—the chaplain's wife kept smiling sweetly.

"Oh, my God!" exclaimed one of the parents. "This is terrible! I'm sorry! How can we repay you for this?"

"Don't worry about it," said the chaplain's wife softly. "Material things are not important. The only important thing is Jesus. We enjoyed it while we had it."

The couple gathered up their children and quickly left. After the wife swept up the remains of the vase, we resumed our conversation, but sensing tension in the air, I decided it would be a good time for me to take my leave. "Thank you so much for having me in your home," I said.

"Oh, it was our pleasure," the chaplain's wife answered agreeably. "God gave us this home to share."

"What a fantastic wife," I thought, almost out loud. When I took my hostess' hand to say goodbye, her palms were moist, and I could feel a slight, stiff trembling.

I went to my car, opened the windows, and took a few moments to study a road map before starting the engine. Borne on the gentle breeze, I heard the chaplain's wife's voice, harsh, angry, sounding almost like distorted slow motion, pronouncing those two handy monosyllabic words so often used to proclaim a stressful situation: "Ohhhh—Shit!"

*   *   *

I managed to be home for Lori's graduation from the eighth grade. A reception and dinner for her were held in an exclusive Westchester catering facility.

As had happened many times before, my adamant objections to having liquor or wine served at dinner caused tension. Rose Marie and I finally reached a compromise, allowing for a special bar to be set up in a separate room, where those guests desiring drinks could pay for them individually.

During that visit, I got to attend my first sectional meeting of New York City area ministers. The "messengers of God" were to meet at Faith Assembly on Hooker Avenue in Poughkeepsie. As I walked in the front door, I heard what sounded like a full-fledged brawl coming from the sanctuary. I supposed that all the shouting had to be the sound track of some film about the tensions of "the world."

As I rounded the corner and got a glimpse into the sanctuary, I was surprised to see that this was no film, but rather the ministers' meeting in progress!

"I'll tell you this much," Reverend Ellis Damiani, pastor of the hosting church and chairman of the meeting, yelled angrily from behind his pulpit. "If they do pass this idiotic measure, I'm walking out of the Assemblies of God and taking my church with me!"

The volatile mix of theology and finances had fired this meeting up to an uncontrollable fury. Everybody was yelling at once, some with fists clenched. Damiani, a short, overweight man who apparently thought he was the only one qualified to speak on the point, had reached such a peak of agitation that his face had turned beet red and the blood vessels in his face were throbbing.

My eyes roamed the sanctuary. Were these really the same men whose faces had been so peaceful and loving when I had seen them preaching Sundays in their respective churches? When the topic turned to district leadership, politics reared its even uglier head and things got still more heated, if that were possible. Outbursts were exploding like artillery shells all over the sanctuary. Quietly, I got out of my seat and made my way up the aisle and out the door. I got into my car, locked the door from the inside, and drove home.

*   *   *

Niagara Falls, New York, was one of the few places where I had had no invitation to preach when the Lipizzan show performed there. I took the initiative and wrote to Pastor Jack Piper of First Assembly of God on South Avenue. I enclosed a copy of the miniature booklet about me and a list of the churches where I had spoken. Pastor Piper replied:

Dear Mr. Miles:

In answer to your letter offering to speak in my church. Quite frankly, people in *this* part of the country would criticize your ministry if you spoke in church on Sunday morning, and then took part in *that* performance in Convention Hall in the afternoon. I'm sorry.

Sincerely yours in Christ,

/s/ Pastor Jack Piper.

Pondering his reply, I dropped Piper's letter into an envelope, together with a note of my own to Reverend R. D. E. Smith:

Dear Brother Smith:

You will be interested in the enclosed letter from Reverend Piper. It looks like a prophet is not without honor save in his own district. I do hope when Christ comes on *his* white horse, he'll have an easier time getting a congregation in Niagara Falls than I did. I'm going there with forty-two of them!

Yours in Him,

/s/ Austin

I felt that this was just another isolated incident. I refused to see it as indicative of the Pentecostal movement generally. Something else happened, though, not long after, that did briefly make me feel like throwing in the towel. The pastor of a church in Macon, Georgia, seemed strangely nervous when he got up to introduce me.

"Our guest speakah," the pastor enunciated in a deliciously slow Southern drawl, " is non otha than Austin Mahles—who is the naar-rate-err of the Royal *Lesbian* show."

*   *   *

The Assemblies of God decided to produce a TV series dramatizing various Christian testimonies, called "The Turning Point." The episodes were to be shot in Canada and hosted by David Mainse, whose national TV program "100 Huntley Street" is by far the most popular Christian broadcast in Canada. "David Mainse is the Billy Graham of Canada," Reverend Riley Kaufman of the Assemblies of God communication department explained to me.

I flew into and out of Canada to do my segment during a single day off. David Mainse was another of that type of TV host with a boyish, innocent quality. We worked well together, and I was happy to agree to return on another date to appear on "100 Huntley Street."

I had begun keeping a daily journal of my experiences in the ministry. It shows that in one year, I narrated 256 Lipizzan shows in 125 cities, preached 109 times in 70 different churches, appeared on 107 telecasts, 250 radio broadcasts, and gave innumerable newspaper interviews. I also taped 100 religious TV spots, carried on full responsibility as chaplain minister to the Lipizzan company, drove 63,000 miles by car, and logged 20,000 miles by plane. On one occasion, I outdid myself creating confusion by forgetting in what city I had left my car!

Reverend Cooke booked me in his church, Bay Shore Assembly of God, for both services of December 14, 1975. Although Rose Marie had reached a new plateau of irritation with me, she agreed to come to the service with Lori and me. I conducted the communion service, as well as delivering a "message" on faith.

I felt the time had arrived to coax Lori to play the piano for the first time before an audience. She took her place at the piano bench, sat quietly for a few moments, then placed her hands on the keyboard. She played the Mozart Piano Sonata #5 in G major. The audience was enthralled by her almost flawless presentation. It was a particular thrill for me.

After the service, we went to the home of Ken and Pauline Bouton for lunch. Ken was a retired police captain and a deacon of the church. After lunch, we went to the parsonage. Rose Marie responded particularly well to the Cookes. Esther Cooke was from Germany, as was Pauline. The three wives talked in German. We walked over to the church.

Reverend Cooke brought his violin with him. "I broke my wrist several years ago, and it never did set properly," he explained. "Because of it, I could not continue as a professional violinist. But I can still play." Lori accompanied him on the piano, and they played classical music together for over an hour.

Rose Marie insisted that I drive Lori and her home before the evening service. Since it is quite a long distance to Forest Hills from Bay Shore, I barely made it back in time for the evening service. That put additional stress on me, which was reflected in my mood. It was 2:00 A.M. when I got back home.

Rose Marie was still up. She was obviously depressed, almost tearful. "I vunder if life is even virth living," she said in a distressed voice. "I did not marry a minister, and I vould only be a hindrance to you."

She seemed to resent my relationship with the church and to be jealous of the church people's affection for me. She showed no willingness to accommodate my new way of life. It was a double-edged sword. The more involved with the church I became, the more I felt rejected by Rose Marie. The more rejected I felt by her, the more I reached out to the church, by way of compensation. It was a vicious circle

XXIII

The PTL Club had captured the interest of not only the Christians, but the population at large. Jim Bakker's winning personality and infectious smile opened the hearts of nearly everyone, regardless of background. People from across the spectrum of American life wanted to hear what he had to say.

In those days, there was still a certain unassuming purity to Jim's message. The guests had moving stories to tell. A sense of peace and love that the show as a whole radiated seemed to reach right out of the television set and caress the viewer. One had to be a hardened cynic not to be uplifted and inspired by the show.

In February 1976, forty-six stations carried "The PTL Club," and more were being added every week. Countless people were making decisions for Christ, and many lives were being changed for the better. It was remarkably easy for Jim to generate a steady flow of contributions, and a surplus of money was quickly built up.

PTL had outgrown the "Trinity Broadcasting System" television studio on Independence Boulevard. The huge volume of mail demanded more office space. Thousands of requests pouring in for studio audience tickets dictated the need for a studio with room for more seats. More telephones for the expanding army of volunteer counselors and pledge-takers were also required.

Jim acquired a stretch limousine and upgraded his wardrobe. I began to detect a degree of professionalism creeping into PTL. "I want you to go somewhere with me," Jim said after a telecast and lunch with me. "I want to show you where our new studio is going to be."

As we walked out to the waiting limousine, Jim enthusiastically told me about the new twenty-five-acre site that had been given to PTL as a tax write-off by the wealthy contractor who had owned it. The property included a luxurious three-story mansion, complete with crystal chandeliers. Construction was underway as we pulled onto the site. "It's going to be a miniature Williamsburg," Jim said. "Now over there," he pointed, "will be our new studio and the Heritage Church." A steeple on top of the studio was under construction, with a crane lifting a section into place while we watched. "The steeple will have the TV antenna inside so it won't look like a television studio."

The limousine had come to a stop. Jim sat quietly for a few moments, his eyes scanning the area slowly. He sat pensively for a few more moments. "Austin," he said, "I—I received—a—bomb threat this morning."

"What?"

"Yes, a bomb threat. They said they were going to blow this place up. I've also received some threatening and obscene telephone calls. And you wouldn't believe some of the mail I've received."

"From who?"

"From—Christians. Not from the world—but from the Christians! I thought people would love us. But they don't. They hate us." He shook his head silently. There were tears in his eyes and a shocked, pained expression on his face. He could not understand how the people he loved the most could feel such hatred for him. An occasional nut letter could be expected, particularly at the beginning. But as he became more successful, the hate letters and calls had become more frequent. They now came steadily.

Jim had been fulfilling his ministry exactly the way he felt God had directed him. Jim was approachable, available to people, and gave of himself unstintingly. His very success made him the object of certain Christians' hatred. It had all built up to this bomb threat. It shook him so badly that the overall outpouring of love and support from within Christianity and outside it seemed no solace. He was too bewildered to think rationally.

The same fragile sensitivity that enabled Jim to reach out to people so effectively was also his greatest weakness. From the beginning, it almost destroyed his ministry time after time. When he preached his first revival in Burlington, North Carolina, in the winter of 1961, he built the service up to a rousing climax with an altar call. He stepped back, folded his arms like Billy Graham, and expected people to cascade down the aisles to the altar. Instead, it became a staring contest. Jim stared at the audience and could scarcely believe that they were keeping their seats and just staring back. Not one soul responded to that altar call. Embarrassed, humiliated, and with a sense of deep rejection and total failure, he retreated in tears to the pastor's office.

Pastor Aubrey Sara, in whose church the fledgling evangelist preached his first revival, was probably the only man who could have convinced Jim to carry on. He did so. Now Jim Bakker was faced with the ultimate challenge to his emotions. But it might not take a bomb to stop Jim Bakker. He could not stand criticism. The little boy in him wanted desperately to quit and retreat to a place of safety.

Instead, nature's built-in mechanism for survival began to manifest itself and overrule the tender little boy. Anger at the Christians—an anger not refined enough to distinguish those who had hurt him from those who had not—began to displace Jim's compassion for them. Henceforth, they would pay him tribute. Didn't he deserve everything he could get from them? Deep down he still loved them. But he would love them from a safe distance. He would keep back far enough not to have to care what they said about him. And he would still be doing God's work.

"We *are* going to make it!" Jim said to me with a new assertiveness and determination. The innocence seemed to vanish from his face, never to return. His posture straightened. "We will not only complete Heritage Village, but one day the PTL Club will reach around the world. And nobody—but *nobody*—will stop us!"

Jim motioned the driver to take us back. February 1976 was a turning point in his life. Jim Bakker had grown up.

*   *   *

Opposition over Heritage Village continued to grow. The agitation had taken the form of a political debate in Charlotte. "Emergency meetings" were held. The entire matter was put to a vote in the city council, which voted to prevent completion of the complex. Millions of donated dollars stood to be lost. The ministry as a whole was now in jeopardy, since Jim had reached a point of no return.

Had PTL been wiped out at that point, it would have seemed tragic. In its early period, its accomplishments were positive and beautiful.

Pastors of competing denominations fanned the flames even higher, preaching partisan sermons against PTL from their pulpits. These were the ones who had mustered the political opposition.

Jim was now toughened up and ready to do battle. Indeed, he seemed to be thriving on the persecution. He added a new dimension to the whole affair by having "all of God's people" join with him in his battle against the devil. "Satan has a definite involvement with the town officials," Jim told his coast-to-coast audience. The political heat those officials soon felt probably did not come from hell.

When I returned for another appearance a short time later, I took another ride out to the Park Road site, with Jim, Tammy, and another guest on the show, Cathy Burrow, a black gospel singer.

"It is good that we have enemies," Cathy Burrow said, "because God says we should love our enemies. If we didn't have enemies, we couldn't follow that commandment. We need to have enemies to love. So, praise the Lord for 'em."

I had never really thought of it that way before. Neither had Jim or Tammy. A smile flashed across their faces as they said in unison, "Praise the Lord, yes, thank you Jesus for our enemies." Jim needed that word of encouragement.

*   *   *

The Royal Lipizzan Stallion Show was booked in Mexico City. Rose Marie took time off from her job and flew down with me. The only people I knew in Mexico City were those involved in putting on the show. I spoke some Spanish, but not enough to announce the show. I worked with a local announcer, who did so well that by the third day I was able to leave him to it. Rose Marie and I had a glorious time together, visiting museums, art shops, dance events, and even the Charros Riders. I wrote in my journal:

> Did mostly sightseeing after 3rd night—really not needed on floor—My wife with me. Away from the pressures of her job we seemed to get along better.

What *really* made the difference was not relief from the pressures of *her* job, but relief from the pressures of the *church!* That was the real barrier between us. Away from it, we regained some of the closeness and intimacy that we had once known so well. I felt a renewal of that zest for life I had not realized I was losing. The setting was perfect, and we were relaxed. We visited every cultural and historic spot, and bought some art objects.

When Rose Marie had to fly back to New York, I knew I would miss her more than I had in a long time. Briefly, we experienced once again what our marriage was meant to be. But in my state of mind then none of the poignant significance of this visit registered with me.

The Lipizzan show returned to the States. The church immediately resumed its place as my first interest.

I did some services for Pastor Arthur Shell in Clearwater, Florida. Pastor Shell could not contain his excitement over a new, rising evangelist. "His name is John Wesley Fletcher. He goes to people in the congregation, and God tells him everything about them, including their house numbers, their doctors' names—he's just amazing."

"Where did he come from?" I asked.

"Oklahoma. He ran topless bars before he was saved. God uses him in ways I have never seen before."

It occurred to me that more and more I was hearing testimonies of people who had come to the ministry from the most sordid backgrounds.

God seemed to use them more than anybody else, and in a more spectacular way. It almost seemed that God favored and rewarded them for their former seedy lives.

"Have you gotten to know him well?" I asked.

Pastor Shell said, "Yes. In fact, we traveled to India together. All he did was fast and pray. You would find him in the dining room at six in the morning, drinking a cup of hot water and reading his Bible."

That evening, after the service, a woman with a seeing eye dog came to the altar to talk with me. She obviously could see. Yet, her eyes were set deep in their sockets, as with many blind people.

"God gave me my sight last month," she said.

"How did it happen?" I asked, with genuine interest.

"I came to one of John Wesley Fletcher's meetings here. I went up for prayer. He put his hands over my eyes and prayed. When the prayer was over, I still could not see. You could hear the people's disappointment. I went home and went to bed as usual. The next morning, when I woke up, I could *see* for the first time! I still keep my dog with me because I am so used to him being with me. I'll always be grateful for the ministry of John Wesley Fletcher!" she said happily.

The woman was well known in the area, and the local newspapers had written detailed stories about her recovery. It appeared that God really did work in mysterious ways.

*   *   *

Growing into a major nationwide show, "The PTL Club" drew a vast audience two hours every weekday, with some weekend reruns. This was unheard of in television. Jim Bakker was the single personality who held it all together, and he was being paid more and more attention. My frequent appearances built my own recognition factor to an all-time high. I had become so well known to PTL's widely scattered audience that even policemen in airports would tip their caps to me in recognition when I walked by.

As Jim's fame grew, he became more and more distant from his public. Rarely did any of his rank-and-file followers get to speak with him in person any more. I was critical of Jim's "aloofness" toward his supporters. After all, they were the ones who had made him what he was. Overlooking the "beam in my own eye," I made the following journal entry:

March 16, 1976

In flight-TWA-NY-Amarillo, Tex.

The combination of my work with the Royal Lipizzan Stallion Show along with my unique ministry is propelling me into national prominence— a position I frankly detest! I cannot move about as freely as I once could. I am recognized now during my travels and am constantly besieged with calls about schemes and angles, and, believe it or not—lonely, designing women. On the latter—never have I met so many forward, pushy women as I have since becoming a minister. It was never this bad in show business. They have out-and-out propositioned me after services and many have sought out my hotel and motel room numbers—some finding my whereabouts under the pretense of an "emergency"—one even passing as my wife to get through the switchboard. One girl who I thought was really a "sister in Christ"—who had recently sent me a gift set of books and had sent some warm letters - now calls me long distance with threats. And I do believe that if one more misguided con man or woman approaches me again telling me they have it all figured out and "how we are going to get rich" over my ministry and this "healing gimmick," I shall no longer contain my outrage toward such a blasphemous suggestion! Everyone seems to have an angle.

Because of so many people intruding upon my time—the insincere— curiosity seekers *et al.*—it has now become necessary to check in and out of hotels in secret, with a "no info" order at the switchboard—only the local pastor being able to get through—my wife and daughter being given secret names so they can get through.

This pains me. I wanted to be readily available and easily accessible to anyone who needed to talk to me about Christ—but now I must close that door because of so many nuts who have gotten my number which was published in the minister's manual. Today, the phone number is changed—unlisted—with an answering service given out. No one will be able to call me direct in the future. Must shield my family and make every move secretly. This is the price one pays for fame.

I spoke to two pastors about this problem—they were very understanding—this is obviously a common problem with prominent evangelists. One of them said to tell anyone who requests individual counseling that God has given me a public pulpit ministry only—and prayer individually will be conducted at the altar and any future contact could only be with their local pastor.

Sadly, this is the way it must be.

Happily—my wife impressed by radio sermon by Unitarian Church— and now interested more in the purpose of being "born again."

She seems for the first time to be genuinely open! Praise God!

The last part of the entry brought me great joy. This gave me the encouragement I needed to carry on the ministry God had called me to fulfill. looking neither to the right nor the left, but keeping my eyes straight ahead.

I settled back comfortably in my seat. Maybe God wanted me in His service full-time. My ministry had certainly proved its worth. There were undeniable results. I wanted more and more to leave show business and its pressures, and enter the tranquil groves of the full-time Christian ministry. The devil had put certain obstacles in my path to discourage me, but I certainly knew better than to let that deter me. Such things were simply further proof that God wanted to do something special through me. And God needed true, honest ministers.

There were frequent news accounts of ministers of the Gospel getting caught in sin. The latest was Billy James Hargis, a high-powered Baptist televangelist who denounced homosexuality, extramarital sex, drinking, and drugs from his pulpit. His enterprises included a Bible university and traveling choir groups. He was also an extreme right-winger. Anyone who disagreed with his politics or theology was denounced as a Communist. He took in millions of dollars from the faithful each year, until he was caught engaging in every one of the sordid practices he preached against—with his own students! The news media got hold of it. His empire collapsed. And many of his students never recovered from the psychological damage done them.

I became increasingly aware of the astonishing prevalence of homosexuality among Assemblies of God ministers. "Why couldn't the people see this?" I wondered. I had resisted seeing it myself, even though my early experiences as victim ought to have sensitized me. But the faithful accepted effeminate characteristics in ministers as examples of the gentleness and tenderness of Christ.

In one large church, the pastor was standing next to the handsome young song leader, near where I was sitting on the platform. During an exuberant congregational song, the pastor glanced over at the young man, winked his eye, smacked his lips, and said, "Oh, you're so gorgeous I could just eat you up!"

During a regional ministers' convention, within earshot of me, a pastor sidled up to a boy who belonged to the Royal Rangers, an Assemblies' youth organization. He said to the boy, "My wife will be gone for the next four days. Why don't you come and sleep with me?"

At a district meeting of ministers in New York, one respected pastor tweaked the cheek of another Assemblies' pastor. The first pastor came back a few moments later and playfully twitched the second pastor's ear with his fingers. The second pastor walked over to me shaking his head. Smacking his lips, he said, "That makes me so *mad* when he twitches my ear like that."

I began to take special note of this sort of behavior in ministers as I went from church to church all over the United States and Canada. I recorded my impressions in my journal. Reviewing my journal, the proportion of ministers I have reason to suspect were homosexually inclined—from whom there had come some sort of clear demonstration of lascivious attention to another male in my presence—is a staggering eight out of ten. Eighty percent! And the great majority of them had what appeared to be good marriages.

The prevalence of Assemblies of God ministers committing—and getting away with—child molestation is a horror of the first magnitude. Reverend E. R. Schultz, District Secretary of the Florida District of the Assemblies, told me of a seventy-five-year-old pastor in his district who had recently been caught molesting a twelve-year-old girl. He had told the girl that it was time for her to learn about sex, that young boys would teach her wrong, so he would teach her about it properly.

"What did you do with him?" I asked.

"Transferred him out of the district," Schultz replied. Later, I learned that the offending pastor had been transferred to Florida from yet another district, where he had been involved in a similar incident. And Eugene Profeta was kicked out altogether for tipping his hairdresser twenty dollars!

Incidents of Assemblies' ministers found patronizing prostitutes were on the rise. But that kind of sordid behavior tended to remain hidden, unless rivalries among preachers provided someone an incentive to expose the offending minister.

Even though I had become aware of the sexual perversion rampant among the ministers, I was still so wrapped up in the church that I rationalized it all away. Perhaps God had let me see all this to impress upon me that He needed true ministers through whom He could work miracles and bring about a revival. And did not Satan come as a wolf in sheep's clothing, or disguised as an angel of light? Looking back, I can see I clearly had lost perspective. Before I was "saved," I would *never* have even *considered* associating with such people!

The ministry built up my ego more than show business ever had, and I ate it up hungrily. The wheels of the jetliner screeched as we touched down in Texas.

XXIV

How can one explain an irrational decision? Especially, how can one explain making a decision when there were so many warning signs beforehand? Ask the woman who marries the known alcoholic or wife beater. Ask the man who sees the unmistakable trouble signs in the flirtatious behavior of the woman he wants to marry. Ask those who begin using tobacco, alcohol, or drugs even though they know the harm those substances can do. There are no happy endings to any of those situations.

For some situations of danger, nature has provided each of us with a built-in warning system, to avert tragedy. In others, it has provided us with common sense. It is a great paradox that the very capacity of humans to think and to decide often defeats these protective devices. The human animal can decide to ignore the warnings, believe only what he *wants* to believe, and plunge wilfully into disaster.

In the face of others' sorry experiences, we all think, "It will be different with me." Then we find something or someone else to blame when our world falls apart. Despite the countless warnings, I made the momentous decision to flee from the worldly life I had made for myself and enter the ministry full-time. I would never have made that decision without abundant "encouragement" from well-meaning Christians. After all, how could I be truly and fully devoted to God's service if I still had one foot in the world?

Four days before my resignation from the Royal Lipizzan Stallion Show was to take effect, I began to feel uneasy about this impending drastic change in my life. "Oh, God," I thought, "if I'm making the right decision, please give some kind of a sign to confirm it!"

Following a performance in Johnstown, Pennsylvania, a woman I had never seen before came up to me.

"You don't know me," she volunteered. "My name is Grace Nicodem. The Lord has sent me to tell you that if you should be available for meetings, I will book you in the Pittsburgh area. My ministry is to help ministers."

I looked at her in disbelief. "I was planning to *leave* show business in four days, to go into the ministry full-time!"

Two other people came backstage to see me. Marge and Andy Krehlik had driven from Latrobe. "We made the trip over to see you," Marge said, "because Andy and I had a strong feeling that it is time that you stop performing in the arenas and start preaching in them." If this wasn't God's confirmation, nothing was!

The four days went by quickly. It was Mothers Day, 1976. While dressing for the show, I became highly nervous. I thought about the good life show business had given me. I thought about Rose Marie. I had no illusions but that there would be a big drop in my income. For the first time, I seriously began to question the matter. Was this really the right thing to do?

A knock on the door interrupted my thoughts. "Phone call," said a voice. "You can take it down the hall."

I took the phone.

"Hi, Austin. This is Grace Nicodem. Guess what? I've booked you to be a speaker at the Pittsburgh Charismatic Conference one week from today. The conference will be held right in the arena where you are performing. It was a *miracle* to get you booked on such short notice. They book their speakers a year in advance. This proves that God is in this!"

That afternoon I said my farewell to show business. I looked at my calendar. The New York District Council of the Assemblies of God was beginning its convention in Poughkeepsie on that very day. I decided to stop by the meeting on my way home and share the good news with my fellow ministers. The first person I ran into when I got there was Reverend Cooke.

"I have some news to share with you," I said to him excitedly.

"You've left show business."

"Yes," I said, a little deflated because he had guessed it so easily.

"I could see it coming," he said with a smile. "How is Rose Marie taking it?"

"So far, she's taking it well. I haven't told her yet. It just happened."

When I got home, I told Lori first. "Oh, Daddy, I think it's wonderful," she said. By now, Mrs. Beck had Lori thoroughly indoctrinated.

Rose Marie was devastated at the news and began to cry. "How can you do dis, ven you know how I feel about it?"

"Rose, please, this won't make that much difference in your life. I will still be on the road and I will still send money home."

"Yes, but I'll know vat you are doing."

"Rose Marie, I know I will be an excellent minister."

"You vould be good in vatever you made up your mind to do," she said. I doubt that she intended the ironic way the compliment came out. "But—I've told you before that I vould nefer be married to a minister. So, you've made the choice."

*   *   *

My first week-long revival was in Fulton, New York, with Pastor Dan Raught. It had been booked hastily in a small church in that small town and I had outlined my sermons at the airport while waiting for my plane. I was so "on fire" for the Lord that I was eager to go anywhere God wanted me. I stayed with Pastor Raught and his family in their small apartment over the church. Pastor Raught's father, a retired Assemblies' minister, lived with them. The simplicity and peace of the whole setting appealed to me. I was excited to be a full-time minister at last.

During the opening service, I glanced down at the third row of pews. A seductive looking woman was studying me with more than casual interest. Just as our eyes made contact, she ran her tongue sensually over her lips. I quickly looked away. She called the church the next day and requested a "counseling" session with me. The pastor's wife took care of that, saying she would be glad to talk with the caller herself.

I spent several hours in conversation with the Raught family during my week with them. They were extremely submissive people, awash in humility and totally obedient to Reverend Thomas Zimmerman. Brother Zimmerman's name came up often in their conversation, both in reverence and in fear. To them, Reverend Zimmerman was a kind of god, to be loved and served. To offend him in any way was unthinkable. His control over the fate of the Raughts' ministry was absolute.

It did not take me long to realize that there were two distinct classes of Assemblies of God ministers. There were the movers and shakers, who jockeyed their way into the upper echelon politics of the denomination, finding favor with "Brother Z" and joining a prosperous elite. Then there were the followers: the fear-ridden, sycophant brigade, held down, kept poor and in bondage. The follower class ministers had lost whatever self-esteem they may once have had. But they were valuable to the church hierarchy. Like little robots, they would do anything for the church leaders upon command. And they could console themselves with Matthew 5:5: "Blessed are the meek: for they shall inherit the earth."

During my visit, the elder Reverend Raught returned home from an outing, holding a pair of shoes. "Look. I bought this pair of dress shoes at the Goodwill store for a quarter," he said. He looked over his bounty with satisfaction and then put them on. In shock, I stared at this retired minister who had served the Assemblies of God for a lifetime. The tired looking furniture all around us was secondhand too, no doubt. The Raughts faithfully tithed, and were expected to give to Assemblies of God missionaries over and above the tithe.

On another occasion, discussing a nearby church, the elder Reverend

Raught asked, "Do they warsh feet there?" I rested my forehead on my palm. Was I really in the right place? This seemed so primitive to me. But through it all, the Raughts manifested a downright spooky kind of inner glow. My mind drifted back to the spotlights in the arenas where I had performed.

*   *   *

The dedication ceremony for Heritage Village took place on July 4, 1976, with great pomp and circumstance. I had been invited to take part in the televised festivities, but was already scheduled to preach in a church in Cortland, New York, that day. Everyone seemed amazed that I wouldn't cancel that appearance in order to attend the higher profile Christian event. The Cortland engagement had been set several months before, and I did not think twice about honoring my original commitment.

"Please stay home with us on the Fourth. It's the bicentennial celebration," Rose Marie said to me. "It's going to be a very important time in New York. The parade of tall ships vill sail down the Hudson. Ve should be together as a family for dis."

"Rose Marie, I'm a minister. The Fourth is a Sunday. The church in Cortland needs me, and they have made a lot of preparations for me to be there."

Rose Marie and Lori went to the banks of the Hudson River with a blanket and some fruit in the small hours of the morning, and staked out a good vantage point to see the spectacle. They saw the river transformed to a bygone era, as the tall-masted ships sailed over the horizon one by one and made their way to the Battery. It was the kind of rare event that a family, having experienced it together, never forgets. Instead of being there with them, I was dutifully preaching the Gospel in a little, out-of-the-way church.

After I preached, instead of making time to be with Rose Marie and Lori, I went directly to the airport to catch a plane for Miami, Florida, to begin a week-long crusade at Evangel Temple. Pastor Martin Luther Davidson picked me up at the airport. "We have an evangelists' apartment right at the church," he told me as we pulled away from the terminal. "You'll be sharing it with a dear friend of mine, Richard Orchard from North Dakota. You'll like him. He pastors a church in Minot. Brother Orchard will be having the morning services and you will be having the evening services."

Suddenly, a car cut in front of us. Reverend Davidson braked sharply, his face contorted. He breathed a heavy sigh and angrily spouted out, "Those Jews will cut you right off to get ahead of you."

"The—Jews?"

"Yes. The Jews. They've completely taken over Miami. Why, if you're in the supermarket and you leave your cart for a minute, some Jew will take out your stuff and walk right off with your cart. They're absolutely no good! The other day a woman from our church said when she sees a Jew she feels like kissing his feet because he is of the chosen race. Aaaargh!" He shook his head stiffly, his jowls wobbling back and forth.

A tall man, Reverend Martin Luther Davidson had stern, judgmental eyes, a long hook nose, and a mouth capable of producing an endearing grin but set in a pious scowl most of the time.

"We've got some problems at the church," he continued, back on track.

"What kind of problems?"

"Well, we're having a problem with our youth pastor. I don't know what's happening with this younger generation of ministers."

"What's wrong with him?"

"Well—he's—worldly. I can remember in my day when the older and younger ministers dedicated themselves to living a life of holiness—praise God! But not today. Not this crop. Especially the one we've got. He's worldly!"

"In what way?"

"Well—among other things—I found out—" Pastor Davidson pushed his chin out. His eyes looked piercingly toward the heavens, as if he were trying to make eye contact with the Almighty. There was a moment of pregnant silence while Pastor Davidson mustered the necessary strength to spit out the shocking revelation. "I found out that he—has—even been going to *picture* shows!"

"Picture shows?" I responded, in surprise. I must have had a stunned expression on my face. I had not heard that term since the 1940s.

"Picture shows!" he repeated, with a smart snap of his head underlining his words.

"You don't mean it!" I replied seriously, looking him right in the eye.

I was relieved to meet Reverend Richard Orchard. He had a kind, round face, and harbored no overt judgmental attitude. He had a jolly personality and enjoyed a good laugh. His unmistakable farm background was becoming to him, and added to his genuine charm. He never wore a regular suit. His wardrobe, both for preaching and everyday, consisted of trousers, shirt, tie, and a short-waisted button-down Eton jacket.

Bible characters came vividly to life in Reverend Orchard's lessons and sermons. He also played the accordion. His rendition of "Let The Rain From Heaven Fall Upon My Dusty Soul" while he accompanied himself singing was moving and unforgettable. I wanted to learn all I could from him, as we shared the apartment and prayed together. He loved God, and wanted only to serve Him.

One night, I woke up in the wee hours, put on my bathrobe, and went out to the sanctuary to pray. I found Reverend Orchard at the altar, prostrate before the cross crying out to God, "Help me Jesus! Please help me!"

Reverend Orchard had a son, Loren, whom he was determined to have in the ministry. He also had a pretty daughter, who had rebelled against the church and her father. She had worked as a go-go dancer in a bar. Her young life had been cut short one night when without warning the bar burst into flames. The symbolic allusion of such a death, in a flaming inferno, constantly haunted Brother Orchard. Ever since then, Reverend Orchard had cried out in anguish to God every night to give him strength to endure the pain and guilt.

I walked over quietly, knelt beside him, put my hand on his shoulder gently, and prayed softly with him. Tears rolled down my face.

XXV

B rother Miles?"
"Yes?"

"I'm Pastor John Bedzyk."

"Praise th—" My voice cracked, and I had to clear my throat. "Praise the Lord!" I responded. It was a phrase that had become more and more commonplace in my speech. Brother Bedzyk was not quite what I had expected. I had looked right past him when I got off the plane at the airport in Ithaca, New York. I had tried to walk past him, and he had blocked my way to get my attention. His clothes were rumpled. He wore a dark-colored shirt that was open at the collar. His elfish, pointed face wore a spaced-out look. A scraggly, institutional crewcut completed the picture. "It's going to be a long week," I thought to myself.

As he drove me to Elmira we became immersed in a conversation about God and the Bible. I began to feel more at ease. His outward appearance no longer troubled me. We were "brothers in Christ." During a quiet moment while we watched the scenery pass by out the window, Pastor Bedzyk suddenly, without any warning, yelled, "OH GAWD!" I stiffened up, tensely holding the sides of my seat. Pastor Bedzyk continued mumbling in ecstasy. I had the uneasy feeling that these spontaneous eruptions of worship would be frequent.

His wife—"Sister Bedzyk," that is—was another surprise. Taller than her husband, she had a good, slim figure, long dark hair, and long fingernails. Her facial features were finely chiseled, with a perfectly sloped nose. She had a quick sense of humor and liked to laugh. Their daughter, Bonnie, an outgoing, pretty blonde, played piano for the church.

The seven hundred seats in the Assemblies' church in Elmira filled quickly for the first of the Sunday morning services. All the services were filled, and I attributed that mainly to my frequent appearances on "The PTL Club." Extra chairs were set up for over one hundred children who had been bused in. "Busing in" was a special custom in the Assemblies of God movement. Early on Sunday mornings, church buses would cruise the neighborhoods looking for children to invite to church. Sometimes rewards, such as hot dogs and soft drinks, enticed them to climb aboard and come to Sunday school. The inducement this morning was to come and hear the circus ringmaster "in person." It all seemed harmless enough to their parents, many of whom were glad to get rid of their kids for a couple of hours.

Before each service, I would seek out a quiet place behind or beside the platform where I could kneel in prayer. Thoughtfully, this church had a designated prayer room located directly off the platform. As I prayed, I felt a gentle sensation of peace flow through my body. Suddenly the words "OH GAWD!" boomed out next to me, jolting me. I grabbed onto the rail of the portable altar for dear life, my concentration thoroughly shattered. Brother Bedzyk had slipped in beside me to join me in prayer.

"Ohhhhhhhhhhh Gawwwwwd," he groaned, "please save those little heathen that have been brought in here this morning. Ohhhhhhhhh Gawwwwwwd."

I opened my eyes and looked over at Brother Bedzyk, who was completely "out of it." I got up and walked silently to the side of the platform and peeked out front at the children. Some had dirty faces—many appeared to come from poor families. They were beautiful, innocent children, open and eager to be molded. I shook my head and returned to the prayer room. Brother Bedzyk was still moaning to God, interceding for the salvation of "the little heathen." After the service, one hundred and eight children came and knelt at the altar to give their hearts to Jesus.

I enjoyed my afternoon conversations with the Bedzyks, particularly Mrs. Bedzyk, because of her lighthearted attitude. Microwave ovens were just coming in, and she had one of the first. I watched with fascination as she heated my coffee in it and a beep signaled that my coffee was "done."

"The Lord has really been blessing these services," she said. I nodded my head in agreement. "I've seen a flow of healing power in these services that I've never seen before," she continued in a tone that had now become quite serious. "You are truly anointed of God. What about your wife?"

"What about her?"

"Well, is she supportive of your ministry? Is she a good helpmeet?"

"She—," I answered uncomfortably, "—Rose Marie's very opposed to what I'm doing. She very much objects to the money I give to the church. She's putting pressure on me to leave the church and the ministry—and return to show business."

Pastor and Mrs. Bedzyk exchanged looks. Bonnie arched her eyebrow with interest and recrossed her legs.

"This really doesn't surprise me," sniffed Mrs. Bedzyk. "God has anointed you with a ministry of miracles. He's had His hand on you from the day you were born. Knowing that God wanted to use you in a mighty way, it's quite possible that the devil put Rose Marie in your life to stop your ministry."

The next morning, Brother Bedzyk took me for a ride to see a waterfall. He took the opportunity to tell me about the fate of ministers in the past who had possessed healing gifts and misused them.

"And then there was Jack Coe. He began to believe that *he* was the healer and stopped giving the glory to God. So, God took him home."

"Took him home? How?"

"God struck him down with polio and he died."

I felt flattered that Pastor Bedzyk would tell me these things. To me, it meant that he saw in me the potential for a great miracle ministry. He wanted me to avoid the pitfalls. I appreciated his concern and support, and was convinced that God had arranged this meeting. We got out of the car at the waterfall.

"The greatest of all time," he continued, "was William Branham. He had a word of knowledge so precise that there was no way it could have been anything but of God. And this was proved! Even the most hardened skeptics would fall down on their knees in front of him."

I was already vaguely aware of the Reverend William Branham. Many "miracles" had been attributed to his ministry, and his "words of knowledge" seemed so uncanny that they made Oral Roberts envious. Reverend Roberts had once complained to a close friend, "I can't understand why God hasn't given *me* the ability to read minds like William Branham!"

"You said that Reverend Branham had a 'precise' word of knowledge, and that it was 'proved.' How did he work?"

"Well," Pastor Bedzyk answered, excitement building in his voice, "as you know, people sometimes think the evangelist can call out anything and someone will respond to it. To prove that this was not just guesswork and that it really was from God, Bill Branham had everyone write down on a piece of paper any illness or problem they wanted God to help them with. This way, it was all on record and could not be altered. They then sealed the piece of paper in an envelope. When they all came up in the prayer line, Bill Branham walked down the line taking all the envelopes, and then stacked them up on the pulpit. As each person came forward, Brother Branham held that envelope in the air. Then—he proceeded to tell that person everything that they needed and wanted from God. He would open the envelope and absolutely everything, word for word, that he had said was right there written down! Miraculous healings took place. Cancers just fell off people! People got 'the shakes.' William Branham was probably the most anointed—"

I did not hear the last part of what Pastor Bedzyk was saying. Suddenly, I felt sick to my stomach. "Pastor Bedzyk—would you mind taking me back to my room? I don't feel well."

"Sure. Sure, we'll go right away."

As we got back in the car, Pastor Bedzyk kept talking: "Brother Branham put such a fear of God in people that one time a couple of men came up for prayer, both claiming to have several serious diseases. They were trying to put one over on Brother Branham. He put his hands on their heads, started to pray, then with great anger yelled, 'You don't have any of these diseases! You were trying to fool a prophet of God! Do you know what's going to happen to you? I'm going to tell God to put on you every disease you claimed to have—right now! And you will be eaten alive by every loathsome disease you lied about!' "

Pastor Bedzyk began to chuckle. "Those rascals fell to their knees, grabbed Brother Branham's feet, and kissed his shoes, begging and pleading with him not to put those diseases on them. It sure taught them a lesson they'd never forget, and this was in front of several thousand people. Brother Miles—you *do* look sick. I'll get you back as quickly as possible."

The first thing I did when we got back was to be sick in the bathroom. Then I lay down on the bed and stared at the ceiling. My mind drifted back to the time when I was twelve years old, in Salinas, California. Like many boys, I was very interested in magic and had managed to accumulate several tricks. I had bought some props with paper route money, and made others from instructions in library books.

During my stay in Salinas, the Foley and Burke Carnival came to town. When they were setting up, I noticed a banner announcing "Señor Lopez—The Magician from Mexico." I introduced myself to Señor Lopez and agreed to be his assistant for the week in exchange for magic lessons.

One afternoon he said, "Today I will teach you the envelope trick." This was a "mind reading" trick that had fascinated me more than all the others. People in the audience would write questions on a piece of paper along with their name and address, and seal the questions in an envelope. During the show, the envelopes would be passed up to the stage, and Señor Lopez would begin to "read the minds" of his audience.

He would take the first envelope with a flourish, tap it against his head, and say, "Where is Mary Johnson?"

Someone in the audience would respond, "Here I am."

"Your question is—'I lost a valuable diamond-studded earring last Tuesday. It has great sentimental value. Will I find it?' " Señor Lopez would then begin to tear the envelope open. "Let's check what you wrote. Yes—here it is—'I lost a valuable diamond-studded earring last Tuesday. It has great sentimental value. Will I find it?' "

Everyone was amazed how Señor Lopez could have known what was written on the slip sealed in the envelope. Then he would continue, "Look in your closet. You have a pair of red shoes there. The earring dropped off while you were in the closet and landed inside the left shoe."

Mary Johnson would now be very animated. "I *do* have a pair of red shoes in the closet. This couldn't have been a trick! You really *can* read minds!"

Enthusiastic applause would burst forth. Señor Lopez would then take the next envelope, accurately describe everything written on the enclosed slip before he unsealed the envelope, and give advice for solving the problem.

"This is one of my favorite tricks," Señor Lopez said to me as he began instructing me in the secret. "The first person whose mind you read is a plant—in this case, Mary Johnson. You do the earring story, or any other one you make up, first. When you open the envelope, you really open the envelope of the *next* person whose mind you're going to 'read.' While pretending to read the information written by Mary Johnson, you're really reading the information for your next subject. You can even get away with putting that piece of paper down on your table and reading from it while you hold the next unopened envelope to your head. You are always one envelope ahead. This is the most effective of all the mind reading tricks."

The renowned Reverend William Branham, faith healer and prophet of God, had been using parlor tricks! He was deliberately staging his supposed messages from God in order to manipulate vulnerable people. Nobody had ever guessed the truth.

When William Branham died in a winter flood that swept through Louisville, Kentucky, his followers would not bury him. They were convinced that God would raise him from the dead on Easter Sunday morning—four months hence. Easter Sunday came and went. Brother Branham stayed dead. Finally, they buried him.

*   *   *

The Bedzyks took me to the airport. "Now remember the dates you're coming back," Pastor Bedzyk said as I handed my ticket to the counter agent. "That's a Sunday through Wednesday."

"There was the greatest movement of the Spirit in these meetings that this area has ever seen," Mrs. Bedzyk added. "We're going to keep you in prayer. And we're going to pray for Rose Marie too! She'd better get herself together and stop trying to hinder your ministry, or God just may have to do something drastic to her—I mean *drastic*—to get her out of the picture. And He'll put someone in your life that will be a real helpmeet for you."

"Praise God!" interjected Bonnie, flashing a big smile.

When I got home, a note informed me that Rose Marie and Lori had flown to Switzerland for a few days. I was disappointed that they were not there to greet me. Rose Marie had felt the need to visit Sylvia, her close friend for over thirty years. Sylvia was a pretty, dark-haired Swiss girl with a deep, husky voice. She lived with her Hungarian lover, Yiatsi, and a daughter from a previous marriage.

Sylvia smoked cigars. "I can only do this at home," she once explained. "If I did this in public, people might think I am a lesbian."

Rose Marie, Lori, and I had once celebrated a belated Christmas with Sylvia and Yiatsi. She had waited until we arrived, a few days after Christmas, before lighting the candles on the tree and having the full celebration.

This time, Rose Marie looked at Sylvia probingly and asked, "Sylvia, do you think that Al is interested in other women? That he would be unfaithful to me?"

Sylvia blew out a puff of cigar smoke and studied Rose Marie quizzically. "Al? Never! He's not that type."

Rose Marie had been uneasy ever since the service at Glad Tidings Tabernacle in Manhattan when that woman had suggested she had something to worry about—a suggestion which the woman had tried to veil with a sanctimonious offer to "pray for her." Rose Marie took comfort in Sylvia's observation.

When Rose Marie and Lori got home, it was their turn to find a note. It told them that I had flown to Charlotte, North Carolina, for another appearance on "The PTL Club." Because of Sylvia's reassuring words, Rose Marie had especially looked forward to seeing me. But now her anger was rekindled. "Your father's off on another ministry thing at that PTL Club," she told Lori, with exasperation.

David Mainse had also come down to be a guest on "The PTL Club" that October 21, 1976. Jim Bakker and David were both overgrown kid types. They had become good friends. Like "The PTL Club," "100 Huntley Street" had grown rapidly, and was now being beamed all across Canada. Between the two of them, they saturated all of North America with the Gospel.

"Look at this new Bible we've produced," said an enthusiastic Jim Bakker over the dinner table after the telecast. Jim took one of the new Bibles out of its box. "They were just finished this morning. Here. Here's one for each of you."

The handsome, rich-looking, leather-bound Bibles came in burgundy and black. I was given a burgundy one. "PTL Counselors' Edition" was emblazoned in gold letters on the front cover. The title page stated that this was an official PTL Bible. A dedication page displayed the PTL logo as well.

"Look at this," Jim said, opening his copy. "This is the best study Bible ever put out! In the front section is a complete cyclopedic index: subjects all grouped together with Scripture passages to do with that particular subject. Look, for instance, here's 'bondage'—and every scripture to deal with that subject. Here's another—'tithing.' And look. On each page there is a commentary and cross references. And in the back, a complete concordance.

"It looks like a fifty-dollar Bible. It costs us less than ten dollars for each Bible. So we can give it out to anyone who sends in a fifty-dollar donation and we make over forty dollars on each one for the ministry."

Instead of it occurring to me that this was a four-hundred-percent profit on an item of merchandise, I felt awed by Jim's vast knowledge of the Holy Scriptures. How impressive, what with Jim's demanding schedule, that he could have put together such a work. Even putting the entire PTL staff to work on it, it must have been a monumental task. "Jim must do nothing but work for God," I thought to myself. "He lives every minute of his life for God. And look how God is working through him!" I began to think that I was accomplishing comparatively very little for the Kingdom, and that I desperately needed more discipline in my life. What a failure I was! Maybe Rose Marie *was* standing in my way.

I asked Jim to sign the dedication page of the copy he had given me. Before he departed, David Mainse arranged for my first appearance on "100 Huntley Street" in Toronto. He could see the tremendous response my appearance on "The PTL Club" had brought.

That night, I held services at Trinity Assembly of God. Hubert Morris had been transferred to New York State, and Calvin Bacon, whose former church in Columbus, Georgia, I had visited, was his replacement.

Jim Bakker had gained additional respect and status when his new Bible was presented to the viewers the next morning. It generated more credibility than ever, and brought in still more financial support. I had accepted unquestioningly exactly what had been implied, namely, that Jim and the PTL staff, as part of their expanding ministry, had developed this new, innovative "counselors' Bible" for the PTL "partners," or contributors. With it, the "partners" would gain a kind of exclusivity to the Word of God, and an advantage over everyone else.

Had I read the introduction, I would have realized immediately the *real* source of the Bibles. Instead, with a classic Christian mentality, I took as truth everything a Christian leader said or *implied,* believing by faith everything I was told. Not until I was exposed to other big ministries did I find out that they, too, had "created" such Bibles. I learned where these Bibles came from. They had been assembled and mass-produced by Thomas Nelson Publishers, out of Nashville, Tennessee, as a fund-raising tool for all comers. That company was simply in business to sell Bibles, and it does hundreds of millions of dollars worth of business in them every year. The gold stamping, the title page, and the dedication page were custom printed to the order of the ministry retailing the product. The rest was "off the shelf." A wide variety of books, study courses, commentaries, hymnals, etc., were mass-produced, to make the maximum profit for the customers with the greatest buying power. Each ministry could assume credit for these erudite works "for the glory of God."

In that carnival where I learned the "one ahead trick" long ago, this tactic would have been called, "the book pitch."

XXVI

Rose Marie made another trip to Europe, this time to pick up a specially ordered Mercedes-Benz 300D from Germany. The arrangements had been made through a dealership in New Jersey. By picking up the car at the factory in Stuttgart-Sindelfingen, West Germany, and driving it in Europe so that it would qualify as a used car, the U.S. customs fees were greatly reduced. As a TWA employee, Rose Marie was able to have the car shipped to New York for free by air freight.

Although I had made the down payment, Rose Marie insisted that the car be titled in her name, to avoid complications when she picked it up and took it through the various formalities. We were excited when the beautifully appointed car arrived at Kennedy Airport. We spent many days touring New England in it and visiting the restored mansions along the Hudson River.

When we got back home, I announced to Rose Marie that I would be spending a few days preaching at Reverend Cooke's church. Rose Marie tensed up. I climbed into bed that night with anticipation and reached over to caress her.

"No!" she said, angrily pushing my hand away.

"But Rose Marie, you're my wife, and I want you."

"You don't vant me. You just vant sex. Dat's all any man vants. Vomen are liberated now, and ve don't haf to do vat any man vants us to do."

I slammed my fist into the mattress in my impatience, even rage, at this rebuff. I kept this childish tantrum up all night, denying us both a proper night's rest.

"What the hell's the matter with you?" I growled. "Why have you changed so much since we got married? But then again, this is typical of a woman, isn't it, to put on a big act to get a guy to marry them, and once you marry one, everything changes!" My assessment of our situation might have been amusing had things not been so out of control.

By morning, both our moods had reached a new low. "Al," Rose Marie said calmly, "I do not vant you to be involved in the ministry, and I cannot be a good vife to you as long as you are."

I straightened up self-righteously. It was all perfectly clear. "The church is right," I said to her in a slow, deliberate voice. "Your women's lib ideas, trying to hamper the great ministry God has entrusted me with—trying to get me away from God altogether—yes, I can see it all now. They are right. You *are* of the devil!"

Rose Marie gasped. That broadside took the fight right out of her. A look of shock and deep hurt replaced the anger. I felt an immediate urge to reach out, pull her to me, and tell her I was sorry. But no, I must be strong for Jesus. I would be falling right into one of the devil's snares if I backed down now. I continued to stand my ground as a minister of God, stiffly glaring at her.

"If you tink dot I am of the devil," Rose Marie said in gentle, sober tones, "den it is ofer between us." Slowly, she took her coat out of the closet, picked up her purse, and left for work.

*   *   *

"So this is your new car," said Reverend Cooke admiringly, as he looked the new Mercedes over.

"Yes," I replied. "I bought this with my show business money, but I don't want people to get the wrong idea. Do you think I should park it around back, out of sight, so people don't see it?"

"On the contrary," he said, smiling, "leave it right here in front, so they do see it. They'll probably put more money in the offering when they see it, figuring that you need more money for your particular lifestyle."

The reasoning seemed strange, even manipulative, for servants of God. I remembered Reverend R. D. E. Smith telling me, "It's up to you to set your own value, your own worth. This doesn't just happen. You have to let people know what you expect of them."

I left the Mercedes parked where it was. That night's extremely generous offering proved that Reverend Cooke knew his business. That elegant car helped convince the faithful that I was one of God's more important representatives. The response to the service was overwhelming. People milled around the church long after the service was over, "testifying" to miraculous healings, being "baptized in the Holy Spirit," and receiving other blessings of God.

"That was a powerful—*powerful*—service last night," Reverend Cooke exclaimed, as we played pool in his recreation room. "The church will be packed to the rafters tonight," he foretold, while he planned his next shot. Upstairs, his wife Esther was taking a steady stream of telephone calls from people inquiring about the service.

My sense of importance as a minister became even more inflated. This set the stage for yet another monster to make its debut in my life: the Pentecostal martyr complex. I looked at Reverend Cooke with solemn eyes. "No one will ever know the price I've paid for this ministry," I said to him in deep, plaintive tones. Then, exhibiting my pastoral humility, I betrayed the sanctity of my marriage in a way that I never had before. I told another person about things that had happened in the bedroom— things that, be they good or bad, should remain inviolate. To my ministerial colleague I complained about my wife, about how frustrating it was living with an uncaring woman who had even cut me off sexually, and how she was standing in the way of my ministry.

"She's absolutely a cold fish. I was tricked! She was tremendously sexually responsive to me before we got married—uh, that is, in the beginning."

Reverend Cooke took these revelations in attentively. He raised an eyebrow in a strange, knowing way. Then, with a clean whack, he sank the eight ball in an end pocket.

*   *   *

Lori performed superbly on the piano, and won award after award for her artistry. After arduous auditions, she entered the New York City High School for the Performing Arts, one of only 225 accepted out of 4,000 hopefuls.

She called me during one of her first days at school. "Daddy," she bubbled, "there are eleven born-again Christians in my high school!" That good news made my day.

In high spirits, I packed for a trip to Savannah, Georgia, to preach a week-long crusade at Bacon Park Assembly of God church. Rose Marie seemed to have simmered down and was more relaxed. For me, the short time I had just spent at home had been peaceful, enjoyable, even delightful.

"You know, Rose," I said, putting my arm around her waist, "I just knew that things would work out between us. There's been a lot of rough spots, but it looks like we are finally going to make it."

"Yes, I guess that's true," she said softly.

A surge of happiness filled me as I thought of the coming holiday season. Christmas was less than a month away. The decorations were already up in the streets of New York City. The year 1976 was winding down, and for the first time in three years I would have a whole month to spend with my family in our home.

The crusade in Savannah would begin on Sunday, November 28, and end on December 5. I had planned to leave the day before and use the layover between planes in Atlanta to visit someone who had written to

"Reverend Austin Miles—The Show Business Chaplain"

Woodcut of Kokomo the Clown by the
Italian-Swiss artist Giani Castiglioni.

Austin Miles in "The Littlest Circus," 1959.
Ballerinas are Alice Shanahan and Betsy
Mann.

News clip from the *Waterbury American*, April 19, 1973.

The Emmett Kelly, Jr., Circus performs at the White House, 1973. Austin Miles, Emmett Kelly, Jr., Tricia Nixon Cox, and Pam Rossaire.

Santa Claus with Rose Marie in Macy's, Herald Square.

Wedding picture with Rose Marie.

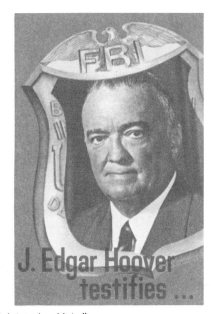

Covers of two Assemblies of God "miniature booklets."

Austin Miles with young Glenn and his family at the Shrine Circus in New Orleans.

Tammy Faye Bakker and Austin Miles with several "little people" on "PTL Club" set at Heritage Village, in the days before Tammy's heavy make-up.

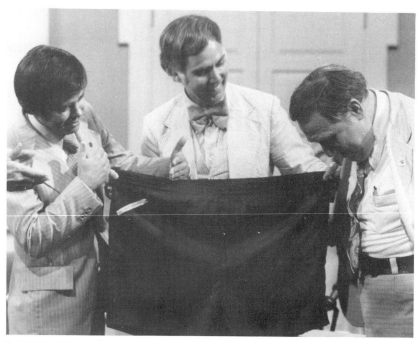

Jim Bakker, Austin Miles, and "Uncle" Henry Harrison on "PTL Club" set at Heritage Village.

September 22, 1982 - My 49th birthday

Many thanks for sharing God's greatness with us. David Mainse
AND THE C.C.I. FAMILY

David Mainse *(far left)* and Austin Miles on set of "100 Huntley Street."

Austin Miles with Bobby Yerkes.

Rick Nelson, Austin Miles, and Bobby Yerkes. Nelson is receiving a ringmaster's whistle from Miles.

MICHAEL GALLACHER

Austin Miles returning to the Royal Lipizzan Stallion Show, 1986.

Lori Miles as Miss Cumberland County, New Jersey, 1978.

me. I responded in some manner to every prayer request and, whenever possible, I scheduled visits to the sick person who needed to be prayed for. I never accepted donations for that kind of visit, and would never even have considered using those names for a mailing list. Often, I took a gift-wrapped Bible to the person I visited, and declined to accept anything in return. I regarded these as sacred missions of healing, where I should be the one doing the giving.

Rose Marie seemed lighthearted as we went down to the parking garage to get the car to take me to the airport. "Here, you drive," she said, smiling as she handed the keys to me.

We stopped in front of the TWA reception desk at LaGuardia Airport. Rose Marie remained with the car while I took my bags in. After I checked them in, I went back outside.

"Can we put the tree up early this year?" I asked.

"Yes, dat ve can do," she said, agreeably.

"Do you think you could have it up when I get back on the sixth? I'd like to have it up for the whole month and just keep December open as our family month."

"Yes, Sveetyheart. The tree vill be up ven you return." Rose Marie kissed me goodbye warmly. Never had she given me a more affectionate send-off.

My flight ran into dense fog and was forced to land in St. Louis. I called home during the wait. When Rose Marie heard my voice, she sounded anxious, almost frantic, to conclude the call. What could have happened in the last two hours to make such a difference? She had been so attentive and loving two hours earlier, and now she acted as if I were the last person she wanted to hear from.

"Ver are you?" she asked nervously.

"St. Louis. We were forced to land. I want you to please call the people in Atlanta that I was going to stop and pray for, tell them what happened, and that I won't be able to come to see them as I planned."

"*Ja, ja,* I'll call them. Bye." She hung up.

The fog did not lift, and I learned that the Atlanta airport was likewise completely socked in. I probably would not be able to reach Savannah at all that night.

Once again, I telephoned home. This time Lori answered. She seemed as strangely distant and uncommunicative as Rose Marie had been. This contagious mood swing made absolutely no sense. "Please Lori, just call Pastor Stanton and tell him that I have no idea when I will get in."

I got to Savannah in time for the start of the crusade and it went well. On Wednesday evening, I called home before the service. There was no answer. After midnight, the lack of an answer began to give me a sick feeling in the pit of my stomach. I tried phoning every fifteen minutes until early in the morning.

The next day, after hospital calls with Pastor Stanton, we stopped by the church. "I just want to check my messages," he said as he got out of the car, "then I'll drive you to your motel." When he returned, he had a letter in his hand. "Here," he said, "this came for you."

The handwriting on the envelope was Rose Marie's. This was the first time she had ever written to me at a church. I opened the letter right there. Tears rolled down my face as I read it.

Dear Al,

Lori and I have moved out. A check came for you and we used it to help us with our moving expenses. I have gathered some furnishings for you so that the apartment is not bare. I am filing for divorce.

I wish you the best of everything in the new life you have chosen for yourself,

Rose Marie

I slowly handed the letter to Reverend Stanton. I got out of the car, walked a few paces toward the motel, stopped, and turned back to him. "Please don't say anything about this. I don't want the people to worry about me. But I will ask you to pray for me, that God will give me extra strength for the service tonight."

During the song service, the tears continued to flow down my face. I looked at Mrs. Stanton, who was playing the organ. She quickly looked away. Tears were flowing down her face as well. Her husband had told her.

Instead of the sermon I had written, I preached extemporaneously on "love." I was unable to sleep that night and threw up several times.

The next day I walked through a shopping center across the street from the motel. The Christmas music, decorations, and families made me feel even worse. For the rest of the week I could not eat or sleep, despite my strenuous preaching Thursday and Friday nights.

On Saturday, just a week after I had left New York, I returned to the Forest Hills apartment. I hesitated before putting my key in the lock, and opened the door slowly. The first thing I saw was a poster Rose Marie had put there to greet me. It said, "Keep Smiling." The beautiful furniture was gone. In its place were sticks of furniture, obviously foraged from the streets. Some cheap, sheet metal bookshelves were propped up against the wall. The oil paintings and art objects had been replaced by TWA travel posters. The floors were bare. Books—mostly the Christian ones—

were scattered loosely everywhere. The ravaged, dust covered apartment gave no indication of the warm, elegant home it had recently been.

Unable to accept what I saw, I closed the door and stood vacantly in the hall. Mr. Siegel, my neighbor, opened his door. "I thought you moved," he said curiously.

"No," I replied haltingly. "My wife and daughter moved."

Mr. Siegel told me that the furniture had been moved out the Saturday before, beginning almost the moment I had left for the airport. Rose Marie's friends from TWA had helped her. A nearby grocery store had been saving boxes for her. Obviously this had been in the planning for some time. It seemed I had been the last to know. I felt betrayed by everyone.

In shock and filled with despair, I wandered out into the street. "Why, Lord, why?" ran through my mind over and over. How could God allow this to happen to me, His devoted servant?

Snowflakes danced in the air, as if to mock me. Brightly colored Christmas lights winked at me through the windows of the homes I passed. I agonized over Lori's having been in on the plot all along. The calls from St. Louis obviously had interrupted the move. Lori had given as little indication as Rose Marie of the planned desertion. How could my own daughter betray me that way? And where was she now?

I wandered aimlessly in the snow. I came face to face with Father Johnston of Our Lady of Mercy Catholic Church and School, where Lori had gone during the height of my FBI troubles. I told him what had happened. He tried to get me to come into the rectory with him. "No—thanks, Father Johnston," I said. "I—I just want to walk for a while."

"Look, I am here, available to you at any time, night or day. Please call me," he added, with genuine concern.

Much later, and soaked with snow, I returned to the apartment. The important Pentecostal teaching "Praise God in all things" ran through my mind. I had never been free in this place to pray or praise God unhindered. I lifted up my hands. "Praise the Lord!" I said out loud. "Praise you, Jesus. Hallelujah! Glory!" As I bounced these phrases off every bare wall in the apartment, I began to feel an extraordinary sense of satisfaction and holiness. A tight smile stretched across my face as I continued to walk through the apartment and "praise God" all night. I felt I had reached a new level of worship. Had anyone seen me, undoubtedly they would have thought I had gone mad.

When daylight seeped through the windows, I changed my clothes and left to catch the subway for Glad Tidings Tabernacle, where I was scheduled for two Sunday services.

"Cameron Stanton called me from Savannah and told me what happened," Reverend Stanley Berg told me in his study. "But I knew you would be here for the services. After all, you've been in show business, and the show must go on." We left the study, climbed up a spiral staircase, and walked through a hidden passage into a room behind the platform.

Seated in the congregation waiting for the service to begin was Van Varner, senior editor of *Guideposts*. He had come to do a story about my "Christian walk" for his magazine. When I was seated on the platform, I looked around the altar. "This is the only *important* furniture, anyway," I reasoned to myself.

As I preached my "You Are Special" message, I sensed a heightened attentiveness from the women, particularly the piano player, Marilyn King. At the end of the service, she hurried to reach me before anyone else.

"I want to talk to you," she said to me.

"What about?"

"I heard your wife left you," she declared.

"How on earth could you know that? It just happened."

"It's all over the church," she chirped.

I looked at her, puzzled. I had said absolutely nothing about it to anyone. Reverend Berg was supposedly the only one who knew about it, and that was because of Reverend Stanton's telephone call. I would have kept it completely to myself. It must have been from Reverend Berg that it spread throughout the congregation. That made me more upset than ever. I did not want this very personal, sensitive matter to be bantered about before I had a chance to deal with it.

"Let's meet for coffee and talk," Sister King persisted.

"No—thank you, Marilyn. This is a very painful time for me, and I wouldn't be very good company."

"What do you plan to do over the holidays?" Reverend Berg asked me when we were back in his study.

"I—don't know. I just don't know. By the way, Reverend Berg—how did everyone find out that Rose Marie had left me?"

"Oh," he replied. "I contacted a couple of strong prayer warriors from the church and asked them to uphold you in prayer during this difficult time."

"That was—very thoughtful of you, Reverend Berg. Thank you."

When I walked out of the empty church onto Thirty-third Street, a cold blast of December air hit me. I turned the collar of my overcoat up against the wind. It was a stark contrast to the cheerfulness of the meeting in the warm church the hour before. As I walked up the dark street, feelings of rejection and loneliness overtook me.

Waiting for the light to change at Eighth Avenue across from Madison Square Garden, a friendly voice behind me said, "Well, hello!" I turned around. It was Sister King.

"Marilyn, what are you doing here?"

"Waiting for you."

"Marilyn, please. I have to go home right away."

"To what? An empty apartment? Let me fix you some soup and tea. My apartment is in the Village. We can take the bus. And it's right near the IND subway to take you back to Forest Hills. Come on. It will be good for you."

"What the hell," I mumbled under my breath. "Why not?"

Marilyn lived in a small studio apartment in Greenwich Village, close to New York University, where she worked as a secretary. Her decor was overstuffed Victorian, with a touch of 1920s flapper look. An upright piano stood by one wall, flanked by floor-to-ceiling hanging beads. A framed record album cover showed Marilyn as a singer in the Revivaltime Choir. The way her dedication to tidiness kept this tiny, overfilled living space from looking cluttered was a marvel.

I looked Marilyn over as she busily prepared the soup and tea in wife-like fashion. Marilyn had just started the transition from youthful bloom to matronliness. Her round face and full frame were still attractive. Some disturbing pockmarks on her face were covered over with smooth, even applications of make-up. Only under careful scrutiny were they noticeable. Her dark hair and beautiful exotic eyes more than made up for that flaw.

A couple of years younger than I, Marilyn was at the point of horrified realization that she might never be married. The first impression she conveyed, of feminine warmth and subtle sensuality, was quickly spoiled by her overbearing, excessive eagerness.

I knew just what she was thinking. Here was the perfect helpmate for a minister—especially one with a high public profile. She was a fine singer and pianist, talents vital to a ministry. Why, she could even make a nonsinger sound good when she harmonized with one. She would be an excellent homemaker—she loved to cook—and she had superior secretarial skills as well. And, yes, she would be a warm, sexually responsive companion.

Surely God knew what she had to give, and would put it in the heart of the right man to sweep her up and give her *status* in the church world, rank that those less blessed would have to look up to and admire. That was what every child of God craved.

While the tea was brewing, she casually changed into a loose-fitting house dress. After we had eaten, she washed the dishes and put them away. She came over to the couch where I was sitting, curled up next to me, and tucked her feet under, making the house dress part over her bare thighs. Now I could clearly see the freckles on the tight skin of her legs. She took my hands in hers. "Please stay the night," she said. "Don't go."

The next morning, I found the IND subway entrance near NYU and went back to Forest Hills. The soup and tea had been satisfying. But I felt uncomfortable about what had happened later, and more unsettled than I did before. What if Rose Marie or Lori had tried to call while I was gone?

XXVII

I had no idea where Rose Marie and Lori had gone. My attempts to reach Rose Marie at work on the phone were met with hostility from her co-workers. The Performing Arts High School would not put Lori on the phone with me.

"But I'm her *father!*" I protested.

"That doesn't mean a thing," the principal answered icily. "If you try to make contact with her here, we'll call the police and have you arrested." What had these people been told to make them to treat me like a criminal?

An attorney named Edward Friedland telephoned me to tell me Rose Marie had hired him to draw up the separation and divorce papers. "We can either serve you with the papers, or you can come to my office and sign them here."

"I'll come and surrender to you in your office," I responded.

Mr. Friedland, with his big, ghoulish-looking eyes, would have been perfectly cast in an episode of "The Addams Family." "Your wife got hysterical—broke down four times while signing these papers," he said, placing the documents before me for my signature, one by one. "I said to her, 'Then why are you doing this to him?' She's a hysterical woman. You're better off without her."

"You ever been married?" I asked him.

"Many times," said the counselor with a shrug of his shoulders.

"Then I guess you know what you're talking about."

Rose Marie had taken the car and cleaned out a small joint account we had in a bank on Queens Boulevard. I wasn't exactly sure just what I had left. In a Christian bookstore, I bought a little plaque that said, "Bless This Mess," hung it on one of the walls, and then set about cleaning up and trying to put my house in order.

Rose Marie's friends from TWA enthusiastically supported her decision to end the marriage, and comforted and encouraged her. At a party, while everyone was laughing and talking, Rose Marie sat quietly on a couch with a filled glass in her hand, but not drinking from it. One of her girlfriends came over and sat down beside her.

"Come on, Rose Marie, cheer up. Live it up! You have a whole new life to live." Rose Marie just nodded her head. Others came over to her. Lori was sitting in a chair next to the couch.

"Look," one of Rose Marie's girlfriends interjected, "you made the right decision. The same thing happened to a friend of mine, and she divorced her husband over it. Once somebody gets religion, it's all over. There's absolutely nothing you can do about it. All they want to do is read the Bible, go to church, and try to save everybody. They lose all sense of responsibility. They go nuts! Al became a religious fanatic, and nobody could live with that."

Lori watched and listened with mixed emotions. She wanted to defend her father, but lacked the courage to speak out in the face of such unrelenting ridicule.

Rose Marie, Lori, and the two cats had taken an apartment within two miles of our original home. When they returned from that party, Rose Marie sat down in front of the empty bookcases, stared at them for some time, and then broke down in tears.

*   *   *

Reverend R. D. E. Smith, now promoted to the National Presbyters, flew into New York and asked for a meeting with me and Reverend Berg to discuss my future. My impending divorce was a matter of extreme concern to the Assemblies of God. The sin of divorce *might* be accepted in my life, so long as I was repentant, adhered to a life of celibacy, and never remarried. I assured these spiritual leaders that I would do exactly those things, and would never disgrace or humiliate the fellowship. That seemed to satisfy Reverends Smith and Berg.

Then I flew to Springfield, Missouri, to attend an evangelists' convention and seminar. I felt the fellowship and encouragement of the brethren would do me a "power" of good. I couldn't help but grin when I walked onto the main convention floor and saw nearly every evangelist there wearing a white suit, as a sign of purity. The theme of the convention was "Walk Worthy." Signs proclaiming that slogan hung everywhere.

Reverend Zimmerman expressed concern for my situation, and made a special point to assure me that all of the ministers were praying for me during this time of trial. That afternoon, with great dignity, he conducted the most elegant, poignant, deeply spiritual communion service I had ever taken part in. It was just the right backdrop for me to reflect on my commitment to God, the ministry, and the world at large.

I was in an awkward and vulnerable position. Word had spread far and wide about my sudden singleness. Church women were literally coming out of the woodwork to offer me their companionship, and making no bones about their intentions.

I sought the counsel of Reverend Paul Markstrom, Director of the Department of Chaplaincies. I had been credentialed as an industrial chaplain, specifically, "Chaplain to Show Business."

"I feel no anger toward Rose Marie," I told him.

He said, "That's not normal. You should allow yourself to be angry. Let it out. Don't keep it bottled up within you. It's not healthy!" That advice surprised me. "What are your plans?" he asked.

"To continue the ministry God has given me."

Requests for me to preach came in over the holiday season. Reverend Cooke called me from Bay Shore. "Something urgent has come up," he said, "and I must be out of town over Christmas. Could you please take my church the day after Christmas, the twenty-sixth? I really need your help." I agreed to do it.

Five days before Christmas the telephone rang. Something inside told me who the caller was. I hesitated, drew a deep breath, then picked up the phone. There was uncertainty in the voice at the other end.

"Hello—Dad?"

"Lori!"

"How—do you feel?"

"How do you think I feel after all this? Was that any way to treat your father?"

"Dad, that's the only way we could have done it. You would never have left on your own."

"Lori, what has happened to you? I've given you the best of everything. You helped clean me out, and left me junk in return."

"Mom said that's all you needed. You don't need better than that."

"Lori, where are you? I want to see you and talk to you."

"Then you'll have to see *our* lawyer," she said coldly, and hung up.

It appeared that not only Rose Marie was divorcing me. Lori was divorcing me too. Maybe the two cats were going to follow suit. Everybody was divorcing me!

Two days before Christmas, Lori phoned again and said she wanted to see me. I dropped everything and hurried to catch the subway. We met in Manhattan and went to a little French restaurant on Fifth Avenue. There was a big, lighted Christmas tree near the entrance. Lights and holly were strung all about. Lori tried to be stiff and proper, as a defense against her nervousness.

"First of all, baby, I'm not angry with you for what happened," I assured her. "You're my daughter, and I love you more than anything in this world. My door will always be open anytime you want to come and see me. As for Rose Marie, I want you to tell her something for me."

That made Lori tighten up, anticipating that she was about to be caught in the crossfire of a battle. Her face relaxed as she heard me out. "Tell her—tell her that I'm sorry for whatever I did that caused her to take this drastic action."

After we finished our meal, I walked with her to the subway. "Let's stop in this store for a moment," I said to her. I checked my wallet to see how much cash I had, then purchased a box of lemon-shaped soaps and had it gift wrapped. "Give this to Rose Marie, and tell her I sincerely wish her a Merry Christmas."

I walked Lori to the turnstile. "Lori—this is a rough time for all of us. But whatever you do—please don't let Jesus out of your life. And please ask Rose Marie to call me. Tell her I feel no animosity toward her, and I would like to spend some part of Christmas with you."

As Christmas Eve drew closer, the loneliness and sense of despair became more oppressive. I wrote in my journal:

December 22, 1976

Beginning this day with a heavy heart—grieved most of the night—finally resorted to a tranquilizer to settle down. Now shall try to address some Christmas cards to close friends.

The expression of love from pastors and people in various congregations in messages on their cards to me has been most gratifying. God will come through for me.

As I sit in this bare apartment, Christmas music in the background, I can only be comforted with the knowledge of other lonely men in history— Jesus—Paul—John—etc. I shall strengthen for my work and prepare for the lonely, lonely walk through this life—that is the price I have been required to pay for this ministry—a price I will have to pay every day.

I must identify with Paul, "to be content in whatever state I find myself." Oh, God, help me to endure this cruel loneliness!

At eleven o'clock, Mr. Friedland telephoned. I broached the subject of Lori's custody, and talked of switching to some other line of work so I could stay in one place and be a proper parent. He pointed out that Lori was now fourteen years old and "formed enough in her mind to come to her own conclusions." The parent who could provide the better home might not be the one to get custody, as would be the case with a small child; so he cautioned me against making any drastic changes. "Just concentrate on living your own life," he advised. "Take it from me: marriage is obsolete in this day and age."

Christmas Eve held the prospect of being the roughest day of all. But suddenly I began to criticize myself for being so selfish. "What's wrong with me?" I thought. "If I'm depressed with Christ in my heart, how awful it must be for those who do not have Jesus. They have to face this season without Him."

I began to see how this entire mess could be an opportunity for great blessings. I looked around me to see what was left that I might have to give. Of course! The Bibles I had acquired from the American Bible Society to use in my work as chaplain. I had a few dollars left in my wallet. I walked into the Forest Hills Woolworth's, bought some Christmas paper, went home, and gift-wrapped thirty-five Bibles. I put the wrapped packages into shopping bags.

In my clerical suit, with the shopping bags hanging from my arms, I headed out in the early evening toward Manhattan to look for some brokenhearted people. They were not hard to find. At Bryant Park on Forty-second Street, I encountered a shabbily dressed, unshaven man walking alone with slow, heavy steps. Although he was weary and obviously down on his luck, he was sober. I approached him.

"Hey, Brother! Merry Christmas in the name of the Lord! Here's a present for you."

Tears welled up in his eyes. He grabbed my hand and shook it warmly. We talked about God. His life had fallen apart, and he had planned to kill himself that night. I gave another Bible to a woman whose clothes were not nearly heavy enough to protect her from the harsh cold. The gesture seemed to make her sad face brighten.

After giving out several more of my packages, I went to Sloane-Kettering Memorial Hospital to visit some cancer patients. They, too, were alone on Christmas Eve. Sharing with them made my burden easier to bear. It gave me a blessing, to feel useful and needed.

In the past, I had always been able to retain my anonymity when walking the streets of New York. But tonight it seemed that everybody recognized me, many greeting me by name. Some had seen me on "The Joe Franklin Show," and others on "The PTL Club." God must have realized how very badly I needed human contact that night.

As I walked up Fifth Avenue, I resolved not to look in the ground floor TWA office where Rose Marie worked. In spite of myself, I stopped and turned toward the window. Inside, an office Christmas party was in progress. Near the back, Rose Marie, a glass of champagne in hand, was laughing at something someone had said. It was the old fun-loving, bright, lively—and, yes, charming—Rose Marie. Through the cold plate glass, I found myself caressing her with my eyes. I could almost hear strains of Bach's "Let the Sheep Safely Graze."

She suddenly glanced up and saw me in my black suit and clerical collar, looking in from the outside. Her expression changed to a look of compassion. She slowly put down her glass and walked toward me. Our eyes met, and in a fraction of a second more, my wordless plea for reconciliation would have been transmitted. But the words of Reverend Markstrom surged through my mind: "You should be *angry*. It's not normal not to be angry." Yes, he was right. What was I, a softie or something? I *must* show her I was angry, and punish her. With a well-acted flourish of indignation, I wheeled around and walked away. Had I followed my first impulse instead, I believe my whole life from that point would have been very different.

Giving out more Bibles and another hospital visit occupied me until very late. I had often thought of attending the famous Midnight Mass at St. Patrick's Cathedral, and now I had a keen desire to be there. Tickets for the event were always gone months in advance. Signs on all the doors declared that there were positively no more tickets to be had.

"I am a Protestant chaplain," I said to the man at the desk. "Is there any way you could slip me in? I'll be glad to stand in the back. It would— mean so much to me."

"Every ticket has been given out. We've even had to turn away some dignitaries who wanted to come. But for *you* Chaplain—" with a twinkle in his eye, the desk man broke off speaking, got up, and vanished into a side office. He came back with an envelope. "Here's the best seat in the house."

I was ushered in and down the long aisle to one of the front pews reserved for dignitaries. With the utmost in Catholic pomp and ceremony, the mass was conducted by Cardinal Cooke. Bishop Fulton J. Sheen delivered the sermon. His theme was that there are really two Christmases: the first, when Christ was born on earth, and the second, when He is born within us. I took it all in like water on dry ground.

When the huge assemblage was instructed to give one another the "handshake of peace," a pretty blonde girl on my left took my hand in both of hers and did not seem to want to let it go. That small gesture of acceptance and affirmation gave me a needed lift.

When I left St. Patrick's, I saw a horse-drawn carriage loaded with children going up Madison Avenue. The driver was decked out as Santa Claus, and everyone on board was singing "Jingle Bells."

On the subway going back to Forest Hills, I noticed the black conductor and studied him attentively. Surely he would rather have been with his family on Christmas Eve than working this train all night. As soon as I stepped off the train onto the platform, I went up to the conductor's window and handed him the last of my gift-wrapped Bibles. "Greetings from the Lord," I said to him. His face lit up in a big smile. He took off his right glove, shook my hand vigorously, and, leaning out the window, continued to wave happily back at me until his car was past the signal.

The clock chimed three times as I entered my apartment. I felt deeply satisfied. "Well, devil, you lost that one!" I said aloud. I knelt beside my bed. "Thank you, Jesus, for one of the best Christmases I ever had."

*   *   *

Rose Marie flew to Zurich on Christmas Day, and Lori came to stay with me for a few days while Rose Marie was gone. I took Lori with me to the various church services I conducted, and she obviously enjoyed them and the overall atmosphere.

"Daddy," she finally said to me, "I want to go to church regularly and be in Christian surroundings." She looked off into space. "Mommy said if I ever decided to live with you, she would never see me again. She said we'd be finished and then I'd have no one to look after me. She said it was my choice—her or you."

"Well, baby, it's whatever you decide. If you feel better living with Rose Marie, you have my blessing and I'll back you all the way. You have the keys to my apartment, and can come visit me any time you want."

On New Year's Day 1977, following services in Poughkeepsie, Lori and I boarded a commuter plane for New York City, where I had services that evening with Pastor William J. Behr at his Bethlehem Church in Richmond Hill, not far from where I lived in Forest Hills. I mentioned that I would like my daughter to play one of her classical pieces before I spoke.

"*No!*" Pastor Behr shot back vehemently. "Your daughter will *not* play classical music in my church. If she's going to play anything, she'll play only gospel hymns, music that glorifies God—not self!"

Lori was shocked and humiliated by the unexpected outburst. From that moment on, she felt a conflict that would subvert and eventually stifle her ambition to be a concert pianist.

Shortly after Rose Marie returned from Switzerland, Lori called me. "Dad," she said in tears, "Mommy and I had a big fight because I wanted to see you and go to church. She slapped me in the face, and I slapped her back. She said she is going to put me out on the street."

"Nobody's *ever* going to put you out on the street!" I declared emphatically. "Come on home."

She came immediately. There were other things on Lori's mind. In order to justify her actions, Rose Marie said nothing but negative things about me and encouraged her friends to speak ill of me as well, which they readily did. As insufferable as my actual behavior had been, what

Rose Marie and her friends were saying about me was extremely overstated. Lori began to see how one-sided and unfair all this was, and she had had enough.

Lori told me that Rose Marie had planned to strip our apartment earlier than she did, but that I had come home unexpectedly, much to her consternation. Rose Marie had told Lori about the less prepossessing aspects of my life, including my trouble with the FBI, and she attempted to convince Lori that I was some sort of criminal. She showed her the documents we had both altered to effect my name change.

I had desperately wanted to shield Lori from my past, but now, in view of these circumstances, she had to be told the whole truth about everything, including her birth mother. It was difficult for both of us, but Lori assimilated the information with exceptional calm and serenity.

*   *   *

When Rose Marie learned that Lori had packed up her things and come to live with me, she became uncontrollably hysterical and briefly wound up in the hospital. She went to stay with a Swiss girlfriend, Elsbate, and her husband Tony Devito in New Jersey to recover. I ached inside when I realized how much she was hurting. That I could feel that with her— for her—showed me that I still loved her very much. And I missed her. When finally I got to talk to her on the phone, she agreed to take a bus from New Jersey and meet me at the Port Authority bus station.

My heart raced with anticipation and excitement as I waited for her. Getting off the bus, she looked worn out and tired. I pulled her to me and held her close, neither of us saying anything. We walked over to Glad Tidings Tabernacle. We had the whole church to ourselves, and talked for a long time. Then I took her to dinner at Brewmaster's on Thirty-fourth Street. It was an agreeable place with a lot of atmosphere. Between courses, I held her hand as we continued the deepest and frankest discussion we had had in years. We were both very open.

"Rose Marie, I believe that we can make a new start. If we could wipe both slates clean—forgive each other—I know we can have a great life. And I think we both want that." We agreed to see each other and to try to put things back together. She wanted to remain living separately in the meantime, and she did not make an issue of Lori's continuing to live with me.

I called Reverend Berg to ask him if he knew an appropriate woman in the church who might be available to come and stay in my apartment with Lori while I was out fulfilling my evangelistic commitments. I had planned to cut down on my traveling so I could spend more time in New

York with Lori.

Within the hour, I received a phone call from Marilyn King, saying she would be happy to stay with Lori.

"I will be able to pay you—"

"No, that's all right," she interrupted. "You don't have to pay me."

"I insist on paying you. This will take up your time."

I prepared my next trip to PTL. In my journal I wrote:

January 12, 1977

Flew to Charlotte, NC—plane late—3 hours. Praise God!—delay allowed me to be at airport to meet Dale Evans also coming in to be on PTL Club. A real gracious lady who loves the Lord.

The next morning I had breakfast with Dale Evans. Then we were taken to the Heritage Village Studios. I loved the new studios, and felt they were a real tribute to God.

"Hello, Austin, remember me?"

I turned to look at the woman who spoke. She was exquisite. Her aristocratic beauty was complemented by the rich-looking clothing and accessories she wore. Anything less would surely have looked out of place on her. I gazed at her for a moment.

"Lyn McMann," she said, refreshing my memory. "We met at Ernie Eskelin's church. I'll never forget that service you gave."

"Yes, of course! Lyn, the actress. Only you look different now. Your hair was in pigtails then. It's styled differently. You seem different, but its becoming. What are you doing here?"

"I work here now," she said. "I'm the guest coordinator. But we have to talk. We have something very much in common." Before I could ask what that might be, she told me. "Both of our marriages split up at the same time, this last Christmas. Isn't that interesting?"

"I am sorry your marriage broke up, Lyn. How did you find out that Rose Marie and I broke up?"

"I read it in the papers," she answered. "But isn't that something! We both got divorced at the same time."

"I'm not divorced yet, Lyn, just separated, and I'm trying to reconcile with my wife. Please pray for me. I need a lot of prayer right now."

A special chapel was located near the TV studio and all connected with the telecast were encouraged to spend time on their knees in prayer before the program. Most of us wanted to do just that.

The telecasts were becoming more and more exciting. The live orchestra gave the production a rousing, professional flair. From the first regal timpani roll, leading into the majestic theme music composed by Gary Paxton, one's blood rushed with invigoration, reaching a high pitch of excitement as the program unfolded. This was no longer just a religious program. "The PTL Club" had become full-fledged, big-time television.

After the telecast, Jim Bakker lingered on the set to talk informally to the studio audience about the goals of the PTL ministry. Jean Albuquerque, a PTL greeter and hostess, came backstage to see me. A gregarious woman, she was well suited to her job and made everyone feel comfortable.

"You were great!" she said to me, with the kind of reassurance one needs coming off such a widely watched telecast. I always felt that it could have been a lot better.

"Thanks," I said to her.

"I want to give you something to give to Rose Marie. Here. It's a PTL Bible. I put a little note inside to her. I'm going to keep you and Rose Marie in prayer, and I believe that your marriage will be put back together."

When I got back to my room, I jotted in my journal:

Jan. 13th 1977

PTL Club

Very anointed—best appearance yet.

I went to the dining room for lunch. "Oh, by the way Austin," an aide interjected, leaning over me. "I was told to tell you that if you like, you can use the health facility. We have an exercise room, whirlpool, steam room. . . ."

*   *   *

Rose Marie seemed genuinely touched by the gift Bible and the note from Jean Albuquerque. To my delight, she told me that she loved God and had started attending a Methodist church with a friend from Scotland, Ellen Bellhaven. I learned that Rose Marie had also asked to have a blessing said over meals, something she would never allow in the past. Rose Marie was on her way to the airport. Uncle Fritz had been taken ill. From Zurich, she planned to go to Monte Carlo.

I also had to leave right away to begin a week-long revival at the Assembly of God church in Farmingdale, New York. Pastor Irving Stevens appeared worried.

"We need this crusade badly," he said. "Our attendance is way down, to about fifty on Sunday mornings and less than twenty-five at night. There's a real falling away."

"What do you attribute it to?"

"That pastor in Massapequa—Eugene Profeta! That money-making scoundrel! He is preaching that Christians *can* be demon-possessed. That's totally unscriptural. But he's confusing and frightening a lot of people who are convinced *he* is the one who can instruct them properly to fight such evil. This church has lost over one hundred members to him!"

The Farmingdale Assembly of God enjoyed big crowds during the crusade, and as so often happened, many people "testified" to miraculous healings. Then it happened again. A woman came up to me and said, "Brother Miles, I want you to know something. While you were praying I definitely saw Christ standing behind you! I have never seen anything like it in my life!" She was well dressed, looked intelligent, and was not at all the usual type that would tell me this.

Another woman walked up during our conversation and said, "I can verify that. I saw it too!"

What was this manifestation that people were telling me they saw? Perhaps this was a "sign." Of course—a sign never to leave the ministry. God would work out my marriage problems with Rose Marie. She had now started going to church, and combined with this sign, it proved that I should not leave the ministry. I had been considering doing just that. I had felt that the main problem in my marriage was my involvement with the church and Christianity. But there was, after all, nothing wrong with Christianity. Or was there? I was thinking about the PTL steam room.

XXVIII

The startling report in the newspaper took me completely by surprise. What next? Investigative reporter Jack Anderson first brought it to public attention in his national column out of Washington, D.C. Other major news stories, particularly in the *Springfield Leader and Press,* spun off, as more light was shed on the scandal.

The Reverend Thomas F. Zimmerman had been exposed manipulating the funds of the Assemblies of God denomination for his own personal gain. The tithes and offerings of the more than 8,500 Assembly of God churches, Sunday school offerings, collections for missionaries, and monies from decedents' estates all came through the Springfield, Missouri, headquarters. A veritable fortune poured in daily.

"Brother Z" had concocted a shrewd scenario for letting the denomination's money work to enrich him. His position as a member of the investment committee gave him virtual unsupervised control over the denomination's funds. He arranged for deposits to be made in the Empire Bank of Springfield, in which he owned 340 shares of stock. At their highest, the Assemblies' deposits in Empire Bank totaled 1.6 million dollars, a conspicuously excessive amount for a "nonprofit" organization to entrust to a relatively small, weak bank. The bank issued "Brother Z" ten thousand additional shares of common stock against his promissory note. Entering into a voting trust with four other Assemblies' hierarchs owning Empire Bank stock (among them, the same Reverend Paul Markstrom who once gave me disastrous, Iago-like marital counseling), "Brother Z" was appointed chairman of the bank's board of directors. Without investing any more of his own money, "Brother Z" took control of Empire Bank. Effectively, he pulled that off with money he borrowed *from* Empire Bank. Even for the most sophisticated Wall Street corporate raider, that would be an elegant coup.

Another high denominational official, Reverend Don Shelton, Secretary of the Stewardship Department, had in his spare time put together a parcel of land in suburban Springfield for some investors from Arkansas. On the parcel, they planned to build a major shopping center. The Executive Presbytery tacitly admitted that Reverend Shelton had let the sellers of the land think it was being bought for church expansion, apparently to keep the prices down. Before the prospect of the shopping center became known around Springfield, Reverend Shelton, "Brother Z," and a third man arranged to buy another hundred-acre tract across the road from the site of the planned shopping center and adjacent to "Brother Z's" house. That tract's value, as well as that of "Brother Z's" house, would skyrocket when the news of the planned shopping center finally got out. One credible estimate placed the subsequent value of the hundred acres, bought by the three churchmen for $155,000, at $800,000.

Conveniently, Empire Bank made the loans to the Arkansas investors to buy the land in Reverend Shelton's package, and to "Brother Z" and Reverend Shelton's troika to buy the hundred acres. An oral promise made by the Arkansas investors to contribute toward a chapel for Evangel College when their shopping center was completed supposedly brought all this wheeling and dealing within the mandate "to properly use God's money for God's work." Reverend Shelton also used his position as a springboard into politics. Casting additional shadows on the integrity of the denomination as a whole, it was revealed that members of the church hierarchy not actively involved had known about the deal and had turned a blind eye to these schemes.

Since there was no clear-cut criminal activity, such as theft or misappropriation of denominational assets, there has always been confusion as to what was actually wrong with these activities. Unfounded rumors about the granting of interest-free loans by Empire Bank and killings made in speculation on Empire Bank stock abounded in Assemblies' circles. I never sorted out precisely what made these events a scandal until I researched the matter for this book.

In hindsight, the trail of dishonest denials, resignations, and changes in the denomination's procedures in the face of public assurances that none were needed provide a good map of the scandal. At first, "Brother Z's" service on the bank board was presented as some sort of civic volunteer work, for which he had been sought because of his financial expertise. When his slender credentials as an expert in banking and finance came under scrutiny, it became obvious that the large deposits of church funds he had brought with him were a more likely reason for his having been chosen. (He did conduct himself very astutely—but the bank's shareholders, to whom a director owes his first duty of loyalty, stood at best well down the list of those "Brother Z" wished to assist by his board membership.)

"Brother Z" countered that he had steered the funds into Empire Bank in order to get the church a better interest rate. In fact, the rate of interest earned by the Assemblies' funds at Empire Bank was competitive with other nearby financial institutions, but no better. A year before the scandal broke, the other presbyters overruled "Brother Z" and instituted a ceiling on how much of the denomination's funds could be deposited in any one bank. For once, the right reason was also the one announced for the change: Because of the risk of bank failure, it is a usual and sound practice to have very large sums of an organization's funds spread among several banks. The new rule caused the Assemblies' deposits in Empire Bank to shrink to about one-tenth of what they had been at their height. (Interestingly, one of the Presbyters who participated in making the new rule and who then declined to comment about it to the press was Richard Dortch.)

The admission that he stood to benefit financially from his involvement with Empire Bank had been particularly difficult to drag out of "Brother Z." Ironically, the Executive Presbytery's claim that the ten thousand shares of common stock "were registered in his name for voting purposes" amounted to an unintended accusation of a far greater impropriety than any it may have seemed to deny. A sham stock transaction—the creation of stock without corresponding investment into the corporation to wrest voting control of a business corporation from the stockholders who have legitimately invested in it—is highly unethical and illegal.

The land deals raised less subtle questions of propriety. At first, "Brother Z" lied, denying that he had a financial interest in the shopping center. Later on, he tried to dodge the issue by emphasizing he had not been party to the shopping center deal itself. Church offices and contacts—the Arkansas investors were prominent Assemblies' laymen—had been used to put together the shopping center deal and keep it secret long enough for private individuals to exercise an unfair advantage in acquiring the land from its unwary owners. While such a scheme in the real estate market is not technically a crime like its "insider trading" counterpart in the stock market, it is a sharp practice, and a highly inappropriate use of the offices of a church denomination.

At its annual meeting the previous August—in 1976—the matter of "Brother Z's" relationship with Empire Bank was discussed in the denomination's two-hundred-member General Presbytery. This elite group is the official policy-making body of the church when the rank-and-file General Council is not in session. The hierarchy would never have allowed this matter to come before the General Council, knowing full well that the ordinary pastors and ministers who make up the larger body would not approve such use of the church's offices and funds. Everyone in the larger body had to be kept in the dark.

In presenting the matter before the two-hundred-man General Presbytery, vague, general terms were used and reference was made to the facts being "public knowledge" as an all-purpose excuse for not giving out the more damaging details. No information was sent or made available to the rank-and-file clergy until after the press broke the scandal.

The story was reported in the media early in 1977. A letter was issued from the Assemblies' national headquarters over the signature of Reverend Joseph R. Flower, then the General Secretary. It was headed:

January 10, 1977

To Assemblies of God Ordained and Licensed Ministers

Dear Brethren:

The letter referred to the statements made by the press as "innuendos," even though everything in them was backed up by documents and facts. It went on to say:

Anderson's column cites a "church official" as his source of information. To our knowledge, no recognized church official has been involved in such unscriptural practices.

The letter further instructed us all to refer any questions from the press to the Office of Information at national headquarters. In the last paragraph, the General Secretary implored us:

Brethren, I would urge you to join us in prayer for our General Superintendent and our Movement. Apart from the personal injury this has brought to Brother Zimmerman, it ultimately does a great disservice to our entire Movement and the work of the Lord.

Accompanying the letter was a legal sized piece of paper, dated January 10, 1977, purporting to answer our questions. It began:

The Rev. Thomas Zimmerman's association with the Empire Bank of Springfield has been a matter of *public knowledge* from the beginning. [my italics]

Also:

Members of the Executive Presbytery, as the church's board of directors, do not consider that the Rev. Zimmerman's association with the bank is responsible for *any special concession to the Assemblies of God or to Rev. Zimmerman personally.* [my italics]

Following the discussion, the General Presbytery expressed complete confidence in Rev. Zimmerman's leadership of the church, and did not request that he disassociate himself from Empire Bank.

Near the end, it stated:

The Executive Presbytery expresses its support for Rev. Zimmerman's leadership of the church and full confidence in his personal integrity.

As the heat continued to be turned up, "Brother Z" sent a letter out to the ministers. Dated February 3, 1977, it began, "Dear Brethren: Warm Greetings!" It went on to say that Reverend Zimmerman was publicly re-validating his commitment to the Lord and His church. Then it got down to the nitty gritty:

> (1) I have taken, at my own initiative, steps to divest myself of all my stock which I have held in a voting trust at Empire Bank.

The next point was even more artfully worded:

> (2) Furthermore, I have notified the President of Empire Bank that I will no longer serve as chairman of its Board of Directors nor as a member of the board.

Nowhere was it written that he had *resigned,* or that his resignation had been accepted or had taken effect. He merely told them that he did not want to serve any more. With a noble exhibition of Christian love and humility that deeply impressed us all, he continued:

> For an error in judgment that involved my participation in a relationship which has brought embarrassment to our Fellowship, I am sincerely sorry. I ask your forgiveness. I solicit your prayers and understanding. At no time would I want to do anything that would erode an impeccable portrayal of a life which is void of offense before God and my brethren.
>
> I want to convey to this entire Fellowship my love and intent to serve always in an exemplary fashion. By the sustenance and refinement of God's grace, I want to draw closer to Him in every aspect of my ministry so as to walk worthy of this high calling.

> Sincerely,
> /s/ Thos. F. Zimmerman
> General Superintendent

I was touched by the letter, and went on to read an accompanying document with the heading:

REPORT TO THE CREDENTIALED CONSTITUENCY OF
THE ASSEMBLIES OF GOD
February 3, 1977

Referring to "innuendos," like the earlier one, the report informed us:

> We shall again, instead, confine ourselves to those allegations which have some foundation in fact, explain the circumstances and *trust to the good judgment of our brethren.* [my italics]

After explaining the charges pertinent to "Brother Z's" involvement with the bank, the report went on:

> The rationale for the above is simply that his expertise in financial affairs was desired by the controlling interests of the bank. *It is not argued that there was no financial advantage for him in this arrangement.* [my italics]

And:

> What has not been said is that this land adjoined the residence of Thomas Zimmerman and may therefore be considered as much an attempt to protect his neighborhood from the unknown impact of the coming shopping center as it could be considered an investment. The Executive Presbytery does not feel that there has been any dishonesty in land or bank dealings by our General Superintendent, but it does believe that there was an error in judgment to which he has freely admitted.

While I was still inclined to see only good in the Assemblies of God church and its leaders, I could not help but gag on the double-talk of this apologia. My head was in a whirl. Where did you draw the line between "misjudgment" and "dishonesty"—especially when the "misjudgment" conveniently just happened to bring in a handsome profit for those who committed it? Why had Reverend Shelton's misjudgment warranted his resignation from church office, but not "Brother Z's"? Why was such a point made of the upcoming audit of the Assemblies' books, when there had been no allegation that any of the improprieties were located there? I went through the three-page report again. It, too, failed to mention whether or not Reverend Zimmerman had actually resigned from his position on the bank board.

The report closed with the predictable summation that Bible-believing Christians resort to when their labors fail to yield good fruit:

> The Executive Presbytery believes this attack, centered at the moment upon the Assemblies of God, is a conspiracy attacking the evangelical society. We expect to see it extended against all who claim a "born-again" experience. . . . Could we ask that you join us in closing our ranks against all the attacks of the enemy that come from within and without?

Let us devote ourselves prayerfully and unitedly to the fulfilling of the eternal purpose: to worship God; to build the church; *and to evangelize the world.* [my italics]

*   *   *

I was sitting with Pastor Edward G. Berkey in his study after the service at Bethany Assembly of God in Springfield, Massachusetts. Another news story had broken about "Brother Z" and the bank.

"Do you have a copy of the constitution and bylaws of the Assemblies?" I asked him.

"Sure," he replied. He got up, went to the bookshelf, and took down the 1973 booklet, *Revised Constitution and Bylaws: General Council of the Assemblies of God.* I flipped through several pages, stopping on a provision on page 141, § 6, entitled "worldliness." It stated:

We urge all believers to "Love not the world, neither the things that are in the world . . . For all that is in the world, the lust of the flesh, and the lust of the eyes, and the *pride of life* is not of the Father, but is of the world." (1 John 2:15-16)

In its teaching regarding worldliness, the Scripture warns against: Participation in activity which defiles the body, or corrupts the mind and spirit; the inordinate love of, or preoccupation with, pleasures, *position or possessions,* which lead to their misuse; manifestation of extreme behavior, unbecoming speech, or inappropriate utterance; any fascination or *association which lessens one's affection for spiritual things.* (Luke 21:34-35; Romans 8:5-8, 12:1-2; 2 Corinthians 6:14-18; Ephesians 5:11; 1 Timothy 2:8-10, 4:12; Titus 2:12; James 4:4; 1 John 2:15-17) [all italics mine]

"Reverend Berkey, didn't 'Brother Z' help to form the bylaws of the Assemblies?"

"Absolutely! It's his leadership that has made the Assemblies what it is today."

"Reverend Zimmerman certainly knows a lot of Scripture. You're a Presbyter, aren't you?" He nodded his head. "Do you think that, as the report stated, this story of 'Brother Z' and the bank is of the devil?"

"No question about it. This is an out-and-out attack of the enemy to try and destroy our great work of God. The devil hates that. Every time a great work of God is taking place, the devil—prowling about like a roaring lion—seeks whom he may devour! Jack Anderson and all the media are of the devil, servants of Satan trying to cause reproach upon our fellowship and bring down this great work of God."

Maybe he was right.

*   *   *

It was late when I returned to Forest Hills. Marilyn King met me at the door.

"You knew I was coming back tonight. I didn't expect to find you still here."

"I thought I had better wait until you got here, to make sure," she replied. "Anything could have happened, and I didn't want Lori to be here alone."

"It is awfully late for you to be taking a subway home."

"How about if I stayed here for the night? I'm really concerned about taking the subway so late."

"Yes, let her," Lori piped in.

"O.K.," I said, resignedly. "You go ahead and use the bedroom, Marilyn. I'll sleep on the couch."

"The couch?"

"The couch."

Just as I dozed off, the telephone rang. "Hello," I mumbled.

"Hello, Austin. This is Lyn McMann."

"Lyn—what time is it?"

"It's late, I know. How are things?"

"Oh, about the same. It's a very difficult situation. I don't know what's going to happen."

"Austin, we *must* talk. Do plan to come and visit my mountain home when you come back for the program. I have some paintings there I know you would like, and the scenery is beautiful."

"Lyn," I said sleepily, "we'll talk about it when I come down."

Marilyn had opened the bedroom door part way and was listening. The expression of jealous rage on her face was just in my line of vision.

"A single woman has no business calling a man at his home at this late hour!" she lectured, haughtily. "This just doesn't look right, and as a *Christian,* I don't like it!" The next sound I heard was the bedroom door being slammed shut.

XXIX

Harold Olshields, one of the PTL chauffeur staff, met my plane in Charlotte and accompanied me out to the gleaming white stretch limousine. The V.I.P. treatment was flattering, and it did give me a feeling of importance.

My PTL appearances, I knew very well, were the main reason why my own recognition factor had reached an all-time high. However, the prospect of seeing Jim, my benefactor, for the first time since the encounter in the steam room made me tense.

"Who's going to be on the show with me?" I asked Harold, looking for some bit of good news to allay my doubts.

"Charles and Frances Hunter," he said with delight.

"Good," I said. "I've been wanting to meet them."

I spent about twenty minutes in the chapel, praying for the telecast, and then went into the studio. I barely had time to say hello to the Hunters when Bill Garthwaite came backstage and hurried us onto the set.

The "Happy Hunters" were to sit on the couch. The producer placed me in the wing chair next to Jim's desk.

"Quick, get me an extra pillow!" Charles Hunter exhorted, with urgency in his voice.

Charles and Frances Hunter were truly the odd couple. He was a former accountant, and would have looked very much at home juggling figures and making entries in ledgers. He was small and scrawny, with thin hair and a narrow face, albeit one that could light up in a big smile when the situation warranted it. She was a tall, big-boned, masculine looking woman who towered over her husband, both in size and attitude. Charles needed the pillow under him to bring his head level with his wife's.

The Hunters, headquartered in Texas like so many big-time evangelists, were heavyweights on the traveling revival circuit. Their high profile ministry always espoused whatever theme was in vogue. Like many evangelists at that time, they had suddenly "caught the vision" and were preaching a "prosperity" message. One could have anything one desired by naming it and then "claiming" it by unwavering faith. In their services, they taught how such faith could be perfected by being obedient to God. The obedience training included a number of different facets. "Sacrificial giving" to God's servants was stressed as one of the most efficacious of those. Appropriate giving would assure the faithful of miraculous "financial blessing" in return.

A trademark of the Hunters' ministry was the phenomenon of having numbers of their audience be "slain in the spirit" during their services. Since the evangelists were so "anointed of God," it was explained, and "filled with His Holy Spirit" as they ministered, one could not stand next to either of them without being knocked flat on the floor by God's overwhelming presence. Sometimes in their meetings the Hunters would walk down an aisle, wave their hands, and entire rows of people would fall out of their seats like tenpins, receiving a special kind of blessing thereby. That show of power became an increasingly important feature of the service, and came to be regarded as a barometer of God's working in it.

Pressure developed over this "gift." Other evangelists and even pastors began to feel that they were failing God if this manifestation did not occur in their services. Some evangelists tried to *make* it happen by planting suggestions in the minds of the crowd or by trying to push some of them down. Others went so far as to put batteries under the carpet where the subject would stand. The preacher would touch the head of the worshiper and step on a button that would cause an electric shock to be administered. Robert Elliott, an electronics expert, revealed to me that he had constructed such an electrified carpet for, among others, Oral Roberts. Only the Hunters were able to pull off this particular demonstration of God's power consistently, and seemingly with little or no effort.

Although I was consciously quite receptive to the Hunters, inwardly I felt a severe conflict when I met them. Jim seemed as anxious as me during the telecast. I had never felt so ill at ease.

"One of our favorite guests on 'The PTL Club,' " Jim began, "is Austin Miles, the Show Business Chaplain who believes that *everybody* is special! Welcome back, Austin."

"Thank you, Jim, and it is true. Everybody *is* special!"

"Austin, what has God been doing in your life since we last saw you?"

"Not enough," I replied with the most cut and dried statement I had ever uttered on television. Jim straightened up cautiously. "You know, Jim, I love God and God's servants, and they all come in different packages with individual ideas. And thank God for that. People aren't supposed to be alike. But I've been slowly seeing things in the ministry I never expected to see."

"I know exactly what you mean," Jim quickly interjected. "Now I don't mean to judge anybody. Only God is the judge, but I've been seeing things being done by certain television evangelists that I just cannot relate to."

"It goes beyond that, Jim. I have been seeing out-and-out fraud and corruption."

The Hunters squirmed nervously, even though I had not been referring to them. At one point, I caught a look of absolute terror on Frances' face, as if she feared all hell might break loose at any moment. Jim got me back on track, and the conversation turned to lighter things.

Following the telecast, Jim had me minister to the studio audience. After lunch, I went with "Uncle" Henry Harrison to a finely equipped radio studio. From it, he broadcast a nightly national radio program called "Night Watch." I had first become aware of Uncle Henry when I accidently tuned in "The 700 Club" on television. Uncle Henry was co-host with Pat Robertson that day. I was a new Christian then, and so excited to discover such a program that I telephoned members of the Royal Lipizzan Stallion Show in their motel rooms and got them to turn it on. Uncle Henry looked like a "good ol' boy," a real huggable teddy bear. Along with Bill Garthwaite and several other key "700 Club" people, Uncle Henry left in 1975 to join Jim Bakker in the fledgling PTL venture.

The move had not been the best for Henry Harrison. Although he lived quite well, he had gradually been reduced to the role of staff buffoon. He was never brought into serious discussions, never asked his opinion on anything that mattered. Eventually, he was reduced to making frantic attempts to interject something—anything—into the conversation, to prove he was really part of the program and not just a bump on a log, programmed to laugh at any joke or say "amen" to any revelation. When he did manage to get a word in edgewise, Jim would either barely acknowledge him or cut him short. Even a groan from the panel or the audience came to signify some small measure of affirmation to Uncle Henry, better than no response at all. To get attention, he made puns at every opportunity. Even then, he would laugh nervously as he set up the pun, obviously struggling, sawing the air with his hands as he spoke, to keep from getting interrupted before the punch line. This had gone way past the point where he could hope to be taken seriously.

Once when John Wesley Fletcher prayed for the PTL audience, Uncle Henry "went out in the Spirit." The audience cheered, clapped, and laughed as Uncle Henry the clown awkwardly fell over backwards. It was a mean kind of fun, reminiscent of the reaction to a knockout at a prizefight. Uncle Henry's wife, "Aunt" Susan, in complete despair over what PTL had made of her husband's image, once told me, "Nobody cares." Uncle Henry had been misused.

Even I got carried away with the PTL Uncle Henry image. He had successfully completed a dieting program, bringing under control a weight problem that seriously threatened his health. I sneaked into the PTL health club facility and stole a pair of his old bathing trunks from his fat days. On my next appearance, I brought in the trunks gift wrapped and presented the package to Jim, to prove to one and all that "nothing is impossible with God." When the package was unwrapped, the sight of the huge, tent-like bathing trunks brought a roar of laughter from the crowd. "Uncle Henry's old trunks!" I triumphantly proclaimed.

"I thought I recognized them," he answered, laughing good-naturedly.

Aunt Susan was not amused. She thought it neither funny nor appropriate, and let me know it in a few choice words right after the telecast, the last she would say to me for several visits to come. She was right. I had tried to be clever at someone else's expense. I had tried to be clever at someone else's expense and I regretted it.

Beneath the bumpkin image Jim forced onto Uncle Henry was a very fine broadcaster. His was the first and last voice heard on "The PTL Club" each day. Uncle Henry timed his announcements perfectly to accompany the opening and closing credits as "voice-over," bringing the show smoothly into and out of format every time. Usually, he composed his announcements on the spot, and material was often added or deleted at the last minute. Uncle Henry never skipped a beat. Never once did I hear him garble or fluff a line. All this was simply taken for granted. The contribution his skilled professionalism made to the overall high production value of the show seemingly went unnoticed, except by a few broadcast professionals attuned to recognize quality work. Henry Harrison enhanced PTL's image tremendously, while PTL made sport of him in return.

Uncle Henry did get a chance to be his best behind the microphone for "Night Watch." He was articulate, smooth, deep-voiced, with plenty to say that was worth hearing. I liked seeing him free to exercise his abilities without restraint. In this setting, Uncle Henry wasn't second fiddle to anyone. He was a star. That hour he and I spent together on the radio gave me more pleasure than any other PTL experience.

That night, I preached at Trinity Assembly of God again. *The Charlotte Observer* had covered a service I conducted there on an earlier visit. The January 14, 1977, *Observer* carried a very favorable article about me, including confirmation of miraculous healings reported to have taken place at the service. The article heightened interest in my meetings for some time.

After the service, Pastor Bacon introduced me to Dexter Yeager, a close friend of Jim Bakker. Yeager had become a legend of sorts. In his forties, he had found himself out of work. He joined Amway and amassed a fortune, eventually including several banks. Now he had the best of everything, including a fleet of limousines for his personal use.

He had the unusual habit of carrying a shoulder satchel. "Take a look inside," he invited me. I reached in and came out with a fist full of one-hundred-dollar bills.

"Good Lord!" I exclaimed. "How much is in there?"

"Fifteen—twenty thousand dollars," he answered nonchalantly. "This is my pocket money."

Jim Bakker so admired Dexter Yeager, his lifestyle, and the money he was able to make utilizing the Amway pyramid sales technique, that Jim let Yeager sign him up as an Amway representative.

Yeager announced that he wanted to take Pastor and Mrs. Bacon and me to dinner as his guests. I very much looked forward to that dinner. One of his posh limousines pulled up, and away we went. Dexter Yeager did take us to dinner—at Perkins Pancake House.

T he note in my motel box read, "The pastor will pick you up at
6:30 tonight."

It had been a long day. A snowstorm in New York had hindered
my travel. The wings of the plane had to be de-iced. When I got to Chicago,
there was no answer at the hosting pastor's phone number. I took the
airport bus to Rockford and checked myself into the Sweden House Motel,
as planned. I freshened up and waited for the pastor to come.

The moment Pastor Ernest J. Moen (he preferred "Pastor" to "Reverend") arrived, I felt a severe conflicting spirit. As I got in his car, the
Bible perched on the dashboard caught my eye. Most Pentecostals who
are having a "deep walk" with the Lord keep their Bibles with them at
all times. This one's owner, an extremely handsome, well-built man, looked
to be in his forties. His natty, gray striped suit was elegant, almost
ostentatious.

As we drove to the church he said, "Now tonight I don't want you
to talk about divine healing, or dwell on Christ. I've been doing that all
week. I want you to talk about your show business experiences and the
celebrities you know. It will be good for the people."

That took me by surprise. "You flew me all the way out here for
that? I left show business to preach the Gospel, and I understood you
wanted me to give my testimony, which is a healing testimony and exalts
Christ."

"Well," he conceded, "maybe you should mention something about
it, but don't dwell on it. Whatever you do, wind up your message with
a salvation appeal. This is a 'salvation' church. *I* can preach on Hershey
bars and people will get saved."

I looked over at him incredulously. "I would like very much to hear
your sermon on Hershey bars."

When we got to First Assembly of God on Spring Creek Road, the
parking lot was already overflowing, and it did not look as if everyone
who wanted to attend would fit into the 1,500-seat sanctuary. Besides my
PTL appearances, a feature story on me in the current issue of *Christian*

Life Magazine had drummed up interest.

"Look at that crowd!" Pastor Moen exclaimed with delight. "This is the best Sunday night attendance we have ever had."

He left me alone for a few moments while the pastoral staff ran around congratulating themselves on the large crowd. I felt I really needed prayer at the moment, to quiet the jangling feelings this environment somehow aroused in me. "Excuse me," I said to one of the staff ministers on his way by, "would it be possible for you to come to the chapel and pray with me for the service?"

"Too busy right now," he said, continuing on his way without even slowing his step. There seemed to be no quiet place in this church.

As the time to start the service approached, Pastor Moen finally reappeared. "Come," he said, beckoning as he walked me to the rear aisle where we were to make our entrance. From there, I got my first look at the interior of this enormous church. The place was alive, every possible space filled with people. An air of expectancy pervaded as the lights dimmed. The choir began with a dramatic build-up, augmented by special lighting effects.

While waiting, Pastor Moen took in the shapely legs of one of his young lady parishioners. There was nothing discreet or subtle about the way he looked her over. She suddenly glanced up at him and flashed him a friendly, familiar sort of smile that seemed as out of place in a church as Pastor Moen's own behavior. He gave a second lady the same sort of ogling once-over as she came up to talk with him for a moment. My discomfort grew. I had been under the impression that a minister was not at liberty to check out any woman's legs except his wife's, and then only in private. I reproved and corrected myself for falling into the sin of judging him, or perhaps, being skeptical of God's servant. After all, he was a high-ranking man of God.

"All right," Pastor Moen said commandingly, "as soon as I give you the signal, walk along side me down the aisle to the platform. Then stand before the seat on the *right* and *wait* for me before you sit down."

The choir segued to "Here Comes the King."

"O.K." said Pastor Moen. "Now."

The beams of the spotlights hit us, and we started our grand entrance. The audience was all keyed up to applaud as we entered. When we reached the platform, all the lights were off, save for a single spotlight shining down on the pastor, who had taken his place in the pulpit.

"People all over the world are watching this church," he began. "This is the biggest, fastest growing church in the world, and I am flying to Canada tomorrow to teach a pastors' school on church growth."

"Where does Christ fit into all this?" I wondered, silently.

The collection appeal was extraordinarily direct. "There's a lot of extra expenses in bringing a speaker like Austin Miles," the pastor entoned, "and we want to be able to bless his ministry with a big love gift. So, dig in deep. You can write checks to First Assembly church, and we'll give it to Brother Miles. So give generously to this love offering for our speaker."

The elegant silver collection plates were quickly piled high with cash, much of it consisting of ten and twenty dollar bills, from the more than 1,900 people who were packed into that church. When he finally introduced me, I began my talk with quips and stories about what God was doing in the world of show business. Naturally, I moved along into stories of healings I had witnessed. A hush fell over the congregation. At the conclusion, there was a noticeable stir as I offered a special prayer for those who were sick. Then, remembering my host's instruction, I cut the healing prayers short and made my altar call. People came from all directions to the front, many of them falling on their knees at the altar wherever space permitted.

Out of the corner of my eye, I could see the expression on Pastor Moen's face become more and more stormy. Then, when his flashpoint had been reached, he rushed up to me and yanked the microphone out of my hand.

"How many of you felt you were touched at this service?" he yelled into the mike. Hands shot up all over the sanctuary. "I mean," he continued leadingly, "how many of you *actually* feel that God *healed* you during this service?"

To his consternation, more hands went up and several people stood up, mistakenly thinking the cue to offer healing testimonies had been given. Furious by this time, Pastor Moen curtly addressed the people who were kneeling at the altar. Then the confused, new "converts" were hustled off to an anteroom. There they were persuaded to sign membership cards and tithe pledges, agreeing to contribute ten percent of all their income to First Assembly. Pastor Moen stalked off the platform to his office.

Before I could get away, I was swamped by a sea of people wanting to talk, shake hands, and ask for special prayer.

"Brother Miles," one man said, "we have been so blessed by this church. They give us so much."

"What do they give you?" I asked, with more than idle curiosity.

"Well, among other things, the men get a free fishing trip to Canada once a year."

"A free fishing trip to Canada? How does that work?"

"Well, that's just for the members, the ones who tithe," he explained. That seemed like a good incentive, and it made excellent business sense, considering the huge profit margin of the amount of the tithe over the cost of the fishing trip.

After I had talked with parishioners for quite a long time, a rather strange man approached me and announced that he would drive me to my motel.

"What about the pastor?" I asked.

"He's in his office."

"My coat is in there," I said. "I'll go get it and say goodbye to him."

As I entered the office, Pastor Moen was sitting at his desk, writing. When he saw me, he slammed both hands down on the desk and glared at me. "I've just written you a note," he said, rising to his feet. "Do you want to see it?"

"Sure," I answered.

He thrust the handwritten note at me and began to pace back and forth across the room. I looked at him. Then I read the note.

Bro. Miles:

Just a Brief Word of My Utter Disappointment in your Ministry tonight. I feel that one of the First obligations of a guest is to be Submissive to the host Pastor. This Church is not Full by Accident but by Design & God's Rich Blessing. I want you to know—the Positive Confession theory Does *not* hold up in totality of all of God's Word. Also one of our Faculty Members has M.S.—Where were the Results for her. I trust you Will be More Submissive To Future Pastors.

Ernest J. Moen

His odd habit of capitalizing certain words for emphasis caught my eye. He spun around to face me in such a rage that I braced myself as if for a physical attack.

"You have caused confusion in my church! You have ruined my church!" He sputtered, waving an accusing finger under my nose.

"I don't believe you will find I've hurt your church," I answered softly. "I think you will find just the contrary."

"And where do you come off with this business of God healing people?" He was now furiously pounding on his desk.

"I come off with it because it is in the Bible and stated for *now*," I replied earnestly.

His face now flushed red with anger, he declared, "I know the Bible inside and out. There is *no divine healing*. That, '. . . with His stripes we *are* healed' [Isaiah 53:5] and '. . . by whose stripes ye *were* healed' [1 Peter 2:24] *is not true!* God does *not* heal people! Job is an example of not getting healed. And Paul's proverbial 'thorn in the flesh' was never removed!"

He pounded on the desk, each thump no doubt accenting a word he would have capitalized had he been writing.

"This is an Assemblies of God church, isn't it?" I asked rhetorically, taking care to maintain the same calm, assuasive tone.

"That's right—and one of the *biggest!*" he thundered.

"And you are an Assemblies of God minister?"

"That's right—for many years."

"And you don't believe in divine healing or even positive faith?"

"There is no such thing."

My mind was spinning. I was well up on Assemblies of God doctrine, and indeed it did stress faith and divine healing. Each Assemblies' minister had to re-ratify the denomination's statement of doctrine, which clearly set those tenets forth, to get his credentials renewed each year.

"You have no faith—and yet, you are a minister?"

"I'll just tell you this," he retorted through clenched teeth. "For what you did I will ruin your ministry. Oh, you're a master on the pulpit. You know how to work up a crowd. But I am powerful and respected, and when I pass the word, your ministry is *finished!*"

"Maybe my ministry should be finished," I said wearily, "but I just want you to understand something. What you are saying is that 'God is dead,' so let's just gather together for a history lesson and I'll be your advisor. Pastor Moen—if you are not giving the people faith to hold onto, then what *are* you giving them for their tithes? No—on second thought, don't tell me. I know: free fishing trips to Canada. And you're traveling around the world conducting 'pastor schools?' " I began to pace the floor. "In other words, success is measured by the number of people in the church no matter what means are necessary to bring them in. You know, Pastor, your methods would never have reached me when I was out in that 'sinful' world of show business." I accentuated the words "show business." The pastor looked at me intently.

"What about that faculty member of mine with M.S.?" Pastor Moen demanded. "*I've* prayed for her, and nothing happened."

"That's it!" I exclaimed, now beginning to see the solution to his problem clearly in terms of my theology. "Because your prayer was not answered to suit you, you refuse to recognize that God will heal anyone, and that others are given this gift. I believe, sir, had God honored your prayer you would have tried to walk on water! You would have taken personal credit for the healing, and Christ would not have been exalted." Pastor Moen's jaw dropped open, as if he had been struck with a club.

"I'm telling you Brother," I said, lowering my voice, "you'd better get on your knees and seek God's will in your life and for this church, or you are eventually going to fall hard and a lot of trusting, innocent people will fall with you."

His eyes dropped, and his combativeness subsided. His voice cracked as he rationalized, "Maybe it's my Baptist background getting in the way."

"No, it's not that, Brother, it is ego. Pure ego. You had better start building a monument to Christ instead of to yourself," I preached to the pastor, who had now become my receptive congregation of one.

"Maybe it's good we had this talk," he said, regaining his composure. "Come on. I'll drive you to your motel."

When we got to the motel, Pastor Moen handed me an envelope.

"If you really feel I've hindered your work, then keep it. You don't owe me anything."

"No," he insisted generously, "it would not be Christian not to pay you for coming."

I accepted the envelope, said goodbye, and went to my room. In the envelope I found a check for 380 dollars out of which I had to pay my travel expenses from New York and my lodging. The "love offering" that had been "taken for Austin Miles" that night totaled more than 10,000 dollars. I was not even treated to a cup of coffee during my stay. At least I was saved cab fare to and from the church.

That night I wrote a letter to the District Superintendent for Illinois. Even though I had never met him, I knew him well by reputation. He was one of the most esteemed members of the National Presbytery, and a leading shaper of Assemblies' national policy. His support and commendation were valuable commodities to anyone wishing to advance in the Assemblies of God. Many saw him as an eventual successor to "Brother Z" as General Superintendent. My letter began,

Dear Reverend Dortch:

After I recounted the events in Rockford, I concluded,

I just want to establish *what* your beliefs are *and are not* in the state of Illinois. If you really do not believe in the Gospel here and do not want to accept it, then I will just shake the dust off my feet and move on.

This last paragraph was hardly suited to pour oil on troubled water or to bring out the best in a man in Richard Dortch's position.

Before a reply could come from Reverend Dortch, however, a note arrived from Reverend Moen.

I just wanted you to know that last Sunday we reached the same peak attendance *without* a guest speaker, as we did when you were here.

Despite the note's intended sarcasm, I smiled when I read it. Inadvertently he admitted that my ministering had helped his church, not hurt it.

His note found me in a gracious mood. I answered the communiqué,

Dear Brother Moen,

Just a note to express my appreciation for being able to minister to your people. There was a good witness of the Spirit on all sides, and I believe you will continue to hear good reports of good things that the Lord did that evening. I was so glad to hear that your attendance continues on the upswing. Even though we are many times different from one another in the ways we approach our ministries, it is beautiful to know that the Lord honors the diversity of gifts of the Spirit, and praise God, He has made us all individuals.

If you are ever in the New York area, I would sincerely invite you to let me know and set aside some time for fellowship, during which time you will be my guest. I believe that God has honored both of these ministries and will do so in an even mightier way as we draw closer to Him. And, too, my brother, I believe indeed that we could wind up becoming very good friends and true brothers in Christ if given half a chance.

My heart is so open.

May the Lord's hand be upon you. 1 Thess. 1:5.

Ready in His Service,
/s/
Rev. Austin Miles
Show Business Chaplain
New York City

Reverend Berg called me and asked me if I could come to the church to talk with him.

"I received a letter from Richard Dortch about you," he said, showing the letter to me. Reverend Dortch had attached a copy of my letter to him. His letter to Reverend Berg said:

See what you can do about this. Have a talk with Brother Miles and tell him just to concentrate on preaching the Gospel.

It seemed that Reverend Dortch could have cared less that Reverend Moen had set himself in opposition to the fundamental tenets of the Assemblies of God—tenets which Reverend Dortch as a District Superintendent was sworn to uphold. The high water marks of his concern seemed to be, "don't rock the boat," and "keep Brother Miles pacified." My first impression of Richard Dortch had been formed.

Back in Rockford, Pastor Moen had been checkmated by the letter from me. He studied it carefully and answered. After a preamble with the usual platitudes, he wrote:

> I accept your invitation of hospitality when I am in the New York area. This is very kind of you, and I have every confidence that we would have a very compatible and beautiful experience of Christian fellowship.
>
> In spite of our differing view on methodology, I must tell you that since I have been pastor in this church, I do not know of any service where more people were healed by the power of God! We have had testimonies in Pastor's Bible Class; people have voluntarily come to me and shared how the Lord touched them that night. Now I have to be honest about this and recognize the miracles of our Lord. I praise God for that. I thought you would like to know this.
>
> May our Lord smile upon all of our efforts for Him. I pray God's blessing upon you and yours.

Next came a letter, dated April 4, 1977, from Reverend R. D. E. Smith in Springfield, Missouri. I had written him a report of the events in Rockford. Reverend Dortch had talked to him about the problem at length: not the problem with Reverend Moen, but the problem with Reverend Miles. Reverend Smith advised me to "just 'keep your cool' and preach the Gospel." Then he summed up the matter:

> Just one word: It is considered unethical to take a stand in opposition to what a pastor believes or teaches—IF you know about it. I think the answer, for you, is to tell those pastors plainly what you feel called to do and if they don't like it, they don't have to call you. I remember when Willard Cantelon took a position on a Second Coming point which was in opposition to the pastor's position. The pastor was a very influential man and it could have hurt Willard except that when he found out about it he wrote a letter of apology. How much better if the two had had an understanding before the meeting.
>
> It's not the last time something like this is going to happen to you. Now is the time to prepare yourself and know in advance what you will do under the circumstances.
>
> You might consider a second type of service which you could fall back [on] if you ran into this again.

It stunned me. Reverend R. D. E. Smith, Executive Presbyter of the Assemblies of God church, was not at all interested in the bylaws and cherished, historic beliefs of the denomination, or even the Bible itself, it seemed. He was informing me that I should preach the very opposite of what I believed if that would keep peace with a host pastor.

My next surprise was on its way. Word had spread throughout the

"Charismatics" in the Rockford area about the miraculous healing that had occurred when I preached at First Assembly. New people were coming to the church, wanting to see more of the same. Many Roman Catholics were coming to First Assembly on that account. Catholics can be the most trusting and vulnerable people of all to that sort of ministry, acclimated, as they are, at an early age to the notion of miracles. They were especially open to accept miracles and support any place of worship giving them credence. An opportunity to greatly expand the Lord's work in Rockford had arisen.

On April 11, 1977, a newsletter in color brochure form put out by the First Assembly of Rockford as Volume 10, Issue 364, was mass-mailed. Together with a smiling picture of Brother Moen, it proclaimed:

Seminar on Healing
(Starts Wednesday, April 20, 7:30)

* Faith Building Series
* Problems in Prayer for the Sick
* Pointers for Prayer, or: Hints for Healing
* Power in Prayer for the Sick
* Popular Approaches to Divine Health
Taught by: Pastor Moen
Each Wednesday 7:30 P.M.

Pastor Ernest J. Moen had obviously had a profound change of heart and the charismatics of Rockford gave him their full support.

XXXI

hree days after that watershed experience in Rockford, Illinois, I was scheduled for a service in New York. Following the service, I wrote in my journal:

Wed—Feb—23, 1977
Bayshore A.G.—Rev. Cooke

It is good I was forced to preach tonight—so turned off by the church and the many phonies who pastor and evangelize that I could well run.

Brother Cooke however is a special brother. My daughter baptized tonight. What a thrill to baptize my own daughter. I wore my collar tonight and felt like I should wear it all the time. I am so tired of these flashy pastors in their $300 suits, most of whom are phonies, that I do not want to be like them. What hot times they will encounter in Hell for trifling with Holy things.

The message very anointed. People in congregation cried as I portrayed the crucifixion of Jesus. Everyone approved of my clerical clothing. Did have to take tranquilizers this week. Such a shock to see more and more of these holy roller wheelers and dealers. Thank God for pastors like Brother Cooke and my N.Y. brethren.

Rose Marie attended service—do not know if she was touched or not.

I pushed my journal aside and began to reflect on the ministry in general. There were, of course, many sincere and honorable ministers in the Assemblies of God beside Leon Cooke.

As I mentally inventoried the pastors who had impressed me, Reverend Jim Jones came quickly to mind. I had been reading and hearing good reports about him. He had risen from his humble beginnings as an Indiana farm boy to a position of influence few other citizens of San Francisco had ever matched. He opened the doors of his first church, the Christian Assembly of God, in Indianapolis in the late fifties. Before long, he moved to Ukiah, in northern California.

Reverend Jones had a special "burden" for people without a purpose in life. People in that category flocked to him. Starting with a bunch of drifters of varying ages, he built a bustling church that drew five thousand people to its morning services and evening sermons each week. Those who knew him during his early ministry in Indianapolis have described him as a dynamic but calm man, and are quick to point out that his concern for the poor and the non-white was genuine by every indication. A majority of his followers were black. Many were ex-convicts and down-and-outers with nowhere else to go.

A soft-spoken man off the pulpit, Reverend Jones' evangelical flair when he addressed crowds seldom failed to bring them to their feet. He moved People's Temple from Ukiah to San Francisco in 1970, and quickly became a force in city politics. The plain sincerity of his concern for the poor and underprivileged won endorsements from many prominent people. Governor Edmund G. Brown, Jr., San Francisco Mayor George Moscone, and Los Angeles Mayor Thomas Bradley were among the many luminaries who called at People's Temple to pay their respects. Mayor Moscone was so thoroughly won over that he made Reverend Jones head of San Francisco's housing authority.

Reverend Jim Jones had a remarkable ability to organize and activate people, turn out campaign workers, and assure a large bloc of votes for the candidate he favored. During the 1976 presidential campaign, Rosalynn Carter swung through San Francisco to make a last-minute campaign speech for her husband. Reverend Jones bused in nearly 600 of the 750 people who showed up to hear her. Reverend Jones received a louder ovation than did the soon-to-be First Lady.

In the prime of his life, and having attained a measure of power and respect equalled by few, Jim Jones felt directed by God to leave San Francisco and start a People's Temple utopian commune in Guyana. The wealth and power within his grasp apparently meant nothing to him. He only wanted to share the Gospel, farm the land, and serve God unhindered, just living for Jesus and building a "good society."

Now, disappointed with pastors who cared about nothing else but power and wealth, I regretted not taking Reverend Zimmerman's advice to go to the People's Temple and take part in Brother Jones' ministry. From all appearances, Reverend Jim Jones was a true man of God. Leaning on my own understanding too much, I had missed out on a rare opportunity.

*   *   *

Before leaving on my next trip to PTL, I squeezed in another date with Rose Marie. I wanted to spend more time with her but my demanding schedule did not permit it.

Rose Marie had been transferred from TWA's Fifth Avenue office to one in the newly completed World Trade Center.

"Vait outside for me," she told me on the phone. "Don't come in. I don't vant anyone to see you."

It seemed as if everybody had been brought into this very personal matter of ours, and few had hesitated to contribute their advice and opinions. What made it harder for Rose Marie was that she had committed herself to some very harsh remarks about me to her friends when she left me. To start seeing me openly would show weakness and make her lose face, something a Swiss heiress could never do. The negative views of one another that we, ourselves, had broadcast constrained us to be secretive about seeing each other.

We took a walk in Battery Park, in sight of the Statue of Liberty. In the distance, we noticed what looked like a circus tent. We walked toward it to find out that it was "The Big Apple Circus." As we drew closer, we could see the balloons and the excited children with their cotton candy, and could sense the general gaiety. The commanding "March of the Gladiators," which I call the circus national anthem, was playing over the loudspeakers.

"Dey play dot at every circus, don't dey?"

"Yes."

We watched the activity for a little while, each of us thinking about happier times when the circus was such a big part of our lives.

"Do you vant to go in?" she asked.

"Yes—but I feel the time would be better spent by ourselves, just talking." I glanced back at the big top as we continued to walk. "Rose, we do love each other and we're both hurting. Why don't we do this? Let's go back to Europe together—go back to the spots that we've enjoyed so much—away from everyone and their advice and opinions and get our life back together."

We stopped. I took both of her hands in mine. "Can we do that, Rose?" We stood there silently for a long time.

"Yes," she finally said, "dot vould be a good idea. I vill start making plans to take some time off."

The next morning, I took an early flight to Charlotte. Harold Olshieds was waiting with a stretch limousine. "Ya know?" he drawled as we pulled away, "I've had a driving ministry for some time." Everything a Christian did was a "ministry." "But," he went on, "there may be a change coming."

"What kind of a change?"

"Well, Vicki Jamison has been talking to me about possibly working for her—to be on her staff—to—ah—be her manager." I had a strong notion that the last part of his statement represented more fantasy than fact.

Vicki Jamison had begun appearing on "The PTL Club," and was building a large following for her singing and healing ministry. Her professed goal was to build a church in each city where she held a crusade. Naturally I was curious as to what *her* story might be.

"Where are we going?" I asked Harold, when, glancing out the window, I realized we were not taking the usual route.

"Oh, Lyn McMann told me to bring you directly to her office." This did not set well with me. I wanted to go straight to my room and freshen up for the telecast.

Once in her office, all hell broke loose. "I cannot understand why you didn't bother to see me or at least call me when you were here last time!" she blurted out as she closed the office door. Her anger marred the beauty of her face. "I feel you're snubbing me and I don't like it! I told you I wanted you to visit my mountain home with me. The least you could have done was acknowledge the invitation!"

"Dear God!" I thought. "How on earth could I have wound up with complications here?"

PTL was an important resource for my ministry. Trouble with Lyn could threaten this vital outlet. The Christian approach seemed the only way to handle it.

"Lyn, I think you and I had better go to the chapel right now and put this before the Lord in prayer." That worked for the time being, but I felt tense and uneasy going into the telecast.

Howard and Vestal Goodman—the "Happy Goodmans"—from Madisonville, Kentucky, were on the show. It seemed they were always on the show. They were excellent gospel singers, a real dynamic duo. Both were overweight, but that was such an integral part of their personalities I couldn't imagine them any other way. Vestal was too heavy-handed for my comfort, with her exorbitant shouting and super-holiness. One never knew when "the Spirit" would come upon her during a conversation or in the midst of a song. Vestal's unpredictable behavior added to the increasing pressure I felt facing this telecast.

"The PTL Club" had become so professional and tightly structured that I began to fear I would get lost in the shuffle. I had to do more than just "share" from the heart. My mind raced ahead as I planned exactly what I was going to say, for how long, and when to pull it in for the punch line.

Before going out, I huddled with the producers and asked them to give the audience an applause cue when I said my opening words, "You Are Special"—my ministry's established trademark. In coining the phrase, I had in mind Bob Harrington, "The Chaplain of Bourbon Street," and the mileage he had gotten from his signature phrase "It's Fun Being Saved." Along with everyone else, I was desperately trying to hold onto my turf.

Today it worked well. But this monster of television evangelism was forcing me to abandon the purity of my message, exchanging it for safe, staged professionalism—for what amounted to another form of show business.

After the show, Lyn, her composure restored, talked quietly to me as I got ready to leave for the airport. "Look, it's Friday. I'm off for two days. Come with me to my mountain retreat."

"Lyn, this just does not look right."

"Well," she persisted, "let them drop you off at the airport. I'll meet you inside and we could go from there. Nobody would know a thing."

"Lyn, that would be a fraud on PTL!" I looked at her searchingly. She was beautiful and desirable, with the sort of immaculate, sophisticated appearance I found irresistible.

"Lyn—I'll probably hate myself in the morning. But I just can't do it. Bye!"

*   *   *

I stopped by my apartment to pick up some things for my next engagement. When I got inside, I found a rug and some pieces of furniture that were not there before. In the kitchen cabinets, I found pots, pans, and utensils that were not mine. I checked the closet, and found that Marilyn King had moved in her clothes. It appeared she was moving in lock, stock, and barrel. Nobody was home.

I picked up the phone. "Hi, Marilyn, I'll pick you up at work. Wait for me." For the next hour, I hurriedly loaded up the car with all her things. I drove to her office, picked her up, and delivered the entire collection back to her Greenwich Village apartment.

"Where's Marilyn?" Lori asked when I got back.

"Never mind," I snapped. I picked up the phone. "Reverend Berg? Would you by any chance know of an *older* woman in your congregation who might help me with Lori?"

The next morning, after speaking at a Full Gospel Business Men's Fellowship International (FGBMFI) breakfast in Huntington, Long Island, I flew to Syracuse for a Sunday service at Grace Assembly, drove from there to Northampton, Massachusetts, for a midweek service, and then flew to Rochester, New York, for a week-long revival crusade.

Word spread quickly that Rose Marie and I were seeing each other, and the newspapers picked up the story. Walter Kaner wrote in his column for *The Long Island Press,* Thursday, March 10, 1977:

> . . . though they recently split up, Rev. Miles' wife Rose Marie attends
> some of his services at L.I. churches. Friends are hoping for a reconciliation.
> The couple dwelt in Forest Hills before the break. . . .

A handful of people read the accounts of our possible reconciliation with more than casual interest. Shadowy figures—not yet known to me—passed the clips to one another in an office full of sophisticated, high-tech equipment. Reverend Cooke, in Bay Shore, was another who took special interest in the matter.

Rose Marie paced the floor in her apartment, a copy of the paper spread out on the table. She picked it up and looked at Walter Kaner's column again. In a way, the news item verified a hopeful development. She sat in a wing chair and stared at the book-filled shelves. She sat with regally perfect posture; even when alone, she never slouched. An aristocrat was an aristocrat, even in one's most unguarded moments.

She had taken the phone off the hook in order to give undisturbed thought to everything about our life together and our marriage. No insoluble problem really existed between the two of us. The entire problem was the church. Could it be the church was right? Could it really hold the secret to a better way of life? She picked up the phone and dialed a number.

*   *   *

Heads popped around attentively as Rose Marie walked into the sanctuary of Bay Shore Assembly of God church with Ken and Pauline Bouton.

"Look!" said a church biddy to her companion, in an excited whisper. "There's Austin Miles' wife!"

"Praise the Lord!" whispered the other, loud enough so others would hear.

Rose Marie, fragile and vulnerable, was at a very low point. During the emotional song service and Reverend Cooke's sermon on love, tears streamed down her face. When Reverend Cooke gave the altar call, Pauline clasped Rose Marie's hand and said, "I think you want to go." Rose Marie nodded her head. "I'll walk down with you," said Pauline, encouragingly.

They walked to the altar, where they both knelt. Crying openly, Rose Marie repeated "the sinner's prayer" while people in the congregation rejoiced over this "victory."

At the conclusion of the service, people came from all over the sanctuary to greet and hug Rose Marie, wishing God's blessing on her, promising they would pray for her. Others invited her to visit in their homes. Now that Rose Marie was "one of us," they no longer hesitated to approach her. She was now "Sister Miles," which apparently gave them the liberty to give her unasked-for advice and to ask her probing, personal questions that would never have been tolerated before. But at this moment, Rose Marie felt a peace such as she had not experienced since before she left me.

"My husband is a good man and sincere," Rose Marie said to Pauline and Ken, as she picked up a freshly poured cup of tea. "I vould nefer haf married a minister. He decided to become dis after ve vere married. I still do not know how I feel about all of dis, but I haf been very unhappy since I left him. If he vants in his heart to be a minister, den I vill just haf to accept dat fact, and try to understand. I'm going to see Reverend Cooke to ask his advice about how I can accept dis and be a good wife to him as a minister."

When she knelt at that altar to become "born again," Rose Marie abandoned her ancestral Swiss pride and strength. Saving face no longer mattered. She had thought her priorities over carefully. She had reached the point where she no longer cared what her friends would think, and no longer minded contradicting her own words. A broken heart was too painful. Especially when the whole dispute revolved around one simple issue: her husband's involvement with the church. What was so bad about that?

Rose Marie could relate comfortably to Pauline, since she was relatively intelligent and they shared a common native tongue. Rose Marie was also impressed with the peace of the Bouton's home and the stability of their marriage. Having a Down's Syndrome son seemed not to dismay them. It only served to enhance their love. This kind of happiness had to be a gift of God.

Rose Marie soon returned to Bay Shore for another service. As she sat quietly seeking the Lord, the whispering of two church ladies seated behind her reached her ears.

"That's Austin Miles' wife sitting there."

"Really?"

"Yes, and have you noticed, she comes by herself. He never goes to church with her."

"Well, it's probably because he's too busy with his, uh, 'other interests.' I've heard that he is quite a ladies' man. In fact, I hear that he has another woman named Marilyn living right there in his apartment!"

"Tch, tch."

Rose Marie never heard the part of Reverend Cooke's sermon that came after that point. She tried to get out of the church the moment the service was over. She heard other whispering voices, and still other voices turn to whispers as she walked by. Others thrust their overbearing expressions of "love" and "caring" on her.

When she made it to the parking lot, she turned and looked up at the church's majestic steeple. She had been rudely awakened. Her first impression and instinct had been correct after all. She should never have allowed herself to become involved in *any* of this.

When I returned from Rochester, I went to Glad Tidings Tabernacle to talk with Reverend Berg.

"How have things been since Rose Marie went to Bay Shore?" he asked with a smile.

"Oh, about the same. I'm not sure if she was touched at the service or not. It's been a while since I was there."

"I'm not talking about the time you preached there. I'm talking about since then."

"Since then? Rose Marie has been going to church there on her own?"

"Then you haven't heard? Rose Marie went to the altar crying and gave her heart to Jesus. Pauline Bouton went with her. She's born again!"

"You're kidding!" Tears of joy started running down my face. "Rose Marie knelt at the altar and gave her heart to the Lord?" He nodded his head, smiling even more broadly. "Praise the Lord!" I went into the empty sanctuary, knelt at the altar rail, and, alternately crying and rejoicing, I prayed and thanked Jesus.

When I got back home, filled with joy and anticipation, I telephoned Rose Marie. "Rose Marie, I just heard the news! I heard that you gave your heart to Jesus! This is wonderful!"

"Oof, dose nosey people. I vish dey vould just mind dere own business and keep dere mouths shut," she said with unusual iciness.

"Rose Marie, I don't understand. I thought you would be very happy for me to know this."

"You know, you haf a very bad reputation," she said, changing the subject.

"What?"

"*Ja,* zee ministers all talk about you. *Two* told me dey do not like vat dey see in you."

"What two ministers? What is there to see? Who are these two ministers?"

"I'm not going to say. But it has to do vidt dot voman you haf in your apartment, Marilyn. I hear she is pretty good-looking."

"Rose Marie, that has already been taken care of. She had things in mind that I decidedly did not! She started to move her things in without consulting me, and I moved her right out! I've gotten rid of her. She's no longer there."

"Dot's good. You had to get rid of her. Dis vas a problem."

"Rose Marie, we've *got* to get away from here, away from *everybody.* Let's go to Europe as quickly as possible."

"It is doubtful dot ve vill ever get back together. But if ve do, I vant you to know dot I hate dis business of you having two names. I just vant to be Mrs. Maddox. Also, I do not like all dis publicity and your name in the newspapers all the time. I vant privacy in our life."

"We'll work everything out. Life is nothing to me without you. I love you, Rose Marie. I have to leave for another crusade in upstate New York now, but can we get together a week from Tuesday?"

"Yes," she agreed. Her voice had become softer and more receptive.

"Great! I have a real special place to take you to dinner. I'll call you Monday and we'll confirm the time."

I flew to Rochester to begin services at the Greece Assembly of God, in one of the city's suburbs.

Rose Marie was puzzled. She picked up the phone and called Reverend Cooke for a counseling appointment. She had great respect for his position as Presbyter of Long Island. He complied with her request immediately. She drove out to Bay Shore Assembly of God.

"Reverend Cooke," she said, "you are Austin's friend. Why does everyone in the church talk about my husband so much?"

Reverend Cooke pondered the question for a moment, then pushed out his chin and said, "Frankly, Austin Miles is his own worst enemy. The brethren don't like what they see. And it's a known fact that he has a mistress in Florida and was seen coming out of a motel room with her."

Rose Marie's mouth dropped open in utter shock and she gasped.

"Just a minute. I'll be right back," Reverend Cooke said, quickly getting up and going out into the hall.

People were coming into the church for the Wednesday service. He walked over to a couple of women, one of them overweight, and talked to them in hushed tones for a few moments. They nodded their heads and followed him obediently into his study. "Here, Rose Marie, you might as well know. Everybody knows it. Ladies, isn't it true about Austin Miles and his mistress in Florida?"

"Yes," they both said, nodding their heads in agreement.

"That's common knowledge," said one.

"Yes, everybody knows it," said the other.

"Thank you, ladies," said Reverend Cooke, dismissing them. The sisters of Bay Shore Assembly of God, the hastily impaneled jury of two who had just delivered their verdict against me in the "court" of Reverend Cooke after hearing no evidence, looked at each other uneasily. Then they left to go join the worship service, which had already begun.

Rose Marie began to tremble. "Would you like to come in for the service?" Reverend Cooke said, with an ingratiating smile. With her hand covering her mouth, Rose Marie muffled her scream, jumped from her chair, and ran from the church, crying hysterically and gasping for breath.

A man and his wife from the congregation saw Rose Marie run from the study. They stuck their heads in the door. "What happened?" the husband asked Reverend Cooke.

"Oh, that is Austin Miles' wife. She came for counseling. She needs a lot of prayer. Pray for her. And pray for Austin, too. He has a lot of problems." The couple shook their heads knowingly in response. With a satisfied smile on his face, Reverend Cooke went into the sanctuary, shaking the hands of some of his flock along the way, and ascended the pulpit to preach about Jesus.

Ken and Pauline Bouton were standing in the hallway near the study also. They had watched the entire sequence of events unfold. Mutely, they looked at each other.

I tried to telephone Rose Marie for several days and got no answer. My revival services at Greece Assembly of God had ended. I wrote in my journal:

> Wed.—March 16, 1977
> Windup—Greece Crusade
> "The Proof"
>
> Started today with another pastor I am to be with—taped eight 4½ minute radio spots for his meeting. Seeing some jealousies and rivalries among the pastors and this is disturbing to me—I feel like anything but a minister these days—would so like to get out of public life—just get away from everything—need an extended rest to try to get self and thoughts back together.

When I got home, I tried again to call Rose Marie. I eagerly looked forward to hearing her voice, setting the time for our next meeting, and completing our plans to go to Europe. Rose Marie, now over her initial shock and outrage, had snapped back into being her old strong, independent self.

The moment she heard my voice, she began to yell and scream at me with abandon. "I should have listened to everybody. You *are* no good!"

That struck me like a bolt out of the blue. We had parted on such a harmonious note the last time we spoke. We had been well along in the process of reconciling. On what basis was "everybody" saying I was "no good?" What had I ever done to warrant such an assessment?

"Rose Marie, what are you saying?"

"Reverend Cooke told me *everything!* You haf the vorst reputation of anyvun in the vorld! Everyone in Reverend Cooke's church and Reverend Berg's church knows everything about you, and dey all talk about you. And it is a known fact that you haf a mistress in Florida, and you vere seen coming out of a motel room with her."

"Reverend Cooke said all this?" I asked in disbelief. "Rose Marie, this is a vicious lie. I was in Florida once in the last several months and I stayed in the evangelists' quarters at the church with Reverend Orchard."

"Reverend Cooke is a good friend of yours. He is a man of God, an officer of high standing in the church, and a man of God would not lie."

Bewildered, I tried to reason with her. "Rose Marie, please, there is absolutely no truth in any of this. I can prove my whereabouts at all times."

By now, Rose Marie's anger had reached its peak. "Don't you ever try to contact me again. Don't you ever come near my apartment or my work, or I will have you arrested. I'm going through with the divorce." She slammed down the phone.

Those were the last words we ever exchanged. To make certain of that, Rose Marie immediately got a new unlisted phone number, and all of her friends and co-workers at TWA were alerted to be on the lookout to help keep me away.

The next day I headed out for Bay Shore to confront Leon Cooke. I was told he was away for an unspecified time, "on the Lord's business."

XXXII

My next shock was being prepared. The service at the Lighthouse Assembly of God church in Glendale, New York, only a mile from Forest Hills, had been "greatly blessed." A worshiper visited with me after the service.

"Detectives are investigating twenty years of your life."

"What?"

My visitor was Vincent Terrenova, a Christian cop on the New York Police Department. "They came to the NYPD for assistance," he continued.

"Why? Who is having me investigated?"

"Reverend Cooke of Bayshore Assembly of God church."

"Reverend Cooke?" By now, a feeling of numbness had become my natural state. "Why would Reverend Cooke have me investigated? Who is paying for this?"

"I guess, his church," Terrenova said with a shrug of the shoulders.

The next day I stopped by the 112th Precinct in Forest Hills. The police verified that they had been asked to assist in such an investigation.

"And what have they found out about me?" I asked one of the cops.

"They found out that you were clean. But—I gotta ask ya somethin'. Don't that church preach against drinkin'?"

"Yes," I answered. "Very much so."

"Hmmmm. We found out in the course of things that Reverend Cooke is a closet alcoholic. He's got quite a stash down in his basement."

I shook my head and started for the door. I stopped and turned back to the helpful cop. "Did you ever notice," I said to him, "that when a person points a finger at someone four fingers point back at him?"

The cop grinned for a moment, quickly resumed a serious face, and said, "Ya know—if this kind of stuff is what Christianity is—I don't want any part of it."

The investigation of me proved to be profitable for Bay Shore Assembly. Sordid details of Lori's birth mother, my problems with the FBI, and my name change provided such interesting gossip for the church that the flock felt that they were experiencing an all-time spiritual high. For them, heaven itself couldn't be better.

Feeling utterly violated, I contacted Reverend R. D. E. Smith, expecting him to be appalled to learn that church funds had been used in such a way. Instead, he coldly acknowledged that he was aware of the investigation. Inventive Christian minds and fiery Christian tongues were busy embellishing the rumors about Austin Miles until they had taken every possible form.

The little Full Gospel Church, out in the middle of nowhere near Alcove, New York, was a welcome refuge for me. The friendship and warmth of Reverend Robert Rosin during the week-long crusade provided a much-needed respite. Spectacular things happened at each service. Then it happened again. Several people in one family reported seeing a halo of light around me.

Next came a very special event, "The Gospel Opry," at the older Carnegie Hall in Pittsburgh. It was refreshingly like old times to be back in a tuxedo, preparing for a stage performance. I wondered why I had ever left my show business career. Relaxed and feeling exhilarated, I was in good form announcing the various gospel groups. I kept the show tied together well, got good laughs with my quips, and had as good a time as anyone in the audience. All of the groups came out on stage together for the finale and received a rousing, standing ovation.

Grace Nicodem, who had arranged several preaching dates for me in the Pittsburgh area in the coming days, came up to me and handed me a note. It said, "Rev. Miles. Please call Rev. Glenn McElwain tonight, after 11 PM." It gave a local phone number. I did not know a Reverend McElwain, and since I was exhausted, I put off returning his call. Immediately, there were several more insistent messages from him. Finally, I called him.

"Reverend Miles," he said, "we've got to have a talk. Could you come to see me tomorrow?"

"Reverend McElwain, I'm very busy with hardly a minute to spare. What is it you wanted to talk to me about?"

"Something very personal," he answered gravely.

"Reverend McElwain, you'll have to be more specific. I cannot think of anything personal between us. In fact, I do not believe we have ever met. Are you an Assemblies of God minister?"

"No. I'm with Pat Robertson's '700 Club,' " he said, haughtily, "and I think you had better talk to us about a problem you have."

"What?"

"That's right, we happen to know about a young lady you've been having sex with, and it's our job to stop your ministry until this thing is straightened out."

I hung up on him, dismissing it as a nut call.

Almost immediately, three large church revivals and the Pittsburgh

Charismatic Conference cancelled me. Grace Nicodem was in tears. "They said it had to do with your moral problems, and they have all the evidence."

The woman in question turned out to be an eighteen-year-old, married, and very pregnant girl named Bridget Short. She was also the mother of an infant daughter still in diapers. Her father, Pastor Richard Serro, was an Assemblies of God minister in whose little church in Bradenville, Pennsylvania, I had once preached. I had only been there at all because of the "burden" I felt for small, local churches. Even though there was little money in such churches, I thought the kind of ministry that truly mattered took place in them, more than in the big, high-volume super-churches.

Pastor Serro had to work in a diner during the week, since his church was too poor to support him. The lack of recognition gnawed at him. Cooperating in this matter would at least gain him a pat on the back, and a credential as one of the righteous.

"Bridget Serro is under counseling by 'The 700 Club' over this thing," a certain Pastor James K. Barrett told Grace Nicodem on the phone. Pastor Barrett, leader of the Greater Pittsburgh Bible Church at 300 Beachwood Avenue in Carnegie, Pennsylvania, had taken me on as a personal foe. "Austin Miles led her on and promised to marry her, and had sex with her on that pretense."

"Reverend Barrett," Grace replied, "this is slander."

"Oh, I would *love* for Austin Miles to sue me!" Pastor Barrett said, arrogantly. Then, with a leer in his voice, the pastor added, "I hear that she's not bad looking!"

"These people are sick!" I exclaimed to Grace when she told me. I dug out the slip of paper with Reverend McElwain's phone number and called him.

"First of all, Reverend McElwain, are you Assemblies of God?"

"No, I am not."

"What church are you with?"

"I'm not with a church."

"What Bible school or theological seminary have you graduated from?"

"I have not been to a Bible school or theological seminary."

"You are using the title 'Reverend.' Who ordained you? What church?"

"No church ordained me."

"Then you are *not* a 'Reverend.' "

"Yes I am. I am indeed a 'Reverend.' "

"Did you tell me you were with Pat Robertson's organization?"

"That's right. I'm in charge of 'The 700 Club' counselors."

"What does 'The 700 Club' have to do with me?"

"It is our job to police ministers. *We* decide which ministries go and do not go!" "Reverend" Glenn McElwain insisted that I should see him privately to discuss this matter.

"Who can I call, down at 'The 700 Club,' to verify that you are a representative of them?"

"James Murphy. Here's his number." He gave me a toll-free "800" telephone number.

To my astonishment, that number got me the Christian Broadcasting Network switchboard in Virginia Beach, which in turn put me right through to Mr. Murphy. To my further astonishment, Murphy advised me that he was on top of the problem and suggested that a group of us meet discreetly in Pittsburgh to work it out in order to "preserve my ministry."

" 'Reverend' McElwain said that it was the job of 'The 700 Club' to police ministries and to decide which ministries go and do not go. Is this true?"

"You better believe it!" retorted Murphy.

I called CBN in Virginia Beach several more times, asking to talk to (then) Reverend Pat Robertson, who refused to take my calls. Finally, I was put through to his secretary, Barbara Johnson, a stern sounding woman who gave the impression of having things well in hand.

"Tell me, Mrs. Johnson, are you Assemblies of God?"

"Yes," she answered sharply.

"I might have known."

This conversation, which I still could scarcely believe was actually taking place, concluded with Mrs. Johnson's admonition, "I think you had better have that meeting in Pittsburgh and make that settlement." That was the first mention of anything to do with money.

"I see, Mrs. Johnson, that the entire matter has come to a 'settlement.' What did you have in mind to 'preserve my ministry?' Maybe a hundred thousand?"

"That would show that you were sincere and of good faith," she replied, failing to pick up on my irony.

Grace Nicodem, who knew exactly where in the vicinity of Pittsburgh I had been and when, managed to corner Bridget Serro Short at a FGBMFI meeting.

"Where did this affair you say you had with Austin Miles take place?" Grace demanded.

"At—his motel room," Bridget said uncertainly.

"And what motel was he staying in?"

"The—Sheraton."

"He has never stayed at the Sheraton."

"I—uh—I meant to say the Holiday Inn."

"No, Bridget, he has never stayed at the Holiday Inn."

Flustered, Bridget made a third attempt to guess where I had stayed. Then she broke down and admitted that the entire story had been a hoax. "But," she said, her face brightening again, "it made my husband jealous and more attentive, so it was all worthwhile."

"And you cost us the Charismatic Conference and God knows what else!" Grace said, tears running down her face.

Angrily, I sent reports of this unseemly pressure to the New York district of the Assemblies, with copies to national headquarters in Springfield, Missouri. I wanted the word to be spread about the heavy-handed conduct of Pat Robertson's ministry. The tactics of some of Robertson's minions had been so professional and well orchestrated that I could not believe I was the first minister upon whom they had preyed.

Reverend Almon Bartholomew, Superintendent of the New York district, and Reverend Zimmerman at the national level, did not do one thing about the matter. They simply put a report in their files stating that Austin Miles had been accused of sexual misconduct with a married, eighteen-year-old girl.

*   *   *

By a unanimous vote of confidence, Reverend Zimmerman was reelected for one more term as General Superintendent of the Assemblies of God. His reign as the Pope of Pentecostalism continued.

Like any political aspirant, he hit the campaign trail at church gatherings all over America. One of his whistle-stops had been Glad Tidings Tabernacle. He timed his visit for May 1977 to coincide with that church's seventieth anniversary. I was master of ceremonies for the commemorative event in which he took part.

"I was amazed about what you said about Ernie Moen," he told me before the banquet. "And, by the way, I appreciated your sending me a copy of the letter to Brother Bartholemew about your experiences with CBN."

Behind the self-assured appearances, Reverend Zimmerman was unsure just where he stood with people after the Empire Bank scandal. He was "testing the waters." I sensed this, and being a "presenter" at heart, I gave him the best possible introduction. When he got up to speak I lifted my hands slowly, which subtly prompted the audience to its feet for a standing ovation. As the applause continued, Reverend Zimmerman turned to me with a smile and said softly, "Thanks, Austin."

*   *   *

It kept getting more difficult for me to function as a minister. I spent more time than ever in prayer and fasting, trying to break whatever mysterious force was coming against me. In that beleaguered frame of mind, I approached the pulpit of the Brookfield Assembly of God church in Milwaukee to begin a week-long revival crusade. It was the first week of June 1977.

The atmosphere felt eerily charged. Then it happened. Everyone In the sanctuary wound up on the floor, "slain in the Spirit." People would approach me for prayer and then collapse on the floor in a heap as I raised my hand to pray for them. Several people said they saw a halo of light around my head.

Word spread quickly about the awesome display of mysterious, spiritual power going on at Brookfield Assembly of God. Skeptics attended out of curiosity and wound up on the floor with all the others. While these manifestations were occurring, I felt extraordinary emanations of energy radiating from my body.

In the middle of a service later in the week, I stopped and prayed that the "anointing of this church" would reach right out into the highway and compel someone "who needs Jesus" to turn around and come into the church. I resumed the service. Several minutes later, a half-dozen barefooted hippies, boys with their girlfriends, two by two, came down the aisle. I interrupted the regular service for a second time.

"What's going on here?" asked one of the hippies. "We were driving down the highway in our van, and something made us turn around and come in here. What is going on?" Everyone in the congregation lifted their hands and began praising God, many in "tongues." I explained what had occurred. Our unwashed guests knelt at the altar and gave their hearts to God. Later they came back to church, scrubbed and combed almost beyond recognition.

When Pastor Sam Peterson took me to the airport, I still felt that odd, surging sensation going through my body. The metal detector sounded as I walked through the security checkpoint. I emptied my pockets. Same results. Even sans belt and shoes, the buzzer would sound each time I passed through the portal. In exasperation, the security people finally let me through anyway. This phenomenon recurred each time I tried to board a plane within a day or so after leading a service.

My destination from Milwaukee was Charlotte, North Carolina, and PTL. Tension hung in the air at Heritage Village. The only one who seemed unaffected by it was Harold Olshields. He seemed to be in a particularly good mood as he arrived with his limousine.

"Ya know? Lyn McMann is a wonderful woman. I've never met anyone like her. I jes' feel so good when I'm around her."

Harold had a big crush on Lyn, and was mentally building castles in the air and inhabiting them with her. He was mustering up the courage to declare himself. Lyn saw this coming, and had thought about how to let him down gently when the time came.

Other romantic feelings, or at least sexual ones, were cropping up all over the PTL complex. Tammy Faye was frustrated and depressed. She and Lyn had become best friends and confidantes. "I just can't get enough of Jim," Tammy confided to Lyn. "I could have sex with him twenty-four hours a day. I want him—I actually ache—I want him so much, but he's ignoring me. What can I do?"

The visit by a former Miss America to the show added to Tammy's insecurity. Tammy hated it whenever a beauty queen was scheduled. Donna Axum, from El Dorado, Arkansas, the 1964 title winner, was a warm, desirable, young woman. "Jim likes tall girls," Tammy told Lyn, and then broke down crying.

When I arrived at the studio, the tension between Jim Bakker and his producer, Jim Moss, was so thick you could have cut it with a knife. "What is happening around here?" I asked Lyn.

She looked at me silently and then hesitantly told me, "Jim Bakker and Jim Moss almost got into a fist-fight yesterday."

"Over what?"

"Over—Donna Axum—Miss America."

Moss' relationship with Donna Axum ended up costing him his marriage. In a jealous rage over her favors, Bakker had Moss' phone tapped and sent tapes of the revealing conversations between Moss and Axum to Moss' wife.

None of this spilled over on camera. "The PTL Club is reaching around the world!" Jim Bakker told his audience. He had been showing clips of the Japanese PTL, African PTL, and Brazilian PTL. The viewers rejoiced at seeing these scenes from around the world. The personable, dashiki-clad host of the African PTL, Benson Idahosa, appeared frequently on American PTL. I wondered how he could get back and forth from Nigeria that often.

After the program, I was asked to return later in the afternoon to tape an endorsement spot for "The PTL Club." I was to walk down a stairway, giving a pitch for people to support PTL with their giving. When the shot was completed, I went to watch some shooting at another set that had been put up in the corner of the studio. To my astonishment, it was the Brazilian PTL program. I felt like someone had hit me in the stomach when I realized that these clips, represented as having been shot and originally aired in different countries around the world, were actually shot in a corner of the Heritage Village studio. I wondered how widely those programs were aired—if at all. The Christians, so trusting and filled with blind faith, would never question.

XXXIII

I had seen enough corruption in the Assemblies of God to make me realize that this was no place for me. In May 1977 I notified Reverend R. D. E. Smith that I wanted to resign from the fellowship.

"Please don't do that," he counseled. "Give it time. Pray on it, and let's get together to talk about this."

I agreed to wait. Within a week, I was notified that a motion had been made in the Presbytery to dismiss me. The bylaws forbade a resignation while such a motion was pending. I had been outflanked.

I called Springfield. "Reverend Zimmerman, it would be much better to just let me resign. Otherwise this will cause a lot of confusion. People know my ministry is of God, and you have no reason to dismiss me. They're going to ask you a lot of questions. You will make yourselves look bad."

"You don't scare me," he hissed.

"I'm not trying to scare you. I'm just saying you won't hurt my ministry. My ministry will continue no matter what."

That was a strategic mistake on my part. I had taken on the great Reverend Zimmerman, of whom it was said, "Hell hath no fury like a woman scorned or Brother Zimmerman opposed."

"Oh," he said confidently. "We'll see about that."

On October 19, 1977, I was formally given the left foot of fellowship by the Assemblies of God. The charge? Having a previous marriage in my background.

I appealed the decision. According to the Assemblies' bylaws, I had a right to a trial by a jury of my peers. I followed the outlined procedure to the letter, sending registered letters to Reverends Zimmerman, R. D. E. Smith, Bartholomew Flower, and Donald A. Richardson, Secretary of the New York district. Even though I had the signed return receipts for these letters in hand, *all* of the addressees denied they had received them. Based on the fiction of my failure to give notice, I was adjudged to have forfeited my right to a trial.

In Bay Shore, Reverend Cooke stood proudly before his congregation and announced, "We waived Austin Miles' right to a trial by jury." Ken and Pauline Bouton sat silently and shook their heads.

With my dismissal, I was immediately removed from the headquarters' mailing lists. I did not even receive my own copy of *The Assemblies of God Minister,* a newsletter for the denomination's clergy. One of that newsletter's functions was to inform the clergy who had been ejected from their ranks and on what grounds. It really amounted to a list of those who had fallen out of favor with "Brother Z." Ministers were forbidden to reveal its contents, so that the victim would not know, and would thus be unable to dispute, what was said against him. I had read numerous accounts of dismissals in the newsletter where I independently knew the facts and the accused minister had been libeled. Now I was the one being libeled, and nobody would let me see a copy. Not satisfied to leave it at that, "Brother Z" published a special "fact sheet" on the sins of Austin Miles and sent it out to all Assembly of God ministers and churches.

A protracted nightmare followed. Hate letters abounded in my mail, to the point that I hated the sight of the mail carrier. The first of that kind was from Pastor Bedzyk.

Bedzyk's letter "rebuked" me for failing to "confess my sins" and for my "unrepentant attitude." My "lack of true humility" was "an abomination to God," who knew "every detail of" my "back-slidden condition." "You may fool others, but you can't fool God—you're on your way to hell!" he continued. I wondered whether it could get any worse than this.

I called Pastor Dan Raught. He said, "I am sorry I can no longer be your friend." That ended the matter. He had received instructions from on high to hate me, and so he did.

Some of the letters were obscene. I thought of the hate mail and bomb threats that had so discouraged Jim Bakker. Ministers all over the country gave out my unlisted phone number so that members of their flocks could do their Christian duty, call me in the middle of the night, and read me out for my sins. It was a war of harassment carried to hysterical extremes.

I kept a speaking engagement with the Women's Aglow Fellowship in Massapequa, Long Island. Seated next to me at the head table was Mrs. Eugene Profeta. Tall and slim, with ash blonde hair, Glenda Profeta had a distinctive face with a strong bone structure. She could have been attractive but chose otherwise.

"Sister Profetta, I'm delighted to meet you," I said, extending my right hand.

"Frankly," she retorted, keeping her own hand far from mine, "I never *heard* of you until this meeting!" Her cold, calculating manner could not have been more devoid of "fruits of the Spirit." The vibrations she gave off settled any lingering question in my mind regarding the Profeta ministry.

The final development for the year came in a letter from Air Force

Chaplain Wally and Anita Pearson, dated December 2, 1977, at their duty station in Great Falls, Montana. They mentioned they sent an offering in my name to Assemblies' national headquarters but received no indication that it had arrived. I never received it. Later I learned that the Assemblies simply confiscated any offerings intended for me that were still on hand. Chaplain Pearson later showed me a letter from headquarters confirming that since Austin Miles was no longer in Reverend Zimmerman's favor, any donations sent to him care of headquarters would be turned over to the Assemblies of God general fund.

*   *   *

The matter concluded much too easily. No fanfare. No publicity. Rose Marie looked around the courtroom. Down deep, she expected for me to be there. To fight for the preservation of a marriage that had bonded together the bodies and souls of two people who should never have been separated. But my inaction confirmed that nothing more could be done.

With the thud of an authenticating rubber stamp that resounded throughout the courtroom, our marriage was no more. "Here you are," said Judge Joseph S. Calabrella. "You are divorced." Rose Marie walked out of the Kew Gardens Court House. She sobbed and gasped for breath as she ran down Queens Boulevard to her apartment.

I was sitting in the home of a Christian family in New Jersey reading my Bible. I looked at my watch, and sickened at the thought that by this time it was over.

"Now don't start looking back," Grace Davis counseled. "The Holy Spirit has worked this all out to your good."

"I know. But this is still rough."

"The trouble with you," Grace's daughter Valerie piped in, "is that you are always swimming upstream, bucking the current. This is why you have never gotten anywhere." At twenty-eight, Valerie still looked like a street-wise teenager.

"Just relax. Relax," Grace entoned soothingly. "Let God do His work, then your life will come together like it should."

"I'm just not sure about all this," I said in an unsteady voice.

"If it's good enough for the Holy Spirit, it should be good enough for you!" Valerie shot back.

This family that Reverend Gerritt Kenyon had introduced me to was undoubtedly right, I thought. Why else did I feel so wonderfully at peace in their company?"

*   *   *

Everybody's excited down here," Harold Olshields gushed as he drove me from the Charlotte airport. "God has anointed the Hunters to impart the gift of healing, just like Elisha giving his mantle to Elijah." Harold had his biblical characters a little mixed up.

This was the first I had ever heard of someone other than God who could confer that power. The faithful were delighted that at last any one of them who wished could now have a miracle healing ministry like Christ after just a few easy lessons. The Happy Hunters had made it possible with a set of teaching tapes and a workbook. To activate each new disciple, the Hunters laid on hands in a sort of commencement service, imparting the mantle. The sheep, now promoted to shepherds, went happily out in all directions to heal the sick.

The grapevine had been pulsating with news of my ouster by the Assemblies. The first person I met at the studio was Bob Gass, a high-powered preacher from Scotland whom I had particularly admired. "Helooo, *Mister* Miles," he said with a delighted, happy sneer. His greeting stunned and puzzled me. Why on earth would he take such obvious pleasure in such a heart-breaking event in another minister's life? On camera, he completely hid his attitude toward me.

Lyn McMann's face revealed that she too had heard the news. I could tell she did not know what to say. "I see Bob Harrington was on the show last week," I said, evading the more loaded topics. "What is he like?"

"I don't care for him," she replied, shaking her head. "He is filled with lust. You can feel it coming out of him."

"Lyn—you know, of course, last year you were very vulnerable because of your divorce. Did you appreciate the fact that I did not take advantage of that?"

"I suppose so. But I am not vulnerable now!"

"Lyn, I'm still very much in love with my wi—, with Rose Marie." I still had not accepted the fact that Rose Marie was no longer my wife, and tears welled up in my eyes. "I'm going to the chapel and pray for the telecast."

"We don't have the chapel anymore," she said, hesitantly. "They've turned it into another office. It has become a madhouse around here."

Jim Bakker took a new tack on the telecast. "Austin," he said after a few moments of dialogue with me at his desk, "I feel the Lord's direction to have you go over to the phones and pray for the people who need prayer." Then he looked straight into the camera. "So call the number on your screen if you need prayer. You might be the one to get Austin's phone and be able to have him pray for you personally."

The cameras followed me as I went to the phone tables, which were in several tiers. Before I sat down, the head counselor gave me some instructions. "First get their name, write it down here, their address, home phone number, where they work, then write down their request here." He pointed to a square on the pad. "Be sure and check if they are a PTL partner or if this is a first-time call."

"Can I pray for them after that?"

As I got accustomed to the routine, I was able to tear off the completed sheet and hand it over my shoulder to a roving counselor while praying for the caller. The sheets were constantly gathered and delivered to the computer room, where the hurting caller's information was entered into the mailing list, all ready to be used for a donation appeal by the time the phone was back on the hook.

Many of the "phone counselors" were recruited from visitors to Heritage Village. These people, with no training whatsoever, some of them with very little education, were suddenly competent to counsel others about the pressing issues in their lives. The impromptu counselors always took great pride in telling the folks in the church back home that they had worked as PTL phone counselors. It enhanced their spiritual status.

After the telecast was over, and the backlog of calls had been cleared, I sat at the phone staring into space. At last, I got up to leave. I noticed a young woman mingling in the crowd, but not really talking to anyone. I had seen her almost every time I had been on the program. She was a tall, trim brunette, who looked to be in her late twenties. She did not have the typical cloned Christian look. On the contrary, she exuded seductiveness. Her skirt, only a bit longer than a mini, alluringly displayed her long, shapely legs. A matching, tight-fitting sweater enabled her firm, superior breasts to make a similar statement. Prominent cheekbones in a youthful but oddly worn face set off her sparkling eyes. She met my approach with a smile.

"Are you on the staff here?" I asked.

"No, just a visitor. My name is Joy Christian."

"That's an easy name to remember: there's Joy in being a Christian." My facetiousness almost curdled into sarcasm.

"Yeah. You've got it." she said, with a big, disarming smile.

*   *   *

Reverend Zimmerman pursued his quest against me resolutely. A letter-writing campaign of Assemblies' ministers denouncing me to various publications was mounted. It got a lot of attention. Chris Stoehr, a syndicated reporter for *The Detroit Free Press,* wrote a feature article that appeared on June 11, 1978.

There are plenty of . . . [controversies] to choose from when talking about the Rev. Austin Miles.

The latest is swirling in the pages of *Christian Life Magazine,* in which members and ministers of the Assembly of God church have condemned Miles and his ministry, saying that show business is inherently evil, and that the performers among his flock cannot be saved.

The charges have taken on un-Christian tones, and his critics point to Miles' background in show business, as a ringmaster and as an actor.

The Austin Miles rumors had reached such bizarre proportions that churches were expressing a vehemence such as I had never experienced before when cancelling my revivals and speaking engagements. In the few I was able to get, there would nearly always be some woman showing up and swearing to anyone who would listen that she had been to bed with me and felt duty-bound to tell. It was always someone who was not a member or even a frequent attender of the particular church.

The Women's Aglow Fellowship proved to be the most vicious of all the purveyors of defamation against me. Obediently following the instructions of their male advisors, most of whom were Assemblies' ministers, they were the foot soldiers in the nasty letter writing/phone calling campaign against me.

One night in the wee hours, I picked up the phone. The woman at the other end had a deep southern accent. "Brother Mahl's?" she drawled. "Ahm with Women's Aglow. Jes' want you t' know that if you ever come to Alabama, you jest may get shot!"

"Is that a word from the Lord?" I responded, before hanging up.

The Canadian-produced Assemblies of God television series, "The Turning Point," had been completed. Since the episode featuring me turned out to be the most professional of the series, it was used as the pilot tape to sell stations on the idea of running the series. In New Haven, Connecticut, the air time would have cost $30,000, but the station wasn't interested in selling the air time to an Assemblies of God program. After viewing my episode, the station *donated* the entire thirteen weeks of time. When the tapes were sent for broadcast, my episode was not among them. "Oh, there's bad things about Austin Miles," the elect of Springfield would tell the station managers, "so we're not letting his segment be broadcast." Without a pang of conscience, the Assemblies' leadership perpetrated this bait-and-switch routine on several stations.

The Assemblies' next kick in the pants was the publication of two books appropriating my trademark slogan, "You Are Special," in the titles and using content from my messages almost word for word. I had registered "You Are Special" as a trademark. My lawyers forced them to withdraw the books.

I made preparations to sue the Assemblies and Pat Robertson for defamation. Both parties hastened to point out that it was "un-Christian" to sue, citing 1 Corinthians 6:5,7-8; and Romans 12:14-17 and 19-21. Since being a true Christian seemed like the only thing I had left, I dropped the matter.

I started my own television series, entitled "You Are Special," which was produced in Detroit. Chris Stoehr asked for an interview about it for her paper. By this time my anger at the Christian world had escalated and I was not handling it very well. My remarks were flippant, but they also reflected my bent-out-of-shape frame of mind.

> I plan to build a Christian "Disneyland." There will be rides, gospel singing twenty-four hours a day, [and] the world's biggest cross with a restaurant in one side and corporate offices in the other. We'll have Noah's Ark and the parting of the Red Sea.

These "revelations" became the crux of a national story titled "Coast to Coast With the Holy Ghost." The caption for my part of the story read:

> Show Biz reverend
> does a great Jesus
> and he's building a
> park with an ark

The story went on with more details of my Religious World-Disneyland theme park concept. My "vision" dwarfed Jim Bakker's Heritage Village ministry, which was also described in the story. Jim read it with keen interest, and preparations to build Heritage U.S.A. began within a month. Even though it was all just a gag, Jim Bakker was not to be outdone.

I gratefully accepted an invitation to hold services at the Fountain Motel in Windsor, Ontario. Jack Mahoney, the owner, had visited me at the television production studio and offered me his banquet room, advertising for the meetings, and room and board. Any offerings collected would go to my ministry. His hospitality boosted my morale after being cancelled by so many churches.

While in Windsor, the sickening news of November 18, 1978, reached me. On that day, Reverend Jim Jones orchestrated the mass suicide of all those members of his cult who were present at the Guyana compound. Nine hundred and thirteen people, including children, died of self-poisoning following the machine-gun assassination of Congressman Leo Ryan and his party. Reports of perverted sex, drugs, and brainwashing masterminded by the charismatic Reverend Jones surfaced quickly.

I became severely depressed. This was the ministry that "Brother Z" had wanted me to become involved in, and I had later rebuked myself for refusing his sage advice. Jones was so smooth and had gained so much political clout that he could have run for high political office and won. He disguised his mental illness by cloaking it with Christianity, the perfect mask for a mad man.

I tossed and turned all night. When I finally did nod off, I had nightmares in which black demon spirits were flying at me. I woke with a gasp. Christianity was evil! It was all phony, a big fraud. These people were all *crazy*. I had driven my wife away, confused my daughter, and lost my life savings—for what?

Struggling financially, with few opportunities to preach because of the vilification campaign waged by the Assemblies of God, my depression got alarmingly worse. I took long, aimless walks. I really could think of no reason to continue to live.

I was still scheduled to go to Minot, North Dakota, to hold a revival crusade for Richard Orchard. I phoned him.

"Brother Orchard, I just called to tell you that I will cancel the meetings we have scheduled before 'Brother Z' convinces you to cancel me."

"What are you talking about?" he boomed indignantly. "*I'm* running this church, not 'Brother Z.' I'm expecting you here as scheduled."

Brother Orchard's welcome at the airport could not have been warmer. As we drove to the church, I asked him, "Brother Orchard, do you own your home, or have anything for your retirement?"

He looked at me solemnly. "I don't own a parcel of land."

"Is it all worth it?"

"Yes. Yes. I could never be anything else but a minister of the Gospel."

While the song service was going on in the sanctuary, I went into the small room off the platform to pray and prepare myself for the service. It was a Sunday school room, with tiny tables and chairs. The sounds of the song service seemed to fade away and become oddly distant. I could almost hear the sound of children's voices singing, "Jesus loves me, this I know, for the Bible tells me so." A lot had happened since I sat at such a tiny table in North Park Presbyterian Church so long ago.

As Brother Orchard was introducing me, I glanced at the placards bearing paraphrases of New Testament verses on the wall. "Blessed are the poor, for they shall inherit the kingdom of heaven." "Blessed are ye when men persecute you for my name's sake. . . ." According to these, I was indeed being blessed abundantly.

I rested my head on the back of my chair in Brother Orchard's study. A sense of peace always enveloped me after a service. Someone gently knocked on the door. Behind the door, a fairly handsome, neatly dressed man who appeared to be in his forties awaited my response. His intent expression communicated urgency.

"Brother Miles, I have to talk with you," he said. "You prayed about a man in the congregation with diabetes. I am that man. It's very serious. I have a farm and property worth one million dollars. I will sign it all over to you now if you will heal me." He was from all appearances a good man; also a trusting, vulnerable, and desperate one.

"Thank God you came to *me*," I responded. "First of all, God is the healer: I'm not. He does not want you to give away your home or your savings. You do not have to pay for healing and prayer. The *only* thing God would expect of you for your healing is your acknowledgement of Him and your fellowship." I prayed with the man, confident that the results would be good.

The next day I opened my journal and began to write:

Tuesday—Sept. 13, 1977—Minot, N.D.

An exceptionally peaceful morning. Lodging in an attractive motel on a hill that overlooks much of Minot. The air is fresh as though it has never been breathed before. I strolled through rolling fields this morning— happily alone with my thoughts—wrestling in prayer—trying to come to some solution.

I watched a cricket crawling along—a butterfly swooped down— the cricket scurried for cover—the butterfly lit on a dandelion bloom to feed. From the grass, the cricket, undaunted, rubbed its legs together giving out its own special kind of nature's music. As the butterfly fed, a bee—with great authority—buzzed down—the butterfly left in haste. The bee settled on a flower to replenish what he needed to be further reproductive.

How busy, yet beautiful, is nature. I am enjoying these moments— sitting here on the terrace overlooking the valley. I've just read—again— a portion of the classical booklet "Power Through Prayer" by E. M. Bounds. Reading again of David Brainerd, how I desire to be more like him. So totally devoted to God—such perseverance—I am so many times ready to give up—toss the gloves in the hat for good—I am not always victorious in discouragements, yet I know—reading of the likes of Brainerd—John Wesley—The Apostle Paul—that I *must* "excel in grace" if ever I am to do a mighty work for God. To do less—to be less— only hinders His purpose through me.

I have certainly had more than a portion of heartache—disappoint- ment—agony—betrayal regularly and out-and-out hurt. I have had a por- tion of suffering. And—living—in this world—there will certainly be more. Oh God—let me take the future over with more *grace*—let me never be ashamed of my testimony. Keep pounding it in my head that "Your

grace is sufficient for me."
    Especially this afternoon as I attempt to talk by phone to the N.Y.
District Superintendent.

    I was amazed that Brother Orchard and I could remain such good
friends. He was a mirror of Assemblies of God doctrine. He vehemently
objected when his son Loren began dating a lovely, blonde Lutheran girl.
She looked to be a very proper, elegant girl who any reasonable man would
be delighted to have for a daughter-in-law. Loren said to me privately,
"My father insists that I should marry only a Pentecostal girl. He says
that if someone does not speak in tongues, is not baptized in the Holy
Spirit, they are not saved and I would be in an unholy alliance. But she
is wonderful! She is a lady. These Pentecostal girls are loose. They'll have
sex with anyone, and I don't want that. I want a lady." Loren's sister
had rebelled against her upbringing, and that had ended in tragedy. I prayed
that Loren would not go off the deep end.
    Another time, Brother Orchard took me to lunch in Keystone, a colorful
Western-theme town. It was closed for the season, with only a couple of
shops open. "Hey," he yelled to a bystander, "is there any place one can
get something to eat around here?"
    "You can probably get a sandwich at the bar down the street," the
man answered. "That's probably the only place open."
    "We certainly would not go to a *bar,*" shot Brother Orchard back
sanctimoniously.
    "I'm sorry," the man said, embarrassed. "I didn't mean to offend you.
I was just trying to help. It's just that there's nowhere else open."
    Despite his straightlaced, letter-of-the-law theology, in which he had
become trapped, Brother Orchard was one of the very few Assemblies'
ministers who remained my friend, swayed neither by gossip nor pressure
from "Brother Z."

XXXIV

D own at PTL, each day was an event. Tammy's new book *I Gotta Be Me* was released. Gary Paxton, whom God had "delivered from womanizing," had written the foreword. In a less exalted corner of Heritage Village, Harold Olshields was trying to mend his broken heart. Lyn McMann had married PTL singer Lee Robbins in an elaborate ceremony.

"There's a lot of hurting people out there," proclaimed Jim Bakker over the airwaves, "and we're here to help *you*. Your contributions keep 'The PTL Club' on the air, and make it possible to have our phone counselors available to you twenty-four hours a day."

On camera, Jim displayed immense compassion and love. From what I saw in private, it seemed he was well on his way to hating the whole human race. And I could understand why. The pressures coming at him from every direction were beyond endurance. *The Charlotte Observer* had begun its fateful series of investigative stories on the misuse of PTL donations. Three PTL vice-presidents who had been Jim's intimates, Roger Flessing, Bill Perkins, and Robert Manzano, gave damaging "insider" stories to reporters Allen Cowan and Frye Gaillard. These personal betrayals hurt Jim more than the revelations.

Kooks of every description descended upon Heritage Village to convey messages God had given them for Jim to guide him in saving the world. Three men with pointed faces identified themselves as "angels" bearing an urgent message. They were intercepted right at the door of Jim's office.

A woman claiming to be the mother of Jesus was determined to get an audience with Jim. Matters finally came to a head when she walked right onto the set during the telecast. The viewers got to see Jim jump out of his chair and exclaim, "Get out of here! I tell you, get out of here!" Security guards rushed in and bodily took the woman out, while she cackled like a cartoon witch.

Jim could no longer make a move unless security guards accompanied him. He was afraid to talk to anyone he did not know. I had the same problem to a lesser extent. A woman named Cheryl Lebbe followed me all over the country with a wedding dress in a box. She said God had told her I was going to marry her. God had neglected to share this news with me.

To add to the clamor, the Assemblies of God tried to tell Jim who should and should not be on the program. I was in the "should not" category. But Jim would not be dictated to that way.

"Nobody's going to tell me who I can and cannot have on this program," Jim told his audience. "God told me that *He* would judge 'em and for me to love 'em." That led naturally into the subject of the Christians' prejudice against the circus. "Tell me, Austin," Jim said after. a telecast, "do you know enough circus people who are Christians to do a complete circus?"

"Absolutely," I responded.

"Do you think you can do it in our new amphitheater? It's almost finished." The amphitheater where the Christian circus would perform was in the middle of the new Heritage U.S.A. theme park, then under construction. Lyn McMann Robbins had been promoted to producer, and she skillfully managed the welter of details needed to bring the project off. Circus Maranatha, presented in a Christian setting with all "born-again" circus artists—each of whom gave their testimony after their performance—would be a first in religious broadcasting. I felt elated to be back in my ringmaster's uniform. It seemed as if the diverging streams of Christianity and circus in my own life were being reconciled. Perhaps bridges uniting church, society at large, and the circus world could result from this. The television special drew such a favorable response that Jim elected to make it an annual event.

I began spending more of my time at PTL. My own television show, "You Are Special," appeared on the PTL satellite network and on a number of regular television stations around the country. I made various appearances with Jim. I preached in the Heritage Church and taught week-long seminars at Heritage Village. I was paid for all of these activities, which helped to lessen my financial problems.

*   *   *

"Angels!" exclaimed Harold Olshields. Another fad had hit the world of Pentecostalism. "The Happy Hunters," Harold explained, "say in their book that there's a lot of excitement in heaven right now. The angels are preparing for the Second Coming of Christ!"

Everybody around Heritage Village was buzzing about this latest phenomenon. The Hunters were pushing a book called *Angels on Assignment* by Reverend Roland Buck as told to Charles and Frances Hunter, who published it with their own company, Hunter Books. Reverend Buck, a rustic preacher from Idaho, told an intriguing story about Gabriel, archangel of Israel, and a band of fellow angels setting up camp on Buck's property. Even his dog saw them, he said.

Angels now accompanied the Hunters wherever they held meetings, and began to favor other ministries with their presence as well. "Everyone be quiet for a moment," said Frances Hunter, shushing the audience suddenly in the middle of a service. "I feel that there's an angel right here in our midst. Let's be real quiet. Maybe we'll see him. There! There he is!" Frances pointed dramatically into the balcony, and everyone lifted their hands and praised God loudly. Some, when they described the meeting later, would say they actually saw the angel. Angel books flooded the religious book market.

The three pointy-faced men made a return visit to Heritage Village, trying to get their divine message through to Jim. Understandably, Jim was getting more and more disgusted.

*   *   *

Pastor Martin Luther Davidson was another of the small minority of Assemblies' ministers who were not swayed by "Brother Z." He asked me back to his church in Miami for a week-long engagement. I wondered what he would do were he ever to find out that Christ was a Jew, but I did not feel up to telling him. At the first evening's service, Pastor Davidson appeared in good form. While the robed choir swayed back and forth clapping their hands, he strutted back and forth with a big grin on his face, singing and snapping his fingers in time to the music of "I've Got Something That the World Can't Give, and the World Can't Take it Away."

I used one of my days that week to visit Pastor Arthur Shell, who had succeeded Pastor Ernie Eskelin at Trinity Assembly of God. An old-timer in the Assemblies' hierarchy, Pastor Shell had even helped to draft its bylaws. I told him about my difficulties.

"There will always be openings for your ministry," he assured me. "There are many, many charismatic groups who have not reached the perfection of the Assemblies who would be glad to have you." I stared at him. When I realized that he was dead serious, I did not know whether to laugh or cry.

When I returned, I found that Pastor and Mrs. Davidson were angry with me. I had no idea that a bitter rivalry existed between Pastors Davidson and Shell, and that they hated each other.

I flew to New England next, to conduct a week of services in a retreat center, looking forward to the possibility of some much-needed rest and relaxation among the spectacular autumn foliage.

"We have a couple spending their honeymoon here at the retreat," the pastor in charge told me. "The bride said she wanted to begin her marriage at an Austin Miles service." At the opening service, the honeymoon couple was called on to stand up and receive the good wishes of the congregation. I almost choked when Cheryl Lebbe stood up with her new husband, a black man. The wedding dress that she had carried so many miles in a box had finally been put to use. The bride insisted on staying in the room next to mine.

At the end of the first day, I went to the apartment of the pastor in charge and his family for coffee. The wife took off her shoes and stretched out on the couch. One of her two teenaged sons quickly slipped over to the couch, took her bare feet in his hands, and proceeded to caress them. The mother breathed a sigh of contentment as her son, excitement shining in his eyes, continued to fondle her feet and ankles. The pastor seemed oblivious to the activity and kept on talking about ministry and soul-saving with me. This ritual apparently took place every night after service. A foot fetish might have been considered acceptable in some circles, but with one's own mother? The Assemblies of God never ceased to provide me with new and interesting insights. One night, the wife gave me a flirtatious look that seemed to indicate I would be welcome to join the proceedings.

Gathered together at that retreat center was a group called Camps Farthest Out (CFO). They were the most contentious people I'd ever encountered. A lady from that group gave me a book of the group's teachings. The book described in minute detail how baptism was conducted in this group. A gourd of water with a hose attached was hung from a tree limb out in the woods. The other end of the hose was inserted in the rectum of the person being baptized. If the appropriate prayer activity accompanied the resulting enema, demons would be washed out of the body at the same time.

"This is a sick cult!" I exclaimed, when I went to the pastor in charge to announce that I would leave early. He prevailed upon me to finish out the week.

*   *   *

Jim Bakker's tensions in his ministry were about to overcome him. The amount of time he spent in the steam room "releasing his stress" increased. Tammy was seen from time to time by various staff members banging on the door, trying to get him to come out. She knew what was going on inside and was sickened by it.

Tammy drew closer to Gary Paxton. When Jim finally learned that his wife had a new soulmate, he flew into a rage and banished Paxton from PTL. Immediately, Jim ordered orchestra leader Thurlow Spurr to compose another theme song for the program to replace the one Paxton had written. "Don't ever—*ever* again—play anything Paxton wrote or had anything to do with in this studio," Jim screamed. Paxton and his wife divorced over the affair.

Thurlow Spurr was a ruthless self-server. The moment I met him, I knew with whom I had to deal. He had involved himself more and more in production discussions and decisions. Undermining the authority of Lyn Robbins was clearly a major objective of his. It did not surprise me at all when I came to PTL for an appearance and he handed me his card: "Thurlow Spurr—Producer."

By now, Jim was going through his own private hell. Tammy's dalliance with Gary Paxton had shaken him profoundly, and he was bitter. When he felt things were back under control, he went to Hawaii, mainly to rest. One morning he tuned in "The PTL Club" and saw Gary Paxton on it as a guest. Jim literally jumped out of his chair. He flew back to Charlotte in a rage and called a meeting of the production staff.

"Who booked Paxton back on this program?" Jim demanded to know, looking each staff member in the eye. His face red and flushed, he glared at Lyn, Jeanne Johnson, and everyone else in turn. "O.K., which one of you did it?"

"I did," said a soft voice. There was a long moment of tense silence as Jim slowly turned toward the speaker—Tammy Faye. Thurlow Spurr took the scene in with great interest, his mind working and turning.

Jim became a little Napoleon. He now felt everyone was plotting against him, and he was determined to keep control over his empire.

Martin Gutwerk, the chief engineer of the PTL television studio, quit. "I couldn't take it any more," he told me. "Jim calls a meeting of his staff every month. He demands that they swear their first loyalty to him, second to God, and third to family. He could become another Jim Jones!" Gutwerk took a job at Channel 40, a Christian television station in Pittsburgh.

My own anger and bitterness over the defamation campaign of "Brother Z" and Pat Robertson boiled unabated. Wherever I could, I retaliated, passing the word about what had happened. Whenever I went to a television station that carried "The 700 Club," I made sure the people learned what really lurked behind Pat Robertson's genial appearance.

This action was self-defeating, and only resulted in more rumors being spread about me. Martin Gutwerk called me and told me that Reverend Russ Bixler, the owner of Channel 40 and a minister I had greatly respected, had started circulating outlandish, slanderous statements of his own about me. Bixler claimed that during my last visit to Pittsburgh I had made advances toward yet another woman who apparently had called me down for it "in the presence of the entire Channel 40 studio staff." He also claimed that I had admitted it.

Against that background, I was startled to find an invitation in my mail to appear as a guest on "The 700 Club." I waded out a little deeper into the waters of hypocrisy by saying "yes." I hated Pat Robertson, and would have loved to punch him in the nose. But I realized that a shot on "The 700 Club" would boost my ailing ministry and puncture many of the rumors that were hurting it. Simple ego, and my drive to be recognized as someone of substance, also played a part in my decision.

My bad conscience about the appearance resulted in a terrific struggle in prayer the night before the telecast. "Oh God," I cried out, "please give me grace for the telecast. Please, God, help me to love Pat Robertson. Let there be healing." I took a Valium before departing for the studio.

The telecast went well. Robertson didn't discuss my Christian testimony or ministry. The main theme of the show was Christian circus performers, and Robertson wanted only to discuss my past circus career.

Gary Paxton, without a beard now, also appeared on the telecast. I found him extremely personable. So did Jackie Mitchem, the attractive guest coordinator for "The 700 Club." No doubt, their conversation would continue after the telecast.

Before the telecast, I had gone from the airport to the swank hotel room reserved for me by CBN. There, I wrote in my journal:

> December 18, 1979.
> Norfolk, Virginia
>
> I felt like I was back in show business—I feel more and more of a desire to get back in arena shows—around real people—decent people again— I have so much anger that I have a desire to go to a comfortable bar and just drink martinis.

After the telecast, while waiting for my plane, I wrote:

> . . . I especially liked Ben. He is so warm, and I feel a real brother in the Lord. I believe there was a real healing here. . . . I feel good—relaxed and anxious to return home.

It was some time later when I realized what forces had been behind my invitation to appear on "The 700 Club." Pat Robertson took a lot of heat for the pressures applied against me. My harping on it to ministers and religious broadcasters who continued to think well of me had taken its toll. After that telecast, whenever the matter came up, Robertson was able to say, "I don't understand how rumors like this get started. Why, Austin and I are friends. In fact, he was just on my television program with me."

Brother Robertson had outsmarted me. He defused the stories about these unfair assaults on my reputation, and now possessed a videotaped telecast that would have made any renewed effort of mine to take legal measures against him look ridiculous. I deserved to be defeated. I had gone against my principles to appear with a man I hated in order to garner extra recognition and publicity for myself.

Jesus Christ, Inc.

XXXV

L ike a sprawling giant, the massive Heritage U.S.A. theme park took form and belched to life in Fort Mill, South Carolina. It straddled the North Carolina–South Carolina border, and spread into three different counties. Like God Himself, it had both a dual and a triune nature.

Jim conducted his first telecast in the new "Barn" auditorium/studio/ church, which was still under construction. I was his first telecast guest there. We sat on bar stools, with a partial set behind us. Workmen and carpenters worked frantically around us. The hammering, sawing, and drilling would stop when Jim and I were on, then resume when the musical and other pretaped segments came on.

"You know, Austin?" he remarked while a taped segment was on, "I always wanted to go into show business."

"Then, why didn't you?" I asked.

"Because the world could never give me what God has." He looked around the mammoth new facility being built. "Look at this. This will be the finest, best equipped television studio in the world. Better than CBS or any of the rest of them. And *God* gave this to *me*. The world could never give what God has."

It had all been built with donations "for God's work," money that need never be repaid. To me, the new operation seemed too big and unwieldy to retain its original noble ideals and goals for very long.

Over at Heritage Village, demons had replaced angels as the latest spiritual craze. Demons were being discovered everywhere. Reverend Russell Olson of the PTL staff wrote a six-page memo briefing everyone on the attack. Reverend Olson had discovered demons in the transmitter tower in the Heritage Church steeple, in all the offices in the complex, in the C.B. radio in Tammy's car, and in the tires of Jim Bakker's car. No mention was made of the PTL health club. Apparently the steam room was demon-free.

Heritage U.S.A. was ushered in with one "financial crisis" after another. Just when one enormous bill had been paid "in the nick of time," another would pop up. "If this bill is not paid by the twenty-sixth of this month, the banks will close down not only Heritage U.S.A., but the PTL Television Network as well," Jim would tell the faithful. "The devil is laughing at you people who are doing nothing to save PTL. One day—one day you will turn on your television set and there will be no PTL. No Christian television! And the devil will have scored his greatest victory!"

Picking up the cue, Tammy would sob, "People, you don't know how serious this is! Jim and I have sold *everything* we have to sell in order to keep PTL on the air, but it isn't enough! You don't know what it's like to see Jim up in the middle of the night praying and crying out to God. One night he couldn't sleep and said to me, 'Honey, I just don't know how we're going to raise that two million dollars.' We're not going to make it unless you do something *now!*"

Remarkably, Jim's followers came through in every announced crisis. There was a genuine crisis going on, however, that Jim did not want the world to hear about.

"Tammy has left me!" a distraught Jim confided to his brother, Norman. Thurlow Spurr, in his quest for power, had used his closeness to Tammy Faye Bakker as a stepping stone. Thurlow had observed how Gary Paxton had been able to move in on Tammy when Jim was away. Worming his way into Jim's confidence, this Sergeant Bilko with a baton encouraged Jim to spend more time away from the "stresses of PTL," to refresh himself. "Besides," Thurlow said to Jim in the privacy of Jim's office, "people will appreciate you more. Johnny Carson does this several times a year."

That did the trick. Jim wanted a star image.

While Jim was away, Thurlow played upon the fragile emotions of Tammy Faye. Although Tammy loved God, the Christians were getting on her nerves too. Thurlow encouraged her to think she could make it in the secular music business and convinced her to go to Nashville with him. There, Thurlow told her, he would make her into a "real star." Thurlow made himself indispensable. He coached and managed Tammy Faye, writing, arranging, and conducting the songs which were to make her famous.

With unmitigated gall, Thurlow Spurr returned to PTL to continue his duties as though nothing had happened. Jim confronted him in a rage. In a cold, calculating ploy, Thurlow went on the offensive and rebuked Jim for neglecting Tammy. The tactic kept Jim from exploding. Several moments of tense silence ensued. Then, calmly and in a subdued voice, Jim fired Thurlow Spurr and immediately issued an order to have all music composed by him banned from the PTL Garden of Eden. Another new theme song for PTL was immediately commissioned.

John Wesley Fletcher's star began to rise at PTL. Fletcher was a mystery to me. Despite his seedy past and noticeable homosexual demeanor, God seemed to use him in a more spectacular way than anyone else.

One day during a telecast from the Heritage U.S.A. amphitheater with Fletcher, Jim said, "You know, I feel that the Lord is telling me that there is a man in the audience who is seriously ill with a lung problem. He has cancer in his right lung."

Jim seemed hesitant as he gave out this divine revelation, as if he were hoping against hope that a sick person fitting his description would identify himself and claim the "word of knowledge."

"My spirit bears witness to that," Fletcher added. "In fact, I'll pick him out for you!" Excitement mounted as Fletcher looked through the crowd. "There—up there, yes—you in the middle up there in the blue shirt, stand up."

Jim took a microphone up into the bleachers to talk to the man. The man's wife was weeping. Everything said about her husband was true, she said, and they had come to PTL hoping for a miracle. Fletcher prayed for the man and everyone was satisfied that a miraculous healing had taken place. After all, since God had revealed it to Bakker and Fletcher, and in such a spectacular fashion, no further confirmation was needed. Nobody bothered to follow up on it.

Jim admired Fletcher so much that he began to take on Fletcher's speech and mannerisms. On one telecast, viewers were treated to the spectacle of Jim shouting out scriptures as he walked with uneven, exaggerated steps, holding his Bible high over his head as Fletcher pranced along after him with a piece of paper, fanning Jim's behind.

They began to behave on camera like two schoolgirls laughing at the world. On one telecast from Clearwater, Florida, Bakker and Fletcher got the giggles. They even giggled during the fund-raising opening of the program. Then Fletcher said, "Jim, you look great. You must have had a good rest today."

"Yes I did," Jim said, with an even bigger smile than usual. "We need more 'rest' like that."

"God really ministered to us today, didn't he, Jim?"

"Yeah," Jim said, gazing at Fletcher. "He really did! We need *more* rest like that!"

They segued from this banter into their serious fund-raising pitch and raised an enormous sum for "God's work" that day. In a motel room not far away, Jessica Hahn watched the broadcast, reflecting on the sleazy sexual encounter she had just had with Bakker and Fletcher—the "rest" they were giggling about.

Something else puzzled me about Fletcher. In his church preaching appearances, he gave the impression of being a devoted family man, often arriving with his wife and children in tow. But whenever he came to PTL, there would be only a male companion with him whose airfare PTL also paid. The word about Fletcher's homosexuality was quietly being spread at Heritage Village. Bakker did not want to hear anything about it. Two young men on the PTL staff came to the front office to complain that Fletcher had made homosexual advances toward them. Jim still did not want to hear. Soon, the entire male security staff came as a delegation to complain about homosexual advances from Fletcher. Jim heard them out politely and did nothing. One day following the telecast, one of the production staff knocked on the door of Fletcher's room in the mansion, then opened it to discover Fletcher's male companion braced up against the wall while Fletcher, on his knees, performed oral sex on him. Jim had no choice but to ban Fletcher from the Garden, citing the severe drinking problem Fletcher also had as the reason.

It is particularly ironic that the "witness" responsible for converting Efrem Zimbalist, Jr., to Christianity was John Wesley Fletcher. Zimbalist and his friends watched Jan and Paul Crouch on Trinity Broadcasting Network (TBN) for laughs. Paul Crouch was so straightlaced and pompous that he could have made reading the telephone book sound like a message from God. His wife, Jan, a ditsy, spaced-out blonde, looked like a retarded Carol Channing. The guests were even more off-the-wall.

One night, Efrem saw Fletcher on TBN. Fletcher's coarse stomp-and-shout antics were the complete opposite of the cultured background and suave manner of the film actor. Yet, something about Fletcher's message so touched Efrem that he suddenly decided to become "born again." Efrem phoned TBN to tell them. Excitement abounded at TBN and throughout its television audience when it was announced that Efrem Zimbalist, Jr., had "received Christ" as a result of the telecast. Many "salvation calls" came as a result. I had often wondered if the truth about Fletcher made Efrem as angry at him as I was at Bobby Yerkes. A lot had happened between me and Bobby that had left a bitter taste in my mouth.

*   *   *

The Fourth of July weekend 1982 promised to be the most impressive week of celebration yet for Heritage U.S.A. The premier personalities of Charismatic Christianity attended. The much heralded "Upper Room" would be inaugurated and dedicated during a festive evening that would be brought to a climax by a huge fireworks display. Rex Humbard, Maude Aimee, Jim and Tammy, Mike Murdock and his girlfriend, Donna Douglas, Dave Lewis, Dr. C. M. Ward, Doug Oldham, and, of course, the Happy Goodmans took part in the ceremonies and were in the platform party. Thousands of spectators were on the grounds.

After the televised rally, the platform party were to lead a torchlight parade to the Upper Room. As we walked toward the Upper Room and a communion service to end all communion services, I suddenly gave in to the impulse to drop out of the march and seek a quiet place to be alone. I spent the time in silent meditation behind some trees at the edge of a lake. The next day, Jim rebuked me for being absent. "Where were you?" he demanded. "I expected you to be at that communion service. You should have been there."

A special viewing area by the lake, for dignitaries to watch the fireworks display, had been roped off. One of the dignitaries waiting there, Efrem Zimbalist, Jr., had just accepted the invitation to be a member of the Board of Directors of PTL, enhancing the ministry's credibility. My chance to ask him the question that had been very much on my mind had come at last.

The actor greeted me with friendliness as a member of the production staff seated me next to him. While fireworks lit up the sky, we chatted enthusiastically about the "born-again" life. He expressed particular excitement over a new, annotated study Bible that Pastor Jess Moody had given him.

"Efrem—I must ask you a question," I said, getting to the point. "How did you feel when you learned the truth about John Wesley Fletcher? Was this an embarrassment to you?"

"Oh, not at all," he responded in his rich, resonant tones. "No matter what he turned out to be, I'll always be grateful to him. It's because of him that I'm a born-again Christian and know Christ."

"I see. I had a similar experience with Bobby Yerkes, and I hate him for it."

"Have you prayed for him?" Efrem asked me, with a probing look.

"No—as a matter of fact, I haven't. I haven't even thought about it."

"Maybe you should," the handsome actor advised as a giant cluster of fireworks exploded all across the sky for the finale of the display.

Late that night, in the tranquil drawing room of the mansion, Pastor Aubrey Sara and I talked quietly. I shared with him some of my incredible experiences with Christians and my disillusionment with Christian leaders. "Yet," I went on, "there is a part of me that demands to preach, to be a minister. But what can I do? All doors are closing to me. It has become almost impossible. God doesn't even seem to know I exist any more."

Pastor Sara looked at me thoughtfully. "When a bird gets ready to be productive, to lay her eggs," he said softly, "she first goes through the ritual of shaking off any loose feathers. It is only when she is free of the loose feathers that the bird is fertile and can produce that egg. Maybe there are some loose feathers in your life that you need to shake free from. It could be loose feathers of anger, bitterness, unforgiveness, looking back—

even pride. It could be any number of things. Whatever it is, when you shake free of those particular feathers, God may be able to use you in a greater way than you ever imagined."

*   *   *

As Heritage U.S.A. made its debut, insanity hit the monstrous complex. "One can hear eighty-six sermons a day here at Heritage U.S.A.," Jim boasted to the television audience. Gospel singing groups could be heard everywhere. The Upper Room, touted as a place for quiet prayer, meditation, and contemplation, became the forum for a twenty-four-hour-a-day marathon of pound-and-shout preaching. The construction noise at the water slide and merry-go-round sites would soon be replaced by the clamor of those carnival attractions in operation. Souvenir shops selling Bibles, crosses, and overpriced jewelry did a land-office business, as did Tammy Faye's "boutique." On "The PTL Club," the message had become a pure promotional travelogue for Heritage U.S.A., which had become the apex of Corporate Christianity. There wasn't a quiet place to be found. God had become hard to find in this atmosphere.

Obsessed with creating a utopian city where he would be Lord Mayor, Jim embarked on an orgy of building that bewildered everyone. The moment one project was completed, he would announce an even bigger one, requiring another fund-raising push and creating still one more financial "emergency." He had plans drawn up for a 25,000-seat indoor coliseum where he would "bring in the greatest evangelistic services on earth," and a stupendous all-glass church. The next phase of building would dwarf Oral Roberts' "City of Faith" and Robert Schuller's "Crystal Cathedral." Anything they could do, Jim could outdo.

The Charlotte Observer began attacking Jim and his operations more regularly. Jim proclaimed it an "attack of the devil upon God's anointed work." The Christians, easily diverted from the real issues with that sort of ploy, were eager to stifle their doubts. Despite the huge cash flow of PTL, Jim Bakker paid only the bills he wanted to pay. Several small businesses and building contractors were driven to bankruptcy because Bakker wouldn't pay them for their goods and services, pleading financial reversal when they presented him with their bills. Bakker did the same thing regarding payments to television stations for air time. Some stations cancelled him or cut him back to one hour a day because of slow payment. Others cancelled "The PTL Club," citing program content as the reason.

The more piteously Jim Bakker cried to his viewers about the impending financial collapse of PTL, the more extravagantly money was squandered on his personal luxuries. Jim had a whirlpool bath installed in his new office at Heritage U.S.A. Since that was the site of many seductions of women, including a former Miss America, some of us referred to it as the "floozy Jacuzzi." During this time of high living for Jim Bakker and selected PTL officials, ordinary full-time PTL employees were paid so badly that many had to get into the federal food stamp program to survive.

When the time for the yearly Circus Maranatha came around, Jim would be content with neither the existing amphitheater nor the Barn auditorium, either of which would have been entirely adequate. Instead, he rented a big top tent for eighty thousand dollars a week. In view of the unpaid debts and the hardships nonpayment was causing the vendors, I thought this inappropriate. I told Jim so.

Tino Wallenda Zoppe felt the same way. Tino was the founder of Circus Maranatha and a descendant of the famous Wallenda high wire circus family. That was not the only area of disagreement between Tino and Jim. Tino had booked his act into the nearby Carowinds Amusement Park, to appear the same week as Circus Maranatha would at Heritage U.S.A. Carowinds had arranged the performance times there in such a way as to allow Tino to be able to perform in both places. For Tino, anything to do with religion occupied a world apart from business and competition, so he could not see why it made Jim so angry.

After a loud argument between the two, Jim, his face flushed, stormed over to me in the huge, empty circus tent. "You'd better tell Tino that he had better straighten up or there will never be another circus in the history of Heritage U.S.A.! Tino has a bad attitude!" he screeched.

Reverend Thomas F. Zimmerman became a familiar sight around Heritage U.S.A. My presence did not seem to deter him, even though he kept up his pressure on the Assemblies' pastors to give me no greeting.

Jim got off on a new tangent that the world was going to come to an end within the year. Even though the Bible says ". . . of that day and hour knoweth no man" Jim had somehow received privileged information about the matter. He was so convincing, that future planning ceased for many of his followers. The end was clearly at hand. Then, on the same telecast, with a perfectly straight face, Jim made a hard-hitting fund-raising appeal to finish the Heritage School of Evangelism, which would take a year to complete and offered a two-year course.

XXXVI

L yn McMann's marriage to Lee Robbins spelled disaster from the
start. It did not surprise me when she phoned to tell me that they
were divorcing. Lyn told me some wild stories about Lee's supposed conduct
during the marriage. Knowing Lyn and Lee, I took them with a grain
of salt.

I understood well what sort of problems Lyn's insecurities must have
created within that marriage. The extraordinarily beautiful former model
saw getting older as cause for panic. Her first husband had dumped her
when she reached the ominous age of forty and had married a twenty-
year-old. Lyn had never fully recovered from it. She felt she had to prove
herself—to *prove* that she was still desirable and receive confirmation that
she was still wanted.

Because I saw all that and could put it in the context of other insecure
models I had known when I was much younger, I knew better than to
form a relationship with her. By now, I too was a poor risk for a lasting
romance. I carried more than my share of emotional baggage from past
disastrous relationships, and was a long way from getting over the divorce
from Rose Marie. I knew I could never give Lyn the constant reassurance
and undeviating admiration she craved. I had no such emotions left to give.

That period, beginning in mid-1978, began the darkest time in my
life. I made regular PTL appearances, my "You Are Special" programs
were being aired, and I preached in a few churches beyond the reach of
the long arm of "Brother Z." The discrepancy between what the public
saw and what was really happening to me could not have been greater.
Inside I was crumbling. I "lost it" in more ways than one.

I have never fully understood how I wound up in Millville, New Jersey.
I still cannot account for most of the time I spent there. It had all started
when Pastor Gerritt Kenyon of First Assembly of God on Wheaton Avenue
in Millville referred me to the Davis family, who owned a furniture store
in the town and supported his church. I was in their home a great deal
after Rose Marie left me.

I had intended to remain in the Forest Hills apartment. I cherished my memories of Rose Marie, and indeed underestimated how much their lingering savor had to do with keeping me going. Lori, still hurting from the loss of her relationship with Rose Marie and the stability she brought, became convinced that she would be better off living with the Davis family. They could provide a more constant environment than I could, Lori reasoned.

One night at dinner, before I realized what was happening, I agreed for Lori and me to move in with the Davis family. Strangely, following meals in the Davis home, I became more compliant than at any other time. Passively, I watched as they moved Lori and me out of the Forest Hills apartment. Just as passively, I signed a power of attorney, giving Mrs. Davis complete control over my finances. A corporation doing business of some kind in my name was formed, with Grace Davis as president. They took charge of my "You Are Special" television series, bringing Robert Elliott, who had filmed and edited it, in from Detroit to complete it. During that period, I entered into an absurd marriage, which was annulled. To be kind, let me just say that my experiences with the Davis family were unproductive—far beyond the normal problems you encounter when you get mixed up with conservative Christianity. By the time my relationship with the Davises was over, I was totally broke.

Lori thrived in that environment. She won every category in the Miss Cumberland County, New Jersey, contest. She aced the talent competition playing Chopin. I fought back the tears as she was crowned and presented with a big bouquet of roses. As she walked victoriously down the runway, the flashbulbs popping, I thought of the insecure little girl with the crooked feet, and the ugly corrective shoes she had worn for so many years. Now she was a beauty queen.

At the state finals, she scored highest in the talent competition. Then, quite uncharacteristically, she fluffed her speech and came in fourth in the overall scoring. She had been distracted by the attentions of a certain young, handsome waiter. I doubt that he had any career ambition beyond seducing beauty contestants. I think his interference cost Lori the state crown and her shot at the Miss America title. He moved on to his next quarry.

My presence as a resident of Millville brought mixed reactions. Reverend Kenyon confided to Luther McDonald, his song leader, how upsetting he found me. "My parents were missionaries. My wife's parents were missionaries to China. We've devoted our entire lives to God, but He has never worked through us like He has through Austin Miles—a former circus ringmaster."

The Kenyons were desperate for recognition. That probably explained their initial interest in me. Pastor Kenyon did everything he could to get his name in the local paper, *The Millville Daily*. The Kenyons had started out in a storefront church in Millville and worked their way up to the good-sized edifice on Wheaton Avenue. Pastor Kenyon's ambitions extended way beyond that church. But his preaching talent did not support his ambitions. He would fumble during the sermon, often reading the wrong scripture or losing his place, and frequently had to correct himself. He spent the whole summer preaching on "the whole armor of God." That armor had plenty of chinks, the way he portrayed it. He never did get it completely on that summer.

Pastor Kenyon tried desperately to *make* spiritual manifestations happen. Whenever someone would babble a few unintelligible syllables, God would immediately give Mrs. Kenyon the "interpretation" in English. This fakery, usually harmless enough, had a tragic outcome. A young girl came to the service with a boyfriend who was a college student. Beneath his seeming normality, the young man was evidently quite disturbed. When he heard the babblings, he became convinced they were from God and somehow he derived hope for his life from it.

"That's a bunch of garbage," the girl commented with a belittling laugh. "Watch. I can mumble out *anything* and Mrs. Kenyon will interpret it." During a quiet moment, the girl yelled out, "Abba coca cola coca cola ruma babba."

Sure enough, Sister Anita Kenyon immediately "interpreted" the babbling, with some portentous phrases in biblical sounding language. The fakery and its exposure devastated the young man.

Pastor Kenyon paid me an unexpected visit. "I just got a call from Reverend Don Richardson from New York. Brother Zimmerman asked him to call me to see if I could think of anything bad to say about you," he revealed. The owlish looking minister peered at me through his horn-rimmed glasses. "I told him that I had nothing bad to say about you, and that I do not want to be involved in this."

Within two months, the worst Austin Miles rumors ever were spewing out of First Assembly of God in Millville. These wild stories ran the gamut of moral sins that only Christian minds could have dreamed up. For me to have had the stamina to commit even a small portion of them would have made a great miracle story. In my state of mind then, I was almost catatonic, and barely did anything, good or bad. Signed denunciations were collected, and Pastor Kenyon mounted an elaborate telephone smear campaign against me, calling every minister he could think of. Every call began, "Brother, we've got to talk. It's about Austin Miles."

"Brother" Kenyon soon became the beneficiary of the sort of "miracle" that a General Superintendent can perform with a stroke of the pen. Gerritt Kenyon, the most boring preacher in Christendom, who could not put one word after another properly, was promoted to Presbyter for the New Jersey district. In conferring the honor, Reverend Zimmerman actually said to him, "Well done, my good and faithful servant." Brother Kenyon had taken his first step toward the ecclesiastical stardom he coveted.

These goings on aroused me from my lethargy. I left Millville and the nightmare that place had turned into. Lori turned against me. She demanded to stay there, where she could "be around *real* Christians." I had reached my lowest point ever. Before me lay the most difficult struggle I had ever faced: To get myself back together and reclaim my life.

XXXVII

I fastened my seat belt and settled back comfortably as the Eastern Airlines jet bound for Charlotte taxied to the runway. From my attaché case, I took a fresh bundle of mail I had picked up before coming to the airport. One letter bore a stamp from Nigeria. The writer of the letter, Joseph Kombat, had written to me before, after reading about me in a magazine.

In his first letter he had written, "I am going to an Assemblies of God Bible school, and I am going to be a minister of the Gospel!" I could sense the feeling of pride and accomplishment in his words. But my heart sank as I read on: "There is one difficulty, that is in raising the money necessary to obtain the study materials."

Surely, I did not understand him correctly. At the Assemblies of God national headquarters, Reverend Zimmerman had made a special point of telling me about the program to train, ordain, and "raise up" ministers and missionaries in their own countries. When I asked him how such a program was financed, Reverend Zimmerman specifically told me that this program, "which furnished study materials and training for these ministers and missionaries," was paid for by special offerings taken in churches in the United States.

I wrote back to young Mr. Kombat, asking him if I understood what he had written. This letter in my hand was his answer. As the jet prepared to take off, I tore the letter open.

"Oh, yes, you understand me correctly," he wrote. "We must pay for *everything*. And this is very difficult. We have very little money; we are very poor and many times we do without food so we can pay for the materials necessary for our study for the ministry."

I began to seethe with anger. That brought on an attack of the physical symptoms that now came whenever something upset me emotionally. I had noticed it more, and it had become worse, since I fled Millville. The thought of talking to anyone or of appearing in front of an audience brought on an extreme attack of butterflies in my stomach. I had frequent anxiety attacks. Sometimes I couldn't eat. Even though I felt hungry when I sat down to a meal, my stomach would knot up and I could take only one or two bites. I thought I was having a nervous breakdown, and consulted a doctor. He prescribed Valium, and some more potent psychoactives, to calm me down.

I had discussed my symptoms with Reverend Leonard Evans, in whose independent Charismatic church in Ohio I preached. I had become acquainted with him at PTL, where he was a frequent guest. He was famous in Charismatic circles for his "Theology of Love" message, and his concern and compassion were genuine. He offered a different diagnosis.

"It's a midlife crisis," he said to me. "I went through it. I got into pornography. At night I would sit there with a Bible in one hand and a pornographic magazine in the other. I knew I was being a hypocrite. I finally realized that I had gone into male menopause. It takes some kind of trauma to set it off. In your case it was no doubt your divorce from Rose Marie and your experience with the Assemblies of God. God will help you through this."

His thoughtful evaluation of my problem made sense to me. Yet, the feeling of terror that rose from the pit of my stomach seemed incredibly severe for such a simple explanation. I took another ten-milligram Valium as the plane touched down in Charlotte.

Lyn Robbins came to the "green room," where I was waiting for the telecast to begin. She had started a radio ministry of her own called "New Beginnings." "Could you tape a couple of radio programs with me tonight?" she asked.

"Sure."

"Good. I'll come by the mansion after dinner at 7:30. What's the matter?" The expression on my face had changed as I strained to catch the sounds coming from the studio.

"I—I see that we have—new theme music again."

I knew what *that* meant. Suddenly, everything seemed funny to me. I began to laugh and could not stop. "Here we go again! Another theme song! 'Darling they're *not* playing our song!' Oh God, and I hear we have another crisis. Jim just can't get enough money to finish that Ferris wheel. I mean—this is *serious!* You can't get to heaven without a water slide or a Ferris wheel!"

"Austin—are you O.K.?"

"Yes, Lyn, I never felt better in my life. Hallelujah! Praise the Lord!"

Our exchange was cut short by the floor manager beckoning me on to the set. As I walked out, I noticed Joy Christian sitting in her usual spot. I blew her a kiss. My contribution to the program that day was anything but spiritual. I told one joke after another, going for the laughs.

"The PTL Club is reaching people from all walks of life," Jim proclaimed to the world. "There is a very famous—I mean *very* famous—movie star who is right now starring in a Broadway show, who calls me every morning before the telecast just to talk about Jesus. He was saved watching this program. I can't tell you who he is. I'm keeping that confidential—but," Jim added as an afterthought, turning to me, "I'll tell you who it is, Austin, right after the telecast."

"Who is it, Jim?" I asked eagerly, as soon as we were off the set.

"Mickey Rooney," Jim responded, grinning proudly.

That evening at the mansion as I tried to eat, I felt my stomach tighten again. Lyn came over later with a tape recorder. "We can tape the shows in the living room," she said. "Are you sure you're up to it?"

After we had taped the radio program, Lyn suggested that we take a ride in her car. Once we were driving, she suddenly asked, "Would you be in the mood to go somewhere to have a glass of wine?"

We went to Bennigan's. "I wonder if we'll see anyone from PTL?" she said, looking around as we entered. We each ordered a glass of wine.

"I didn't think you drank wine," I said when our order had arrived.

"Lately I have been," she said, fingering the rim of her glass. "There are times I get sick of the ministry and the Christians. I've been seriously thinking about taking a secular job."

"Doing what?"

"Phil Donahue would like me to work for him as a producer."

"I'm getting sick of the ministry and Christians too. Sometimes I wish I had never heard the name of Jesus Christ."

"Austin, don't say that. God is real and Jesus loves you. Besides, God has ordained you to preach. I will never forget that service you had in Ernie Eskelin's church, the first time I ever saw you."

"Lyn—who is Joy Christian? She's always in the studio. There's something strange about her." I wanted to change the subject, and satisfy a nagging question in my mind. From her hurt expression, I realized this went deeper than I imagined. Lyn loved Jim and Tammy, and was probably closer to Jim than any person on earth except for Tammy.

"Joy Christian is—'Bambi.' She works in a massage parlor. She is a—friend—of Jim's."

"She is in *that* profession and comes here? Why?"

"Because—she says that knowing Jim like she does, she gets a kick out of watching him preach."

That made my stomach knot up even more. "How long has this been going on?"

"Several years."

"Come on. Let's get out of here," I said, my discomfort growing.

*   *   *

Marvin Gorman's was another familiar face around PTL. A powerhouse of a preacher, he pastored a mega-church in New Orleans, drawing over five thousand worshipers every Sunday. He also had a television ministry that had moved from a local telecast to a number of major broadcast markets. His success made him a lightning rod for the jealousies of other pastors. Not wanting to believe that ministers of the Gospel—co-laborers for God—could be rivals, I overlooked it.

When Pastor Gorman came to PTL, he always brought with him his pretty, young secretary. PTL picked up their travel and lodging tab. Before one telecast, I tarried in my dressing room to pray. Pastor Gorman and the secretary, thinking they were the last people to leave the dressing rooms, remained in the sitting area outside my closed door. After praying, I briskly opened the door and stepped out, finding myself face to face with the two of them locked in an embrace, with Pastor Gorman's right hand of fellowship inside his secretary's blouse, caressing a breast.

The encounter seemed to embarrass me more than it did either of them. "Praise the Lord," I said, weakly.

"Praise the Lord!" Pastor Gorman responded, taking his hand out of his secretary's blouse and raising it in the air with impressive poise.

Jean Albuquerque walked in on Bob Harrington and his secretary in a similar clinch during one of their visits to PTL. She promptly reported it to Jim, who warned her, "Don't you ever—*ever*—say anything about this to anybody, or you will be fired."

During that same period, a popular young pastor of PTL was caught having an affair with Tammy's maid. Both the pastor and the maid were married to others. With Godly indignation, Jim removed the man from his position, but allowed him to remain at PTL as a clerk in the Fort Heritage General Store. It was a strange code of moral ethics that I watched unfold.

A new spiritual trend swept PTL: "prophecy scriptures." "The Lord just gave me a scripture for you," an evangelist would say to someone he picked out. The scripture, selected at random or by some sort of divining ritual, would be recited and was expected to have some deep, personal meaning to the person given it, relating to some problem or situation in his or her life. Even though it closely resembled Gypsy fortune-telling, prophecy scriptures took off among the Christians. Suddenly, everybody had the "gift."

Even Marilyn Hickey, a well-respected Bible teacher, jumped on the bandwagon and began showcasing the "gift" at her meetings. The results were embarrassing. At a Full Gospel Business Men's Fellowship International convention in Indianapolis, while walking among the crowd in a packed ballroom, she suddenly interrupted what she was saying as she stopped in front of an intense looking man and announced: "God is speaking to me about you. God is giving me a scripture verse for you—it is—Romans 12:19. 'Dearly beloved, avenge not yourselves, but rather give place unto wrath: for it is written, Vengeance is mine; I will repay, saith the Lord.' "

The man looked confused, and reluctantly responded, "I don't see how that scripture applies to me."

"Oh, yes, it is for you," Marilyn insisted. "Someone has done something to you that angered you, and God is saying He will fight your battle for you."

The man looked even more puzzled. "There's no way that can apply to me. I'm not mad at anyone."

Marilyn squirmed. "But somewhere along the line, someone you trusted took advantage of you, and it has bothered you."

"There is nothing even remotely like that in my life!" the man protested.

"Well, keep thinking of that scripture that God gave me for you," Marilyn stammered, "and He will reveal the purpose for you. God bless you." She moved hastily back to the platform to do the thing she did best—teaching the Word.

Ben Kinchlow, of CBN, was another speaker at that convention. He was the last to speak, coming on after several displays of faith healing. He made no effort to go the others one better. Rather than attempting to fake anything more dramatic, he simply said, "Everything that can be accomplished has been done. Let me just share a message about Jesus." At least I had been right about one minister: Ben was for real—Praise God!

At that time, a scandal broke that the press ignored. Some officials of a West Coast district of the Assemblies of God went into the retirement condominium business. Several model apartments were built. The contractor showed the district officials how a few feet of floor space and some other items could be omitted from the apartments actually sold to the retirees and how, with the savings, some additional, freebie apartments—like the full-size model ones—could be built for the district church officials. One high official still has his ill-gotten condo in the mountains, the fruits of a kick-back scheme at the expense of the most trusting and most vulnerable of their flock—the elderly.

At another Assemblies' church on the West Coast, an elderly woman turned to her pastor for help. She was wealthy but had no family to look after her. She wanted her pastor's assurance that she would never be put in a nursing home, a prospect she found terrifying. One pastor, an older man with a kindly face, said he was eager to assist her. He took charge of the woman's affairs and money, promising to see to it that the lady would be cared for at home, and that her estate would go to the church when she died. The woman trusted her minister implicitly. This trust had been built up over a period of years. The moment the papers were signed, he hustled her off to the cheapest nursing home he could find. Then, like a vulture, he ransacked her house for valuables. He discovered a safe, which he blew open with dynamite to get at the jewelry and other valuables it contained.

A deacon of that church, who had accompanied the pastor to the house and witnessed the entire episode, called me. His voice cracked as he told me the story. "This really hurt me, Brother Miles. I don't know *what* I believe any more." An older retired man himself, the deacon was shattered by what he had witnessed.

"Where is the reverend now?" I asked.

"He's gone," he answered sadly. "He took off with all her money. He got almost a million dollars from her."

This pastor had earlier been president of a theology school, but he left under a cloud of accusations about "financial irregularities." I had dismissed it as some sort of misunderstanding. Now I had a different view.

I still took what few preaching dates I could get in Assemblies of God churches. The same Brother Zimmerman who had whined about how unscriptural it was for ministers to speak out against him during the Empire Bank scandal was determined that no Assemblies' church door should remain open to me. Like clockwork, about a week after I had conducted a service somewhere the pastor who had hosted me would send me a hate letter. Reverend Ray Rachels of the Christian Life church in Long Beach, California, started the rumor that I had been charged with attempting to rape a girl in his congregation. Another rumor had it that I had once been jailed for embezzlement. I suppose I would have fared even worse had they been able to agree among themselves what manner of criminal I was.

"Mainline" denominational churches began asking me to speak because they liked the decorum of my services. The Assemblies of God had no compunction about continuing to interfere with my preaching, even when they had to cross denominational lines to do so. One day the phone rang in the pastor's study of the Presbyterian Church in Harrison, New York. Pastor Don Theobald, a former armed services chaplain, answered.

"Hello, Pastor Theobald?"

"Yes."

"This is Reverend Winston Schmock, pastor of First Assembly of God church in White Plains." Reverend Schmock was a close friend of Reverend Cooke.

"What can I do for you, Reverend Schmuck?"

"The name's Schmock, not Schmuck."

"I beg your pardon."

"What I called you about is that I heard you have Austin Miles coming to your church."

"That's right."

"You don't want him in your church," Reverend Schmock said, in stentorian tones.

"Oh? Why not?"

"Because there's bad things about him."

"Oh? What king of bad things?"

"Just—bad things."

"Well, you will have to be more specific about what's wrong with him."

"Well, nothing specific," Reverend Schmock stammered, now on the defensive. "But I'm just telling you that you don't want *him* in *your* church."

Reverend Theobald sat shaking his head. It was obvious to him what was going on. "Listen," said Reverend Theobald, his own voice calm and resonant, "I've seen him conduct a meeting, and I've also seen God work through him. I've seen results. If he is good enough for God to work through, then he is good enough for me and my church. But thank you for calling me—Reverend *Schmuck!*" He hung up the phone with a satisfied grin on his face.

*   *   *

The rites of mating were not confined to the spring at PTL. I began to understand what Saint Paul may have meant by "be instant in season, out of season. . . ." An intense sexual energy could be felt around both Heritage U.S.A. and Heritage Village. "Seducing spirits" may have been the culprits that kept most people at PTL in a constant "turned on" state.

Young people who came to attend the school of evangelism quickly paired off. It became a common occurrence to round a corner and interrupt two young people in an intimate embrace. These couples were not just girls and boys. Boys and boys were even more prevalent. Hushed talk about "the pretty boys" could be heard in many corners of the complex, especially the executive offices.

Gospel groupies came to Heritage U.S.A. in droves, to take jobs and try to make it with the visiting evangelists. One morning, a security guard informed me that a nineteen-year-old girl who worked in the kitchen had tried to slip past the guardhouse into the mansion where I was staying. The next day a different guard told me he had caught the same girl halfway up the stairs in the mansion, making her way toward my bedroom.

"Then why don't they fire her?" I asked.

I never got a sensible answer, although one guard told me, "She causes a lot of problems whenever a prominent evangelist stays in the mansion."

Determined in her quest, she tried it again the next night and—made it.

The overall atmosphere of strange contrasts at PTL affected all of us in some way. My relationship with Lyn developed into a deep love affair. The intimacy provided relief from the general stress that we both were under. But more than that, I began to realize that we were incredibly alike in many ways, with the same tastes and ideas. I enjoyed her company and was stimulated by her. I realized that she now occupied a permanent special place in my life.

A popular singing and faith healing evangelist was constantly flown back and forth to PTL with her boyfriend. Even though not married, they slept together in the mansion with Jim's and his staff's complete knowledge and apparent condonation. Lyn shook her head. "She has broken up two marriages. Now this. And the PTL partners are paying the airfares."

*   *   *

A handsome singer-evangelist was angry over a divorce action which had ruined him financially. He and his wife had had a successful televangelism program. To all appearances, they were the ideal, happily married Christian couple. His side of the story was that, at the peak of their success, his wife decided she wanted to leave him. He said the judge at the divorce trial was antagonistic toward him because he was a television evangelist. With one stroke of the gavel, he was separated from $90,000 in savings, his house, furniture, and car. "All I was left with," he said, "was a fourteen-year-old bed." The case attracted the attention of the IRS, which swooped down, demanding thousands in back taxes. He was wiped out and bitter.

This singer-evangelist began dating Donna Douglas, the actress who had played Elly May Clampett in the TV series "The Beverly Hillbillies." Things went well until she fell in love with him. I suspect that he was falling in love with her too and, in his determination not to make the same mistake again, broke the relationship off. Heartbroken, Donna went to Oklahoma and enrolled in Kenneth Hagin's "Word of Faith" Bible school.

When word got out that he was unattached, women fairly fought each other for his attentions. He enjoyed their favors on his own terms. Once when he came to PTL, one of Jim Bakker's secretaries went to the airport to pick him up. She took him to a wooded area she had staked out in advance, stopped the car, and attempted to unzip his trousers. He pushed her away, and demanded that she drive him to the complex at once. The secretary was attractive, but such aggressiveness was too much, even for him. Both he and Lyn told me this story.

A "down home" singing evangelist had become popular through "The PTL Club," and now had his own program on the PTL Satellite Network. One day while I was talking to Helen Headley, the greeter in the studio, I noticed an attractive, leggy blonde pleading with the former coal miner to let her sing on his show. She was convinced it would be her passport to Christian stardom. "Ah jest don' have any guests on mah show," the good ol' boy told her politely. The woman persisted, and the two went into an empty office to talk.

Later, continuing our conversation, Helen and I started to pass through the same office. Opening the door, we found the blonde practically sitting on top of the rustic evangelist, rubbing what had developed into a huge bulge in his trousers. They were so absorbed in their "discussion" that they never noticed us. We quickly closed the door, and figured out another route to take. The next week, the willowy blonde was singing praises to the Lord on the former coal miner's television program.

Amidst these goings on, we all exchanged questioning glances when Jim Bakker hired David Taggart as his personal aide. Taggart guarded Jim like a mother hen and seemed jealous if anyone else received any attention from him.

Lyn Robbins became distressed at this. "Austin," she asked, "do—do you think there's something—something sexual between Jim and David Taggart?"

I looked at her for a few moments, carefully keeping a neutral expression. "What do you think? You've seen Tammy banging on the steam room door."

Soon Jim and his aide reportedly were having a full-blown affair. Jim and Taggart held many a "private conference" in the office with the floozy Jacuzzi. Jim's personal bodyguard, Don Hardister, guarded the door, unaware of what was taking place behind it.

According to Jim's peculiar reasoning, flings were merely to relieve stress and didn't represent unfaithfulness to Tammy like his heterosexual dalliances did. Homosexuality was becoming more and more usual around Heritage U.S.A. It amazed me that, with multitudes of willing women of all ages around, gay sex was preferred.

Severe personal problems and family break-ups erupted throughout PTL.

Renowned gospel pianist Dino Kartsonakis and his wife Debbie, frequent guests at PTL, were divorced amidst sordid charges. Just a month before they separated there had been no hint of anything wrong between them. They arrived at the Heritage Village mansion with their baby daughter in the wee hours one morning and I joined them in the kitchen for a snack. I had long been eager to meet Dino, and to work out my mixed feelings about him.

A graduate of the Juilliard School of Music, Dino was a superb concert pianist. He had been "discovered" by Kathryn Kuhlman, who had featured him on her national television program and in her revivals for many years. When he had been with Miss Kuhlman long enough to become a fixture in her entourage, he claimed he had proof she was a fraud and threatened to expose her unless she gave him a $10,000 raise. To me, this maneuver brought Dino's moral, ethical, and Christian testimony into question. He seemed willing to be a part of a fraud as long as the price was right. For the record, there has never been any evidence suggesting fraud on the part of Miss Kuhlman or her ministry. It was widely believed that the stress caused by Dino's attempts hastened Kathryn Kuhlman's death. Tragically, this brought to an end what very well may have been the one, true, anointed-of-God healing ministry of all time. I wanted to get to know Dino so that I could form a valid opinion of him. This was important for me, since I had admired Miss Kuhlman so much. I got along with Dino better than I expected. When I told him about Lori's accomplishments as a pianist, he gave me a book he had written containing classical arrangements of gospel standards for her. I liked him, and greatly respected him as an artist. But his Christian side did not convince me. I sensed that Debbie was the more sincere of the two.

Debbie had come from the southern California entertainment world, and when she divorced Dino, she returned to that world, moving into the Playboy Mansion with Hugh Hefner. She felt there was more honesty there than in the world of "born-again" Christianity. Their divorce, the latest, was the chief topic of conversation around PTL.

Raleigh Bakker, Jim's father, chatted with me every time I went to the studio. "Pop" Bakker always had a subdued smirk on his face, as if he had just sold a lemon of a used car to someone he disliked for cash. After one telecast, he came up to me.

"You know," he said, "I've gotten to like you."

"Well, I'm happy to hear that," I answered, unsure what he was leading up to.

"When you first started coming down here, I said to myself, 'What would a *circus* man have to say about God?' But now that I've gotten to know you, I've gotten to kinda like you."

I stared at him. It's a wonder he couldn't hear my mind yelling out, "Go to hell, you old codger! Who are *you* to judge the circus? We've *never* had anything *like* the problems that you people have in this Christian Mecca!"

I returned to my room, and aimlessly flipped television channels. I came across Richard Roberts' televangelism program and paused to watch.

Roger McDuff—Coleman's brother—was a guest. I was curious to hear what he had to say.

"Our church was failing—going under!" Roger testified. "So we decided to hold a revival crusade. Before the crusade got started, we all got together and prayed, 'Oh God, we pray that a millionaire will come and get saved, to save our church!' And who should come into our church that first night and get saved? Colonel Sanders!"

The salvation of Colonel Sanders was the McDuff brothers' main claim to fame, and nobody they talked to escaped hearing it at least once. But this time, his approach to the story had changed. This greatly interested me.

"And we have photocopies of the checks Colonel Sanders gave us," Roger boasted. Colonel Sanders had his vulnerable spot. He had once shot a man over the affections of the future Mrs. Sanders. People in Kentucky had never forgiven him, and even after fifty years, their rejection still nagged at him. Finally, he turned to the church for comfort.

It is well that Colonel Sanders died without knowing that the McDuff brothers did not care one damn about his hurts, or his soul. Obviously, the *only* thing about Colonel Sanders that the preachers were interested in, according to McDuff's own words and actions, was his money. Without meaning to, Roger McDuff had revealed the true, self-serving motive behind the celebrated conversion of Colonel Sanders.

I clenched my fist, and slammed it down on the table next to my chair. "Those no good bastards!" I mumbled while getting to my feet.

I switched off the television set, walked over to the desk, and picked up a paperback book from it. The book was titled *How to Live Like a King's Kid,* a rambling essay by another PTL guest, Harold Hill. Hill, a "recovered alcoholic," was one of those Christians who should answer to the name obnoxious. He had just created a lapel pin with the words "King's Kid," and had introduced it that morning on "The PTL Club." He wanted to present one of the pins to me just before the telecast. Hill would not be content just to hand it to me. Before I could stop him, he had grabbed my lapel and jammed the extra-large pin through the fabric of my good suit. He wanted the viewers to see me wearing his pin. I found everything about Hill and his self-serving ministry offensive. He had given me the copy of his book that I now held in my hand along with his autograph on the front page. I love books, especially those that have been given to me by their authors, but I was so turned-off by Hill that I threw it across the room with full force. It landed with a loud "plump" in the wastebasket, a perfect shot.

At that moment I hated Christianity and everyone associated with it. It dawned on me that the least palatable Christian I had ever met was the very man who had led me into the whole mess, Bobby Yerkes.

Bobby Yerkes had presented a very flattering side of himself to me when the mission of recruiting me into the Christian army was his aim. As I sank deeper into the quicksand of Christianity, I began to see at the same time the true character of my "Christian witness." While Bob had led me to believe that Christians do not drink, chase women, or get into brawls, he was at the same time doing those very things when I was out of his sight. Everybody in the circus seemed to know it but me.

Bobby had a trailer, parked with those of the other circus people, and everyone became well acquainted with his activities. Still, whenever I heard anyone make fun of Bobby or his Christianity, and this was frequent, I simply passed it off as an attack of the devil. By that time, my new Christian perspective had thoroughly closed my mind to reality. There was a constant stream of stories about mayhem in the Yerkes' trailer. Then, I began to see things for myself.

I once got Bobby booked on "The PTL Club." He wasted no time in trying to hit on Lyn. He boasted to her about his Hollywood contacts, telling her that he staged all the numbers and tutored the stars' circus feats for the annual television special "Circus of the Stars."

"Why don't you come out and see me for a couple of days, and let me take you up on the riggings. You would be great." He made this pitch to her again and again.

Bobby's Bible-filled house in Northridge, California, was always a beehive of activity. During one of my visits in his house, he threw a party. Bob mixed himself a drink, looked at me mockingly and said, "I guess you will just have milk, Austin." The same man who had induced me to abstain from liquor was now ridiculing me for it! On another occasion, Bob put porno movies on his television in the presence of my daughter Lori.

Bob's behavior disturbed many Hollywood people, especially when they saw how he gave huge donations to Pat Robertson and Jerry Falwell, as he did to many missionaries. Bob let everyone know that his giving so generously was his way of serving Christ. He also financially supported the Contras because the leader confessed to being a born-again Christian. Enterprising preachers found Bob an easy mark. He seemed to be trying to buy his salvation.

Bob was a friend of Pat Boone, whose Christianity was another marvel. Pat's career was over. His white buckskin shoes had started to fade. He had an expensive mansion across from The Beverly Hills Hotel to keep up, and few prospects for work. He suddenly got "saved," a well-publicized event. Pat wanted to share "the good news" with everyone. To hear of the glories, blessings, and humility of Christ through Pat, however, required a $10,000 fee for each appearance. Whoever booked him (and his calendar filled quickly) had to send him a $5,000 deposit before he had even set foot outside his mansion.

Bob Yerkes eventually divorced his good wife Dorothy after twenty-seven years of marriage. Now he would be free to swing with the young starlets without interference. And they were more than willing to "get to know" Bobby because of his professional film contacts.

Then, it happened. During a week-long stay in Bob's house with my daughter, he made a pass at Lori, who was then fourteen years of age. When Lori told me about it, I wanted to kill him. "Don't worry about it, Dad. I've taken care of it," Lori told me. "I got him good in the stomach with my elbow. I don't think he will try it again."

I paced the floor for a few minutes, then, with growing anger, picked up the phone and called the man who had been so determined to bring me into the Christian way of life.

"Bob, it's Austin. If you will meet me at the airport, I will fly back out there and punch you in the nose!"

"What?" He was taken aback and shocked.

"You heard me. How dare you talk to anyone about Jesus Christ and tell people how to live their lives, when your own life is a scandal! Thanks to listening to you and getting involved in this Christianity crap, I lost my family, everything I owned, and in return I've received the most horrible hatred I ever knew."

"Look, pal, I—"

"Shut up and listen! You are a *joke*. The greatest service you can do for Jesus Christ is never to mention His name! You did me the worst disservice of anyone on earth by getting me into all this, and I believed you and trusted you as someone who had it all together."

"Please, pal, let me talk." It was a fair request. "Look, Austin, I never claimed to be perfect. Besides, you never look at the man, you look at Christ. All of us are weak and have sinned. Yes, it is a daily battle against the flesh, and I suspect that you have the same problem."

"That's where you're wrong, my friend. I am *responsible*. That's the problem with Christians. You all judge everyone else by your own standard of conduct. I can accept you for what you are, Bob, but I cannot, nor will I, accept you for what you are *not!*"

"But," he pleaded, "don't blame Jesus for what has happened to you. Remember, man is weak and will fail you every time, but Christ never fails you."

"Bob Yerkes, the darkest day in my life was the day I heard the name of Jesus Christ. The most wretched people I ever met came into my life through the name of Jesus Christ. It was in *that* name that my marriage fell apart. Every hate letter I receive is signed, in the name—and love—

of Jesus. Every obscene phone call I receive from Christians starts with, 'I am making this call in the name of Jesus.' The whole thing is sick and vicious, and I curse the day I ever got involved in it."

"Please, pal," Bobby answered. His voice cracked. "I am your friend. I love you like a brother. I respect you, and you know my house is your house. I want you to come and stay with me when you can."

I began to calm down. I couldn't deny that Bobby had, in the past, reached out to me in many ways. "O.K., Bob, I'll make a trip out and visit you again some time—but only on one condition: that we talk only about professional things. That's where we are at our best. You're not even to bring up the name Jesus Christ while I'm there."

"Sure, pal," he said, hesitantly. "I'll respect your wishes."

XXXVIII

I sent the book of concert gospel music Dino had given me to Lori. As accomplished a classical pianist as Lori was, gospel was not her forte. She simply had no flair for it. The Christians pressured her relentlessly to be only what they wanted her to be, and to play only music they said glorified God. Since that included none of the music that Lori had any feel for, she quit playing altogether. Thanks to the church of Jesus Christ, another fine artist bit the dust.

Reverend Richard Dortch joined PTL as a salaried executive. Once I met him, I liked him immensely. The bad first impression of him I got when he was Superintendent of the Illinois district of the Assemblies was quickly erased. He had a great passion for preaching and teaching the Word. Whenever he taught a seminar, I'd attend.

I approached him for help in making peace with the New York district. I was forgiving to a fault. I liked people, and did not want to be in conflict with anyone.

"They would be very much in the wrong if the New York brethren would not respond favorably to a sincere effort of reconciliation," Reverend Dortch said to me when I outlined my plan. He was held in such high esteem in the Assemblies—even talked of as a potential General Superintendent—that I felt his assistance and counsel would bring about the desired result.

"If you were the Superintendent," I said to him, "things would be very different between me and the Assemblies." He was the only person left in the Assemblies' hierarchy whom I trusted.

Optimistically, I wrote to Reverend Almon Bartholomew, Superintendent of the New York district:

Dear Brother Bartholomew:
    Greetings in the name of Our Lord Jesus Christ!
    I respectfully request a meeting with the Presbytery for the purpose of reconciliation between me and the New York district of the Assemblies of God in the truest Biblical sense. "And *all things* are of God who

hath reconciled us to Himself by Jesus Christ, and hath *given to us* the ministry of reconciliation.

"To wit, that God was in Christ, reconciling the world unto Himself, not imputing their trespasses unto them: and hath *committed unto us* the word of reconciliation."

2 Cor. 5:18-19

I went on to offer to come to Syracuse in person, to put an end to the battle. I received the following letter in reply:

Dear Brother Miles:
    Cordial greetings in the name of Jesus Christ our Lord:
    We have read your letter to the presbytery respectfully requesting a meeting with them for the purpose of reconciliation between yourself and the New York District of the Assemblies of God.
    While the brethren appreciate your request to appear, they do not feel that such a meeting is necessary. If you feel from the standpoint of conscience that you have amends to make, you can be assured by the presbytery that your letter would be received in the same spirit with which it was sent.

Sincerely in Christ,

Almon Bartholomew
District Superintendent

The lack of a signature completed the cold impression the typewritten letter had been calculated to make. There was nothing more to be done.

*   *   *

Grim news poured out of PTL. Jim and Tammy were locked in the fiercest struggle with the devil yet. Tears were flowing. The way they presented it, was very simple: Either the "partners" came up with several million dollars by a certain date or else ". . . they will pull the plug of the satellite," Jim Bakker wailed, "and this will be the end—the finish—of Christian television, and the devil will have won!"

Jim and Tammy looked so frantic that I called Lyn in Charlotte. "Things are just fine here," she assured me.

I watched the telecast the next day. Jim and Tammy portrayed a state of frenzy. To hear them tell it, the end of everything they had worked for was drawing nearer and nearer. Every day brought more tears and renewed cries of panic. I called Lyn again and marveled at how calm she sounded in the face of PTL's impending doom. "Lyn's quite an actress,"

I thought.

Jim and Tammy ground out a solid month of their "Emergency Save-the-Satellite" telethon. Their plaintive cries filled the airwaves. "This is a *crisis,* people!" sobbed Tammy. It looked serious to me. Rising to the challenge, I got on a plane for Charlotte on March 12, 1982, to help out with the telethon.

Surely Harold Olshields would be able to fill me in. I noticed the limousine was a new one since my last visit. The first words out of my mouth when I got in were: "Harold, what is happening down here?"

"Oh, haven't you heard?" he answered, cheerily. "The Happy Hunters have learned the secret of teleportation! They've been able to leave their bodies and visit places around the world in a flash to deliver the message of Jesus! It's biblical, and they are teaching about it!"

I thought, "Dammit! Another money-making *trend!*" Not a word about PTL's financial apocalypse. At the studio, everyone went about their business as usual, seemingly unconcerned about the approaching collapse of the network.

After my appearance on the emotionally charged telecast, Jim's brother Norman invited me to lunch. He pulled his big car into a handicapped parking space at the Wagon Wheel Restaurant."You'll never know what it's like to lose a leg when you're a teenager," he said to me. Norm was bitter, not only about his handicap, but about sharing no more than a flicker of the limelight in which his famous brother basked. Norm filled an undefined but obviously low-ranking staff position. Norm's wife, Dorothy, a tall, attractive brunette, was closer to Jim than her husband, and had a more important job. She worked in production, booking guests and gathering information on them.

Norm Bakker maneuvered his artificial leg over the sill and out the door of the car. He pulled himself out, deliberately bracing himself as he straightened up, gaining his balance with difficulty. We proceeded at his laborious pace into the restaurant.

"Norm," I said after a sip of coffee, "do you think we'll make it through this emergency?"

"There's no problem," he said with a shrug. "The money's all there."

"What?"

"We have the money."

My mind reeled. There were still two weeks of telethon to go and on camera, at least, everyone was in a tizzy. That very morning, Jim and Tammy were crying hysterically, wailing about the end being near. And the money was—all there?

"What—what about the crisis you had about four months ago, when they were going to shut down Heritage U.S.A.? How did you come out of that crisis?"

"Oh, there was no crisis." Norm spoke unconcernedly, and somewhat unclearly because his mouth was full. "We had the money all along. It was in another account. So, when they demanded money over here, this gave us a tool to raise money on, and something for the people to rally around."

"You—had the money all along?" I kept on, fatuously flogging the dead horse. "There—was—no crisis?"

"That's right," Norm answered. He expressed no shame when he told me. This was business.

I began to understand the significance of the direct mailing phase of PTL's fund-raising efforts. My stomach knotted up a bit more when I learned that the emotional "personal" letters that the "partners" received over Jim's and Tammy's signatures were never written or dictated by them. They were carefully composed by highly skilled, psychologically trained professionals at a fund-raising corporation. Careful statistical monitoring of the response to previous letters made it possible to predict the effectiveness of each ploy in stimulating the faithful to give, and to give generously. The ministry paid $20,000 for each of these scientifically designed letters. The "PTL Club" ordered four and five of these letters at a time, and pre-determined the exact month to declare a "financial crisis." What sickened me even more was to learn that these "emergency" fund-raising appeals were skillfully timed to arrive in the mailboxes of the faithful at the same time that their social security and welfare checks would arrive.

Later that evening, I told Lyn that this was my last appearance on PTL. "Wading through the other problems here is one thing—but this! This is *fraud*, and I will not be part of it. Little old ladies and pensioners are eating cat food and buying secondhand clothes and shoes in order to have money to send to PTL, thinking it's for God's work. I will come back to see you and some of the others on the staff, but I won't go on the program anymore."

I felt sad as I left. What had begun as a blessing had become a cesspool of Christian corruption.

*　　*　　*

My health broke. The horrible attacks of anxiety and fear became more than I could handle. My self-confidence was shattered and my spirit was broken. I had no home and very little money. I missed Rose Marie more everyday, so much that when something reminded me of her, certain music, or a scene that brought back memories, I would actually cry out in pain.

I wound up in Bobby Yerkes' house in Northridge, to try to get myself back together. I was broke, discouraged, and had nowhere else to go. Bob welcomed me warmly, telling me I could stay as long as I wanted. I had a love-hate relationship with Bobby. I accepted his hospitality, feeling that I would never have been in such a position in the first place had he not convinced me that I would have a better life with Christ.

My condition worsened while I was there. The constant parade of movie stars in and out of the house was more irritating than stimulating to me. At that point, I had no desire to even try to work in films. In my condition, it would have been professional suicide to attempt it. I couldn't work up an interest in developing contacts. I had no energy at all. All I wanted to do was sleep.

Whenever I would wake up from sleep, I would be terrified. Before going to sleep, I would carefully set out a glass of water and a ten-milligram Valium so that I would not have to spend the few extra seconds it took to open the pill bottle in that frightful post-sleep state. These were absolutely the worst moments of my life. It was a serious question whether I would live through it.

One day I ventured out of the house in a beat-up truck Bobby let me use. I went to Los Angeles to visit Coleman McDuff who had figured so prominently in the early days of my life as a minister. The Bell Gardens Assembly of God church he pastored was thriving. It was outfitted with expensive carpets, chandeliers, and other opulent furnishings. Coleman and his wife had his-and-hers Cadillacs.

His manner with me was distant and condescending. Like the rest, he had accepted the rumors and the lies about me. His face, which had once expressed such warmth and love for me, was now cold and devoid of compassion. As I told him of all the injustices and viciousness meted out to me by the Assemblies of God, his face simply got more impassive. Finally, I said to him, "One day, Coleman, the Assembly of God will destroy itself with its evil."

His expression changed to smugness. "Austin—there will *always* be an Assemblies of God church," he responded with self-complacent arrogance.

I studied his face for a moment. "Yes, Coleman, I guess you're right. There will always be a chicken out there waiting to be plucked."

Coleman changed the subject, attempting to bring out the positive things that were happening in his church. "Tonight," he said cheerfully, "we are having a 'will clinic.' " I groaned. A "will clinic" involved having highly polished salesmen from Springfield, Missouri, with some training in estate planning come into the church and persuade the faithful of their duty to leave their earthly goods to the Assemblies of God. That way they could still be helping with God's work after He had "called them home."

I got up to leave. "Coleman," I said, standing by the door of the pastor's study, "how much does a prayer cost? What price tag did Christ put on a prayer, that we can use as a precedent?" I stared at him for a moment, glanced around at the foyer of the church, and left in disgust.

Back at Bobby's house, another party, in what seemed an endless round of parties, was underway. Mark Yerkes, Bobby's grown son, and I talked. Bobby was too busy with his movie star guests to pay attention to his son. Mark, in his early twenties, seemed destined always to be pudgy. A fine athlete, Mark could appear as light as a feather doing somersaults on the trampoline despite his bulk. His father had gotten him some stunt work on the movie sets and Mark had branched out into acting, including some speaking parts. He did so well that he had been able to make the down payment on the house he lived in nearby. He also aspired to write, and was working on a play.

I had watched Mark go through his teen years and even attended his graduation from Christian secondary school. Then it had looked as if he would become a minister. But as he progressed and his view of his father's poor Christian example matured, he had become turned off.

A lonely young man, Mark had subscribed to a computer matchmaking service to find the right woman to marry. "It costs $2,500 to sign up with the service," he confided in me, "but if I found the right woman to marry through it, it would be well worth it."

Mark tried several times to talk to his father that evening. Clearly his father had no time for him. Mark said to me, "Tell my father good-bye for me," and left. That got me. I went to my room and wept.

After seven months, I reached the point where I could no longer tolerate Bobby's house—Southern California—or anyplace. Only one thing remained to be done. I would return to Forest Hills where the memory of Rose Marie still lingered, get an apartment in the same building where we had lived together, and in that setting put an end to a life that had become too painful to endure any longer. I returned to New York to die.

XXXIX

eing in Forest Hills brought on a feeling of unexpected exhilaration. Rose Marie's presence was everywhere. I could feel it, and almost hear the music of Bach.

I recreated the home I had shared with my family as best I could in the small apartment that had become available in our old building. It was a smaller version of the original. Familiar records played on the stereo. Some of the same staff still worked in the building, among them Louie the doorman.

I took long walks in Forest Hills, retracing the routes I had taken with Rose Marie and Lori in happier times. Hardly a day went by when I did not walk past Our Lady of Mercy Catholic school, where Lori had attended, and fight back the tears.

Lori had married a man in Millville, sixteen years her senior, named "Smokey." I had attended the wedding but was treated like a complete outsider. When I asked about getting a wedding picture of the couple, my daughter shot back, "Then you'll just have to go and buy one from the studio."

Smokey owned a factory and was financially secure. He made it clear from the beginning that he was his own man and wanted no part of Lori's family. "Smokey just wants his privacy," Lori informed me, snippily.

The romance of Lori and Smokey was enthusiastically championed by the Davis family, who had taken over completely in Lori's life. What they seemed to like best about Smokey was his money. "You'd be *crazy* not to go after him and marry him," Grace Davis drummed into Lori. I had not seen Lori since the wedding.

I never felt so alone in all my life. The air turned crisp. Even though Thanksgiving was still a few days ahead, people had already begun to put up Christmas decorations. The approach of the holiday season brought me both inordinate pain and a curious solace. The time had come. I obtained a bottle of tranquilizers, emblazoned with a stern warning never, *never* to exceed the prescribed dosage. I put the bottle in my top dresser drawer.

Two days before Thanksgiving, and the official start of the Christmas season, the agony I suffered became so great that I felt I would not make it to Christmas Eve. It had been eight years since Rose Marie had left. Eight wretched years.

Mustering my last ounce of resolve, I made myself get on a subway for Manhattan. Being part of the Christmas celebration, rather than merely a spectator, might pull me through this. The best Christmas display in the city—perhaps the best anywhere—took place at Macy's at Herald Square, on West Thirty-fourth Street. I applied for a job as an elf.

"What do you normally do?" the stern personnel director asked.

"I—I'm an *actor,*" I responded. That explanation was all that was necessary. Actors were always out of work.

I was given a psychological test to fill out. I looked at the questions. "Do you feel that if it had not been for others, you would have been more successful? Do you feel that people are staring at you while you work? Do you feel that God has given you a mission?"

"Oh, shit!" I thought, "I will never pass this test." I gave the answers I knew were considered "normal."

The day after Thanksgiving, I took my place in the magic Christmas wonderland that thousands of people would walk through on their way to visit Santa Claus. The background music was "Have Yourself a Merry Little Christmas." I looked around at the charming setting, with its mechanical figures, dozens of evergreen trees, hundreds of lights, little streets, buildings, and bridges. The first time a family with a little girl in tow came through, my heart grew heavy. But soon a real spirit of Christmas was kindled inside me, and my elf character began to develop many facets and come to life. I evolved into "the toy maker," telling stories to the children as I escorted them to Santa.

There were two routes to the Santa house. The longer one wound its way into Santa's house. The shorter one went by the house, to a vantage point where, through a one-way mirror, one could see the children talking with Santa.

"Would you like to see Santa?" I said, automatically, to the next man in line.

"No, I would not!" the man shot back, piously. I turned and got a good look at him, standing stiffly, a big Bible clutched in his hand. "I don't believe in Santa Claus! I believe in Jesus Christ!"

The slow boiling I felt inside made it hard for me to keep in character.

"Tell me something, sir," I said, making the maximum effort to control my voice. "Do you believe in children?"

"Why—ah—yes," the man of God stammered, trying to figure out the point of my question.

"Good!" I said, cheerily. "Come with me." I took a firm grip on his arm and guided him roughly around the lines of people to the one-way window. "Look in there!" I commanded. Uneasily, the Christian turned his head to look. Inside he could see a delightful scene of several happily smiling children talking to a jovial, beautiful Santa Claus. "Let me tell you something—*brother!*" It was an effort to say it firmly, yet in a low enough voice not to cause a scene. "Santa Claus has *never* caused evil, nor has he ever *divided* people. Santa is *love*. Now, sir, you take your Christianity, your Bible, and all the hatred that goes with it and get the *hell* out of this place! Don't you ever let me see you here again!"

He left hastily. Without doubt, that is one Bible-thumper who will never mess with an elf again.

During a break, a man known as "the Santa boss" told me, "You really should be in the red suit." I had never even considered the possibility of being Santa.

One morning a few days later, in the thick of the season, the Santa boss hurried into the dressing room just as I finished getting into my elf costume. "We've got an emergency!" he said to me. "Santa just called. He's sick and can't come in, and this is our busiest day. I need you to do Santa for us. Come with me."

The Santa dressing room looked like something from Grand Opera, with elaborate costumes, magnificent beards and wigs, and a special hairdresser to look after them all. I stripped off my elf costume. They handed me each piece, one at a time, starting with the fat frame. The beard, hair, and bushy eyebrows were carefully applied with spirit gum. The stocking cap completed the magical transformation. As I rose from the chair, I did not merely feel like Santa Claus, I *was* Santa Claus. A deep "ho Ho HO" came out of me, which reverberated through the room.

The Santa boss hastily briefed me. "You've got to get them in and out quickly. Get the child in your lap after greeting him, give him a toy from the bag beside you, pose for the picture, and send them on their way."

"Oh no," I boomed out in deep, Santa tones. "I'm going to spend twenty minutes with each child. Then I'm going to give away every toy on this floor. When they're all gone I will give away everything on the seventh floor. Merrrrry Christmas!" Word spread throughout the store that the real Santa had taken up residence on Thirty-fourth Street, and various people who worked at Macy's came up to see for themselves.

After a lunch break, I was back in the little chalet house to greet the children. The background music changed to "Let the Sheep Safely Graze." My mind drifted for a few moments as I thought of Rose Marie. How I missed her. I could almost hear her delightful laughter. I suddenly froze in place. I *did* hear her laughter.

"Isn't dis adorable!" said the voice I knew so well. From there, it was as if everything became unreal and happened in slightly distorted slow motion. I thought, this can't really be happening. It felt like a dream.

I slowly turned my head in the direction of the voice. Rose Marie, with a delighted expression on her face, had two small boys by the hand. I felt paralyzed. "When she sees me, she'll leave," I thought. I reached up and felt my false beard. "No," I reassured myself. "She won't even recognize me."

Using every shred of acting skill I possessed, I brought my Santa character closer to independent life than ever. The photo elf looked puzzled as I kept the conversation going, trying to keep them there as long as possible, relishing every word Rose Marie spoke. I had not heard her voice for eight years!

"Are these your little boys?" Santa asked jovially.

"No," she responded. "Dese are little friends of mine from New Jersey." God, how I wanted to reach out to her, to hold her. She was still so pretty, so elegant. How had it all happened? How did I ever let our marriage break up?

"Shouldn't we take a picture?" the photo elf finally interrupted.

"Oh yes, yes, of course," Santa responded, motioning for the little boys to come and sit on his lap. After the photo, Santa said to Rose Marie, "Santa should also have a picture taken with you."

"Only if I can sit on Santa's lap," she replied, in her distinctive lilting tones.

I fought to keep my eyes from betraying me. "That will be just fine," Santa answered. I had stayed in character perfectly, through one of the most emotional moments of my life. When Rose Marie sat in my lap, the charade ended. I put my arms around her, pulled her close to me, squeezed her, and held her as the picture was taken. Rose Marie pulled back, looked in my eyes, and put her hand over her mouth. She got to her feet, hurried to the door of the little house, and stopped to look at me, tears running down her face.

"Merry Christmas, Rose Marie," I stammered, struggling to savor this fleeting last look at her. She grabbed the two confused little boys by the hand and ran out, crying. Everyone wondered what had happened.

"Close the house for a few minutes," I instructed the photo elf. I sat quietly by myself for a few minutes, tears streaming down my face. Then, I said, "O.K., reopen the house. I'm ready to greet some more children."

When the day's work had ended and I got back into street clothes, I walked into the Christmas wonderland. I needed to have it all to myself for a few minutes. Arthur Fiedler's sentimental orchestral version of "White Christmas" now played in the background. I lingered a few minutes, then walked out of the store and into the subway at West Thirty-fourth Street. On the platform waiting for the train, I leaned against a steel beam, crying softly. It was a moment of big city privacy, being alone in a crowd.

Back in my apartment, I sat in a wing chair with a glass of wine. I let out a sigh, got up, and took the fateful bottle of pills from the dresser drawer. I slowly walked toward the kitchen, then past the kitchen, through the front door, and down the hall to the incinerator chute. Down the chute went the pills. I went into the bathroom of the little apartment and took out the Valium and the other assorted prescription psychoactives I had accumulated and threw them down the incinerator chute as well.

The meeting of Rose Marie and Santa—literally a one-in-ten-million chance—became a human interest news story. A reporter contacted Rose Marie at TWA.

"I haf no desire of going back," Rose Marie told the reporter. "I vent through a lot. I almost lost my health. I haf started a new life for myself. I've gone back to school—regained my health. No—no, I vould nefer go back to him. Dot is all ofer."

Rose Marie took an early retirement from TWA. She moved back to Switzerland, probably never to return to America again. Nobody had to tell me. I could feel that her presence had vanished from the city. I knew she was gone.

*   *   *

If I were allowed only one word to describe circus people, I would pick: "Extraordinary!" Not one of them asked me where I had been for the last few years or what had happened to me. They just welcomed me back with great love. I appreciated and respected the circus more than I ever had before. In my red tails and top hat, I stood waiting to go on. One of the artists walked by and squeezed my shoulder with affection and a warm smile. Not a word was spoken.

My days of horrible nervousness and anxiety attacks were over. I had gone off the tranquilizers cold turkey. After the ordeal, my insides felt clean and refreshed. Distancing myself from the ministry and the church was another positive move. I felt like a captive released from prison. The break had been difficult, but once it was done, I felt free.

I began to see colors again and relearned how to appreciate the beauty in scenery. Everything looked remarkably different. To be sure, I had plenty of lingering hurts to work through.

Waiting to go on, I thought of the time I told my daughter the story of the ringmasters clicking their heels and flying. Before making my entrance, bringing that happy little memory to mind, I clicked my heels smartly.

I made that a little ritual and did it before every performance.

There were some beginning difficulties when word got out that I was making a come-back in show business. The church wanted me silenced forever. In Toronto, Ontario, a woman who identified herself as a Women's Aglow member grabbed me by the arm. Fortunately, security guards were close at hand and threw her out. More Women's Aglow members intervened with the Shriners to try to convince them that I would be bad for their circus. In Detroit, when the newspaper reviews mentioned my name, a group of Christians rented an entire box of seats at the front. When I made my exit at the end of the show, they all stood up with their Bibles in their hands and made a thumbs-down gesture at me. But these tactics fell flat. Most intelligent people witnessing them simply had their notions about Christians being mentally disturbed reinforced.

My work had a new zest and distinction about it. My press notices were excellent, and new prospects seemed just over the horizon. Then something happened that I would never have expected. I received a call on my answering service from Walter Kaner, the columnist for the Queens section of *The New York Daily News.* When I returned his call, he informed me that my daughter had called him.

"She told me to put no credibility in anything you say."

"Lori?"

"Yes, Lori. She also said you were mentally unsound and were in need of psychiatric care and medication. She said you have a lot of problems. There must be *something* wrong with you for your own daughter to call me about you. Anyway, don't contact me again!" It was his way of telling me that his column was closed to me.

I had not recovered quite enough to handle this. My own daughter had joined the vulture flock, to try to keep me from making it back into public life. Nothing less than driving me into the gutter to die would satisfy these insatiable people.

Slowly, I dialed her number. She answered. I asked her about the call to *The New York Daily News.* "Why on earth would you do that?" I asked, bewildered.

"Because it is my *duty,*" she replied, icily.

"Your duty? To whom? The church? Your duty to Jesus Christ? To God? To destroy your father? I don't know what has happened to you, Lori, but you are no longer my daughter. You will never hear from me again."

I went into the bathroom and coughed up blood.

*   *   *

The 1985 national convention of the Assemblies of God in San Antonio produced an unexpected jolt for Reverend Thomas F. Zimmerman. He was overwhelmingly voted out as General Superintendent. The action caught him by such total surprise that he jumped up screaming, "It's over! It's *over!*"

One would have thought that God Himself had died.

This "humble man of God" left the General Superintendency a wealthy man. Within the year, he landed another board of directors gig—at PTL. He had been appearing frequently as a guest on the telecast for some time. At PTL, he could again control more millions of dollars, obediently handed over by the meek.

Happy as it made me to be back with the circus, I yearned to be with the Royal Lipizzan Stallion Show again. That would be like picking up my life where it had left off. I officially rejoined the Lipizzan show on May 4, 1986, at Radio City Music Hall—exactly ten years to the day I had left it to join the Christian chamber of horrors fulltime. My gut reactions, which Christianity had taught me to ignore, were the right ones after all. I began to find answers to many questions.

When the show appeared in Ann Arbor, Michigan, a visitor found his way to my door. "I checked every motel and hotel in the area," he said. "I had a feeling that you might be back on the Lipizzan show." The tall, big-boned man with the protruding teeth, one eye slightly crossed behind his glasses, with his hair blown in every direction, was a welcome sight. Bob Elliott had worked on my "You Are Special" television show in Detroit. I had last seen him in Millville.

"I've been trying to find you for five years," he continued. "I've been looking for you everywhere. I even went to the convention of the National Religious Broadcasters in Washington, D.C., and asked Tom Zimmerman if he had any idea what had happened to you. And—would you believe it?—he said, 'The last I heard is that he's back in the circus with all the rest of the freaks.' "

My mouth began to quiver. Then I broke out in the healthiest burst of laughter I had experienced since going into the ministry.

Bob's expression remained serious and intense. He told me that, like me, he had experienced some strange emotional and physical symptoms after partaking of the Davis family's hospitality in Millville. That pointed toward a conclusion I had been loath to reach. I got up from my chair, and paced the room for some time, mulling over what I had just learned. Maybe my prescription drugs were not the *only* ones that had dragged me down during that dark period.

"Let's take a walk," I suggested. We walked to a nearby lake.

"Do you remember that cameraman who shot your TV series in Detroit?" Bob asked. "He was a real good looking young man."

I nodded my head.

"As you know, he was hired by PTL to be a cameraman for their program. They said they were impressed by the work he did on your series. He was thrilled at the opportunity. When he got to PTL he found out that his *first* job was to be a 'pretty boy' for the executive staff. His *second* job was to be a cameraman. He left PTL and came back to Detroit. He's working in a motor plant now and won't even touch a television camera. The whole experience was a trauma to him. They destroyed him."

"Dear God!" I groaned, stopping and leaning against a tree. I shook my head in despair.

"What about your ministry?" Bob asked, when we were underway again.

"Oh, there is no more ministry. I'm not involved with any of that anymore. I wish I never had been."

"But you still have a relationship with Christ."

I shook my head no.

Bob stopped. He looked hurt. "But you *must*. I've seen how God worked through you. You—do—still believe in God, don't you?"

I looked at him expressionlessly, without answering.

"Austin, I heard about things that happened when you ministered. People saw a glow around you. You were so anointed of God that you set off every security device you walked by. I've seen miracles of healing take place in your ministry that defied medical science! They've written about it in the newspapers. You've got to believe in God! How else could these things have happened?"

"I don't know. I suppose I will never know what really happened. But that is all behind me now. A part of my past."

"Ashes to ashes . . ."

XL

The Christmas tree lights and displays had become a major attraction at Heritage U.S.A. I drove there to see them late in November 1986 and stayed over to be in the studio audience for the telecast the next day. Helen Headley spotted me in line and ushered me to a front seat. Before the telecast, a message was brought to me, inviting me to one of the dressing rooms. There, I enjoyed a friendly visit with Uncle Henry, like in happier times.

The Happy Goodmans were still there. Jeanne Johnson had developed an attitude of superiority and coldness toward me. Reverend Philip Bonjiorno, the District Superintendent of the Assemblies' Pennsylvania district, was there to teach a seminar. He received me cordially. As always, Richard Dortch reached out to me with a warm handshake and a welcome. When the program opened, Jim and Tammy looked at me in the front row and waved to me first thing. I did still like them very much—and, frankly, I missed them.

"I never know who I am going to see when I look in that front row," Jim said to his worldwide audience. "There's always a celebrity there. Sitting there this morning is a good friend of ours, Austin Miles, who is the greatest circus ringmaster in the world. Austin, stand up!"

I appreciated that hospitable greeting, and it felt good to be with Jim again. I took a walk around the vast Heritage U.S.A. grounds. An eerie feeling surrounded the place. The colorful, covered "Mainstreet U.S.A." seemed strangely funereal. It smelled like formaldehyde. I normally love Christmas decorations, chalet houses, lakes, and the like, such as Heritage U.S.A. offered in abundance. But somehow the feeling had turned uncannily uncomfortable, if not downright sinister.

Lyn Robbins still radiated her perennial loveliness. "I run five miles a day," she told me. Some stress did show in her face. She had become entangled in a painful relationship she could not handle.

I felt drawn back to PTL two months later. The air of tension had thickened. Security personnel put me in an aisle seat near the front as part of an obvious effort to rim the audience with people they knew. Then, a closed-door meeting of all the staff took place backstage just before the program went on the air.

Jim and Tammy made their entrance through the audience with security guards much closer at hand and more attentive than usual. One could sense Jim's anxiety behind his mask of composure. During his opening remarks, he came close to where I was sitting, as if he would have liked to speak with me but did not feel at liberty to do so. The rumors swirling about me in Pentecostal circles had never been worse. A demonstration of friendliness toward me could have hurt Jim, and he had more than enough problems of his own at that moment.

Jim had just sent his aide David Taggart off to Europe on vacation and had given him $37,000 for "pocket money." That seemed utterly excessive to me, especially after I learned that Taggart's base yearly salary as an "aide" was $360,000 and that he had just received an additional $45,000 "bonus."

"The devil is really at work," Jim told the audience. "Efforts are being made to destroy this ministry. Someone has called and said they are giving a story to *The Charlotte Observer* about so-called sexual activities regarding us, and have threatened to name names!"

"What the hell is going on?" I wondered. The atmosphere settled down somewhat as the telecast continued, but resumed its strangeness when Jim blurted out, "People have been asking me why I haven't gotten into politics, and I said because God had not called me to do that. I started praying, 'Dear God, I hope you don't call me to run for president.' Oh my! I don't know what I would do if God told me to do that."

"Oh no," I groaned inaudibly. "I don't believe it." Thoroughly impressed by Pat Robertson's making a stab at becoming president, Jim was setting his own stage to try the same thing eventually. I knew his thinking all too well.

When the telecast ended, Tammy Faye, without speaking a word to Jim, went off by herself. Their daughter, Tammy Sue, came on the set, hugged her father, and just held onto him tightly. Something was about to explode. But what?

I went back to the dressing room area and sat down to write Jim a note:

Dear Jim,

I would have liked very much to have a talk with you today. I can feel that something is very wrong here. I also have a gut feeling that you should put extra security around Tammy Faye. I am worried. As I watched you today I thought about your first studio in the furniture

store, when I was your guest. How I wish I could turn back the clock
to those days when things were much happier and less complicated.

Austin

I handed the note to Jeanne Johnson and asked her to give it to
Jim. "I think you should know something," Jeanne said to me, as she
took the note. "Lyn has cancer. That's why she isn't here. It happened
suddenly. It's—extremely serious." Two months earlier, Lyn had seemed
perfectly healthy. I felt as if I had been hit by a truck.

I was invited to join the staff for lunch at the Grand Hotel. I sent
word to Richard Dortch that I needed to talk with him. He was running
around talking quietly with a succession of people. At last, he joined me.
He did not really hear one word I had to say. Clearly, there were more
pressing matters on his mind.

As I walked around Heritage U.S.A. it hit me that I felt death itself
around the complex. Lyn had been stricken. Uncle Henry was seriously
ill—in fact, dying before everyone's eyes. They refused to see it. In the
evening I attended the passion play. An opening announcement dedicated
that night's performance to a cast member who had just died. This was
no place of healing anymore. It had become a place of demonic destruction.

Two more months passed before I could bring myself to call Lyn.
I could not handle the reality of her illness.

"I thought you would have called me before now," she said over the
phone.

I went to her richly furnished townhouse. Aimee, the young woman
caring for her, let me in. Aimee went upstairs to help Lyn get ready.

"O.K., here I come," Lyn said in her clear speaking voice. I watched
her ride down the specially installed stair elevator. She tried to look strong,
even though it was obvious that she had lost a great deal of weight. Her
hair was gone, as a side-effect of the chemotherapy treatments, and she
wore a wig that exactly duplicated the hairstyle that had been uniquely
hers. I gently helped her into the car. We drove to Bennigan's. I knew
that after this night I would never see Lyn again.

"I'm prepared to die," Lyn said when we got back to her townhouse.
"I'm making all the arrangements now. I want you to pick out something
you want from the house, so I can make sure you get it when I go."

"No, Lyn, I can't." Even though I realized that her death was inevitable,
I could not confirm it by taking something.

"Austin," Lyn asked, "why didn't we ever get together?"

"Your life was established here at PTL. There was nothing for me
here."

"I would have gladly given up my position here and become part of your life and ministry." This took me by surprise. I had never dared to think of the possibility of her willingness to do that. If only I had known!

The phone rang. "I'll just let it ring," said Lyn.

"No," I replied on impulse, "I think you should answer it. It may be important."

With difficulty, Lyn made her way into the kitchen. "Hello?" she said into the mouthpiece. "What? *What?* I don't believe it. This can't be—Jim resigned from PTL? . . . A sexual situation? . . . I don't believe this!" After a few more minutes, with whoever was at the other end doing most of the talking, Lyn came back to the living room. "They just announced at the studio that Jim has resigned—that he got involved in a sexual situation—"

"My God," I interjected. "They found out about the homosexuality."

"No, it wasn't that. It was with a church secretary from New York, and it's all going to be hitting the news."

"I don't believe it," I responded. "These church women are always claiming they've been seduced—especially when they haven't been."

"Jim has admitted it," Lyn added sadly.

"Let's turn on the news," I suggested. The telephone continued to ring nonstop. Lyn's mouth dropped open when the first report that Jim had put the PTL operation in the hands of Jerry Falwell came in a newscast. "No—there's *no way* this could be. This is a mistake. They're giving out false information," she protested.

The phone rang again. It was Jim. He had wanted to get the news to Lyn before she heard it from the news media. He genuinely cared about her, and didn't want her to be upset.

"Hello, Lyn."

"Jim!"

"Are you O.K.?"

"Yes, Jim—but how about you? I don't like what I hear."

"It's true, Lyn, I have resigned. I just want you to know that I really love you. I don't know what's going to happen."

"There will always be 'New Beginnings,' " Lyn assured him, borrowing a line from her ministry by that name.

"Yes!" Jim said, in an optimistic tone. "And there will even be new beginnings in Heaven!"

"Austin Miles came by. He's been very comforting to me, and has had some good words for me. He also has some good words for you. He says he loves you and wishes you the best."

"Austin said that?"

"Yes he did—Jim—I'm going to miss you guys." Lyn began to cry. "Bye."

After a little while, Lyn regained her composure. "Austin, I've got to talk to you. There are some things I want you to know. Things I feel I should tell you." Lyn knew she was dying and wanted me to know every secret of her life and of what she had witnessed at PTL.

She did not need to tell me about her love affair with a prominent—and married—Assemblies of God minister in Charlotte. I already knew about it. This affair was absolutely wrong from the outset. The minister deceived Lyn, promising he would divorce his wife for her. Lyn had fallen deeply in love with him. When she realized he had simply used her, the disappointment was too much for her. Many of us connected that extreme stress with her sudden illness. The Assembly of God minister could not have cared less. His ego was boosted from the conquest and that's all that mattered to him.

I took care not to let my shock at Lyn's revelations show. At one point I interrupted, "Are you sure you want to tell me all of this?"

"Yes," she maintained.

"Why?"

"Because I must know if you would still think the same about me if you knew all those things."

"Lyn, you have been a very special part of my life. You are very dear to me, and that will never change."

*　　*　　*

The next day, the scandal made headlines around the world. I felt numb as I drove my car through Charlotte. Soft music played on the car radio. I stopped by the furniture store on Independence Boulevard that had been Jim's first studio. How I wished Jim and Tammy had remained there! I drove by the site of Heritage Village on Park Road, but could not bring myself to go back to Heritage U.S.A.

The developing news gained momentum. A few days later I did go back to Heritage U.S.A. Despite the press releases claiming that the Christian Disneyland was still drawing huge crowds, I could find only slim ones. In the cafeteria-style restaurant in the Grand Hotel, one man told me, "In all the times I've been coming here, this is the first time I've ever been able to just go through without standing in line."

A woman server, handing me a plate of food, studied me intently. At last she asked, "Didn't you used to be Austin Miles?"

Uncle Henry burst out laughing when I told him the story. I had stopped by the Upper Room, where he was scheduled to hold a worship service, to visit him. I paused by the grave of Pastor Aubrey Sara, just by the doors leading inside. "If only a *small* percentage of Assemblies of God ministers were like Aubrey Sara, things would be different with that denomination," I thought to myself.

The Upper Room was packed with bewildered PTL supporters. They desperately wanted someone to tell them what to do and what to think. Uncle Henry called me to come forward and minister with him. We sat casually on a big table and exchanged stories. For a little while, it seemed like old times. Then Uncle Henry led me into a more serious discussion, soliciting my thoughts on what was taking place.

"On the way in," I said to the assembled people, "I stopped by the grave of a good friend, Pastor Aubrey Sara. I remember one night in the mansion. . . ." I told the story of the loose feathers, concluding, "Maybe some loose feathers are being shaken off. Then PTL can grow bigger and better."

That's what the gathering wanted to hear, and they responded with heavy applause. "We still do not know the complete story of what actually happened to Jim and Tammy, and until we do we should stand by to help them in any way possible."

A profusion of news stories surfaced about plots, subterfuges, and take-over conspiracies that kept everyone confused. I continued to be very protective of Jim and Tammy for a long time. Gradually, the sordid truth about the greed and lust of the televangelists came out, making all of us who had cooperated with them look like fools.

Meanwhile, smaller scandals in the Christian community continued to break almost daily. A person high in the leadership of a large women's Christian fellowship was caught in a lesbian affair. Her husband came home unexpectedly and found her naked in bed with her female paramour. He subsequently divorced her.

In Schenectady, New York, smoke continued to rise from Calvary Tabernacle at 1840 Albany Street. Pastor Al Fisher had been exposed participating in a barrage of sexual activity, involving the wives and daughters— some underage—of his flock. In the midst of these shocking revelations, Reverend Fisher conveniently died of a heart attack.

I could not contain my amazement over the secret sex life of this pastor. Reverend Fisher was so overweight that during an emotional sermon on self-discipline, his pants broke loose at the waist and fell down around his ankles. He did not even realize it until a deacon hurried to the platform and whispered the news in his ear. Pastor Fisher quickly commanded the congregation to bow their heads in prayer, as he, with difficulty, managed to pull his errant trousers back up into place. Church-sex knew no boundaries.

The biggest surprise for me came from David Mainse of "100 Huntley Street" in Canada. He announced that his program had been approved to be shown in Italy. "We are the *only* Christian program allowed to telecast in Italy," he proudly told his Canadian and U.S. viewers. He also raised money for the project, stating that his program was on the air forty hours a week in Italy, reaching a potential audience of 45 million people weekly.

At that time, David Mainse's was the only televangelism program I would appear on. I trusted him above all others in Christian television. In a private conversation in his office following a telecast, he discussed his overseas ministry outreach with me, and said he desperately needed one million dollars to carry on his work in foreign countries that needed the Gospel. Obviously, he hoped I would make a substantial contribution. He also pointedly asked me if I knew someone of wealth who could give him this amount.

On a trip to Italy shortly afterwards, I did some checking. No such program could be found anywhere in Italy. An acquaintance of mine there, heavily involved with television programming throughout Italy, told me no such program had been broadcast, "and there never will be." Others, including Father Joseph Anthony Barrett, who works in television communications at the Vatican, confirmed that the program had not been shown in Italy. In this case especially, considering the love I have for David, I continue in the hope that there is an explanation that might put a different light on this matter.

The smooth-talking, "possibility-thinking" Robert Schuller was not to be left out of tried and proven fund-raising gambits. In the early 1980s, he sent his flock an "urgent" communiqué, informing them that—Praise the Lord!—Reverend Schuller was in Red China, and the way had opened for him to confer with Red Chinese leaders. Jesus Christ could be brought to the Chinese! For such a door to have been opened had to be of God! Of course, it would require a lot of money to carry out God's mandate to seize this one-time opportunity. If it were lost, China was forever doomed to hell! The mailing included a photograph of Reverend Schuller standing before the Great Wall.

As the *Los Angeles Times* and other papers reported, Reverend Schuller had been nowhere near China at the time the photo was taken. The photo had been taken in a studio in Orange County, California, before he went to China, in front of a stock photo background of the Great Wall. Schuller managed to explain the whole thing away as an "unfortunate misunderstanding." This "misunderstanding" certainly made for an effective fund-raising mail piece.

Being still further tempted by the root of all evil, Schuller decided to enter the competitive world of show business, staging theatrical productions. Tickets for Crystal Cathedral concerts and productions were sold through Ticketron.

Then, a muffled explosion rumbled throughout the glass house. Schuller's handsome minister son, Robert A. Schuller, groomed to be his father's successor, became embattled in a divorce scandal.

There seemed to be no end to the revelations. On a radio call-in show with Joe Woodburn on CHOW Radio in Welland, Ontario, a listener told how his brother had once been approached by Ernest Angley just before a big crusade and offered $120 to be brought to the front in a wheelchair, and then to stand up and walk when Angley gave the command.

Reverend Eugene Profeta, who had been the cause of so much concern to Reverend Leon Cooke, reached a new height of celebrity as the PTL scandal continued to unravel. Jessica Hahn, who had burst into the news, worked for Profeta at Massapequa Tabernacle. Profeta had introduced her to John Wesley Fletcher, who in turn arranged the fateful liaison with Jim Bakker that toppled an empire. To make the story even more intriguing, the news came out that Profeta, who had become known locally as "the pistol-packing preacher," had himself carried on a torrid sexual affair with Jessica for more than eight years. In a jealous rage over Jessica's favors, Profeta threatened one of Jessica's lovers in Long Island with physical harm. To top off his problems, according to press reports Profeta had to plead guilty to federal tax evasion.

The name of Richard Dortch became a household word as more news of the PTL scandal developed. Reverend Dortch had arranged the hush money payoff—from contributions the faithful had given "sacrificially" for God's work—to Jessica Hahn. That $265,000 of viewer-contributed money, put aside "in trust" for Jessica, may have set a record for the most expensive roll-in-the-hay in history. In arranging the deal, Richard Dortch must have set another record for the number of moral and ethical obligations ever broken by a minister. Blinded by greed, he threw all caution to the winds to protect his own $360,000 per year "ministry" position at PTL. There were persistent rumors—later substantiated—that Dortch planned to double-cross Jim Bakker and muscle his way into total control of the lucrative PTL operation. My experiences with the Reverend Richard Dortch taught me to pay closer attention to my first impressions.

Reverend Marvin Gorman lost his church in New Orleans after Gorman's adulterous affair with his secretary was exposed by rival televangelist Jimmy Swaggart. Swaggart claimed that Gorman had had *many* adulterous affairs. Mustering up his holiest and most righteous indignation, Swaggart spearheaded the push to have Gorman defrocked by the Assemblies of God. Then Swaggart hit the headlines. The king of the fire-and-brimstone preachers had been photographed coming out of a seedy motel room after an assignation with prostitute Debra Murphree. To make matters worse, Murphree claimed that Swaggart wanted her to bring her nine-year-old daughter in to watch, and then to take part in, the sex.

Swaggart was the next to be kicked out of the Assemblies of God, in a move led by the man who arranged for the tell-tale photos outside the motel to be taken—Marvin Gorman. Gorman's son Randy may have provided the initial information about Swaggart and the prostitute. It came out that Randy himself had been paying to have sex with Murphree.

The Happy Goodmans dealt so dishonestly with the William Morris Agency in Nashville that word spread through the secular talent agencies to keep clear of them. "In all the years I've been in this business," Dolores Smiley, an agent with William Morris told me, "I've only been screwed royally by *one* act. The Happy Goodmans, the Christian act. They are *not* nice people."

*   *   *

Warfare broke out, between my feeling soul and thinking mind. A part of me remained deeply spiritual, and wanted to commune with God. Another part of me had been driven to outrage and revulsion by what I had witnessed and experienced in the name of Christianity. I wanted to strike back, denounce the church—even denounce God. From the beginning this appeared to be a war that could never be won. I knew both sides of the issue too well.

I found solace in each performance of the Lipizzan show. Those were the best two hours of my day, when I concentrated totally on running the show and pushed all unpleasant thoughts out of my mind. From my earliest days in show business, I never allowed my personal thoughts or problems to interfere with my performances. Perhaps this is why I loved show business so much. It had always brought out the best in me.

When the show played in Massachusetts, I remembered a certain Mrs. Wirkkala who had written me a lovely letter of encouragement during some dark days in my relationship with the Assemblies. There were always a few good people standing out among the Christians.

The Assembly of God in Leominster, Massachusetts, where I had met Mrs. Wirkkala, still evoked happy memories. I had been on a week-long revival crusade there when the big blizzard of '78 slammed into the area. One hundred and thirty-eight people showed up for the service that night, when supposedly nothing could move in the deep snow. It made national news.

I called Mrs. Wirkkala and invited her to bring her family and some friends from the church to be my guests for the Lipizzan show's performance in nearby Fitchburg. She seemed reticent. It soon became clear that her small talk, mostly about churchy things, was building up to something fairly heavy. Then she came out with it.

"Nelson Benedict came by to see me. You know him."

"I can't place the name."

"He's a deacon with the church. His wife was healed during one of our services in New Hampshire. Anyway—he came into my house and—knocked me across the room!"

"He did what? What on earth got into him? Are you O.K.?" It took a few more volleys of dialogue before I realized she was speaking in parables. Then she got down to business.

"He told me that he came to see me—to tell me—that he had talked to people and learned that you—have been having—sex with my daughter Karen and her friend Pamela. He said he knows this for a fact."

I sat dumbfounded for a moment. "I—I've been having sex with *your* daughter?—and her girlfriend—here?"

"That's right! And at the same time in the same room."

"Did your daughter and her friend tell you this?"

"No. As a matter of fact they both said that such a thing never happened. I talked to both of them—but there must have been something to it."

Once the initial shock of her words passed, I almost exploded with anger. "I've not even *been* in this area since the blizzard of 1978! Who is the man who said all this? What is his name?"

"Oh, I'd rather not say. No—I won't say who it was who said it."

Fortunately, I had scribbled the name "Nelson Benedict" along with my doodling on the phone pad as we spoke.

I called Pastor Otis Stanley of Leominster Assembly of God. He was also the Presbyter of the New England district. My feigned friendliness did the trick, persuading him to agree to meet me at church.

After some initial small talk, I went right to the heart of the matter. "There is hatred coming out of your church," I told the pastor, looking him searchingly in the eye. "And at long last I know the name of one my accusers, and I insist on talking to him face to face."

Pastor Stanley hesitated for a few moments. Then, apparently finding no easier way out, he picked up the phone, dialed Benedict's number, and handed the receiver to me. I repeated what Mrs. Wirkkala had told me. Benedict flatly denied that he had ever said any such thing.

"So you are saying that Mrs. Wirkkala, a respected member of this congregation, is a liar? Frankly, I believe her. There is no way that she could have come up with such a story on her own. Do you realize, Mr. Benedict, that you are not only guilty of bearing false witness, but also of lying before God? And *you,* a born-again, Spirit-filled Christian?"

"I—I think I had better get dressed and come over to the church," he conceded. I knew I had gotten him out of bed but didn't care about the inconvenience. I had waited a long time for a moment like this.

It was just after 10:00 P.M. when Benedict came through the church door. He was an older man, but sturdy and hearty looking. He looked vaguely familiar. If I had seen him before, it had been eight years ago. "I—I—uh—guess you won't want to shake my hand," he blurted out defensively.

"No, Mr. Benedict, I will *not* refuse to shake your hand. I am still a gentleman."

After sitting down, Deacon Benedict continued to deny ever making accusations against me, and he was remarkably convincing. Pastor Stanley interjected that everybody in his church loved me, and he had heard nothing bad about me in New England.

"Why, Brother Miles," Benedict effused, "my wife was healed under your ministry."

"What kind of healing?" I inquired.

"It was when you were ministering in Jaffrey, New Hampshire. I brought her up for prayer. She had cancer and a lump in her chest. She was very sick. Well, you prayed for her and the lump dissolved and disappeared right there. Everybody saw it. We were so excited. When we got back, we stood up in church here and gave our testimony, and when I said your name, well, that just went over like a lead balloon."

I looked at Pastor Stanley.

"They love me here—eh? So, Mr. Benedict, your wife gets healed in my service and you repay me by trying to destroy me?"

"Brother Miles," Benedict whined plaintively, "I just cannot understand this hostility that you have toward me. Why, I have never *ever* said any such thing against you or your character."

"Good," I said. "I'm relieved to hear that." I walked to the desk, picked the phone, and handed it to Benedict. "Call Mrs. Wirkkala right now and tell her to come to the church—that you want to straighten up this mis-understanding right now!"

Benedict froze in place. Having failed to think ahead more than one move, he had been checkmated. "O.K., Brother Miles," he said, now speaking in a far softer tone of voice, "let me explain to you what happened. I had heard these stories about you being circulated. Now, I love and respect your ministry, and I don't like this. So I decided to ask some questions about all this, so that I could get to the bottom of it and set things straight."

"Bullshit!" I thundered. A book toppled off the shelf behind Pastor Stanley and landed with a thud, startling him. It may have been the first time in the history of that church that such language had been uttered the pastor's sacred study. "Checking on these things, my butt! You were out there starting and spreading these rumors!"

"No, Brother Miles—I had heard this—"

"From *whom?* Name the source!"

"Well—everybody was talking about it—it came to my attention."

"Who is *everybody?* Name someone—*anyone*—who specifically told you this." Benedict sat mute. "Tell me the name of *one* person who told you this."

"Well—there's really no one I can name."

"Then tell me, Mr. Benedict, what is this story *based* upon? What *facts* do you have to support it?"

Benedict looked over at the pastor uncomfortably, and then dropped his eyes. "There—I—uh—guess there—is no basis for the story."

I turned and faced Pastor Stanley. "There it is in a nutshell. The basis for every Austin Miles rumor is just that—nothing. You've seen this and heard it. I expect you to take this to the Presbytery of New England and tell them everything that was said here tonight. *And* I expect you to present this before the congregation here on Sunday morning, and everybody had better get on their knees and ask forgiveness from God. I *was* one of His servants. And *you*—" I turned to face the deacon. "Nelson Benedict—they should have named you Benedict Arnold! You people are sick. Why couldn't I see this in the beginning? Why is it that Christians always repay kindness with evil?"

"Brother Miles," Benedict interrupted, "something disturbs me—just now you said 'was' one of God's servants. You're still in the ministry, aren't you?"

"No, Mr. Benedict, I left the ministry and the church a long time ago because of people like you. But you didn't know that, did you? Gossiping about a *minister* would give you more importance. So that's one thing that tripped you up. Furthermore, Mr. Benedict, I haven't stepped inside Massachusetts for over eight years. Yet, you convinced people that I've been here all along, having sex with those two girls. By the way, what ever happened to your wife?"

"She—died last year."

"Then *you* are responsible for her death!" I fired back. "I was indeed one of God's servants, totally devoted to serving Him and His people. God healed your wife as a result. Then you turn around and viciously attack the instrument God used to bless you, actually trying to destroy that instrument. His anger was kindled against you, Mr. Benedict. *You* killed your wife! And the fires of Hell will be extra hot for you, for what you've done!"

I had always been offended whenever I heard a minister use that particular spiritual kick in the groin. I always felt that such statements were cruel. But in this case, the statement seemed entirely fitting. If there were a God, He would have been furious at Benedict and all the rest of them for the way they treated me. *If* there were a God. The "if" crept in to my thoughts more and more.

"Brother Miles, I still just can't understand the hostility you are showing toward me," Benedict insisted, trying to change the mood.

"You can't understand it? It was just this kind of false rumor about me, started and spread by people like you, that was responsible for breaking up my marriage. I lost my wife, daughter, home, savings, everything—and you can't understand why I am hostile? My whole life was destroyed because of getting involved with people like you and this cult."

"Now see here!—" Pastor Stanley interrupted, rising from his seat.

"*You* see here," I shot back, pointing a finger in his direction. "The Assembly of God *is* a *cult*. The most dangerous, vicious cult in the world—destroying families, reputations, turning children against their parents, drug-gings, sexual perversions, homosexuality, child molestation, bilking old people out of their life savings, will clinics, brain washing—Jim Jones—Jim Bakker—the lies, lies, LIES. The Assemblies are a cult and you know it! I'm going to write a book about all this, so that people will know the truth and protect themselves."

During my tirade Brother Benedict became "baptized" with a surge of indignation. "It is quite clear what you think of the Assemblies of God," he burped piously, "and I have no desire to read any book you write, and I won't."

"Oh yes, you will buy and read my book, Mr. Benedict—from cover to cover—because it will be filled with lots of nice, juicy *gossip,* and that will certainly appeal to the likes of you!"

The clock on the wall chimed midnight. Nelson Benedict and Otis Stanley had been my captive congregation for two hours. I felt great. I had gotten things out of my system that had been stored up for years. It was like a mental enema.

"Goodnight, Mr. Benedict," I said, dismissing him unceremoniously. Benedict slowly got out of his chair and turned toward me with a piteous expression. "Please understand, I *do* love you, Brother Miles."

That was the last straw. I almost yelled at him, "Don't tell me you love me! Words—empty words! That's all that comes out of the mouth of any Christian—empty words! Don't any of you ever tell me you love me again. I find it offensive. And, furthermore, *don't call me brother."* My voice had reached such a pitch of intensity that it sailed right out the church windows and down the cold village streets. Nelson Benedict walked to the door, opened it, and left. He did not look back. I turned slowly toward Pastor Stanley, who was sitting at his desk with his face in his hands. He got up and walked toward the door. Then he leaned back against the door, facing me, a pained expression on his face. "You know, Reverend Stanley, I feel sorry for you. You are still in this thing.

You're stuck here, in bondage of the worst kind. But I'm *free*. I've escaped. As a result of tonight, I'm not only free—I'm reborn—into real life—and that is wonderful!" His eyes moistened and he nodded his head. He knew that I was speaking the truth. I had once felt a deep affection for Otis Stanley. But he, too, had betrayed me with lies, and it hurt.

"Goodbye, Otis."

I did not sleep that night. Early the next morning, I quietly made a side-trip to Reading, Massachusetts, and stood before the pretty town hall where Rose Marie and I had been married. My anger from the previous night now turned to grief.

That night I called Art Harris of *The Washington Post*. I had spoken with him before. "Art, there is no reason for me to protect these people. I'm willing to tell you some things. Maybe this will help keep other people from being taken in by these charlatans."

*   *   *

Lyn died. Nobody from PTL let me know. They were angry with me, after seeing the steam room story in *The Washington Post* and the resulting wire stories. By not telling me, they successfully punished us both. I later learned that in her dying coma Lyn had called for me.

"I think you should know something," Art Harris said to me in a telephone conversation. "According to some reliable sources who were there, Jim and Tammy tried to take over Lyn's funeral. They cried, carried on. All the media could see that they were using her death to try and gain sympathy for themselves. Everyone was disgusted."

"You know, Art," I replied, "in all fairness I believe that this was one time when Jim and Tammy were for real. There was real love there. They made a couple of trips to Charlotte to visit Lyn, and never told anyone who the friend was that they came to see. And Jim did call Lyn the night the scandal broke to try and ease her pain at the news. I was there and heard it. No, Art, this time the tears were for real."

There is something I will reveal now for the first time: Jim Bakker paid every penny of Lyn's medical expenses and hospital bills, from the time she first became ill until the end.

XLI

H aving made the final emotional break from the world of the Pentecostal church, I found that everything about Christianity, the Bible, and even God took on a whole new perspective. I began to *listen* and *analyze* what the preachers were saying. How could I ever have been duped into accepting such absurdities?

The religious news of the day became a continual "Saturday Night Live." In his quest to become President of the United States, Pat Robertson abandoned every one of the Christian teachings he had preached. When former Congressman Paul N. ("Pete") McCloskey, Jr., revealed that Robertson had used the influence of his late father, Senator A. Willis Robertson, to keep him from dangerous duty as a Marine lieutenant in Korea, Robertson lashed back with a 35-million-dollar lawsuit claiming defamation. When it turned out that Robertson could not prove his case, he dropped the suit. The whole thing confused me. If, as Pat informed his followers, it was indeed God's will for him to be President, then why worry about McCloskey's story? Also, I remembered when Pat told me, through his secretary, Barbara Johnson, that it was un-Christian to sue. This was when *he* was about to find himself on the *receiving* end of a legitimate defamation suit.

The public got a demonstration of the Christian rumor process in action in February 1988 when a UPI wire story took Pat Robertson's wife Dede to task for bearing false witness against presidential candidate Gary Hart. When asked if voters would forgive Senator Hart for his involvement with Donna Rice, Mrs. Robertson said, "I don't know whether they will or not. After all, Mr. Hart is still carrying on these affairs." When pressed to back up her damaging accusation, she finally admitted that she had no special information, and could not back up her charge. This good Christian woman gave no thought to the damage such a rumor could do to Hart's marriage and family. It made me think of my confrontation with Nelson Benedict. Since the Christians preach so loudly about morality, we should be able to expect better than this from them.

To the good fortune of us all, Pat Robertson's political star sank rapidly in the west. I couldn't help but feel sorry for God. First, Oral Roberts made Him out to be a hit-man, requiring Oral to raise eight million dollars ransom, or else be taken "home" by way of the graveyard. Then Pat Robertson showed us that God must either be a liar, a failure, or a bumbler. Even though Pat announced to the world that God had ordained him to be President of the United States, it didn't work out that way. In God's defense, I respectfully submit that this was another case of God being misquoted.

In December 1988, the IRS announced that Robertson's ministry was under investigation to determine whether tax-exempt ministry donations had been misused to support his political campaign.

There were many interesting sidelights to the infamous presidential campaign of '88. One of the most popular candidates, *Reverend* Pat Robertson admitted he got his wife pregnant before marriage.

Another fascinating observation of that overall mess concerns Donna Rice, the Jessica Hahn of the political world. The sexy model, whose liaison with Senator Hart made his presidential aspirations end with a thud, professes to be a "born-again," Spirit-filled Christian. After her headline-making affair with Hart, Rice retreated to the ministering arms of—Bobby Yerkes! While Bobby "counseled" her and helped her find a proper church to attend in the Hollywood area, Donna was spending her nights with Bobby on the boat he docks in Marina del Rey. They even had a photo taken of bikini-clad Donna sitting in Bobby's lap, mocking the infamous news photograph of Donna on the lap of Senator Hart. A gloating Bobby Yerkes told me that Donna Rice was about to enter his stable of movie stunt girls. Born-again Bob has a good life.

Some evidence that quietly passed among a few of us suggested that Pentecostal preachers are beyond repair. Shortly after his classic "I have sinned" televised speech, there were reports that Jimmy Swaggart was back cruising the same seedy motel strip in New Orleans. Since Oral Roberts had cast the demon of lust out of Swaggart earlier (by phone), many of us found this extremely perplexing.

Facing the possibility of 120 years in prison, Jim Bakker was indicted on twenty-four counts of mail fraud, wire fraud, and conspiracy in December 1988. Related indictments were returned against Richard Dortch and the Taggart brothers.

Heritage U.S.A. was sold by the bankruptcy court on December 12, 1988, for $65 million to a Canadian developer, Stephen Mernick, who is also an ordained Orthodox Jewish rabbi. He and the present staff of the "Heritage Ministries" successor to PTL immediately began exploring possibilities to keep the telecast on the air and to preserve the Christian character of the park. Before the gavel came down and the real estate went to Mernick, "Heritage Ministries" managed to raise an incredible five milllion dollars cash in a telethon, attempting to put together a down payment to buy the complex for itself. I frankly would have preferred to see the whole monster dismantled. Heritage U.S.A. was ill-gotten, and at least for me, can be nothing more than a monument to stained Christianity.

During this period of sadness for the conservative Christian world— and rejoicing for the free, real world outside—the duo of Fletcher and Hahn provided some comic relief. John and Jessica slugged it out on national television with such gusto that they became a modern-day Punch and Judy. Jessica still claimed she had been an innocent church virgin deflowered by Bakker. Fletcher, while admitting his own shortcomings, denounced Jessica as a Jezebel, whom he, himself, had bedded months before the Bakker tryst. A fuming Art Harris took part in some of the public debates. He too had been conned into accepting Jessica's virgin story and writing some national articles in her defense.

A memorable time was provided for all observers when the former church secretary posed for *Playboy,* facing the camera stark naked, with her legs spread wide, to show her treasures to the world. All the while, she continued giving interviews to the rest of the media repeating the sad story of her exploited virginal innocence. In the Gospel according to Hahn, the *Playboy* session "just happened" in the course of the unfortunate events that had caused her such grief. Her mother gave interviews to the supermarket tabloids about how the family had been devastated by all that had happened, and how shocked they were when Jessica wound up on the pages of *Playboy.* Those interviews also stated that Jessica's stepfather Eddie Moylan, an ex-cop, just sat for hours staring into space, and would probably kill Bakker if he could get his hands on him, for corrupting his little girl. Next, in a cover story interview in *People* magazine, Jessica said her family had been in favor of her *Playboy* spread, and had looked the layout over and approved it before it was published.

The first *Playboy* photo spread did not "just happen" as Jessica led us all to believe. Attempting to capitalize on the scandal in which she played a key role, Jessica went to the *Playboy* offices in New York to sell her body to the magazine. A source close to *Playboy* told me that Jessica was so plain and frumpy looking that nobody was interested. As the news from the PTL scandal progressed, persistent Jessica succeeded in making the sale.

Before the second *Playboy* pictorial, Hugh Hefner had Jessica made over, including lifting into place and tightening her boobs, giving her a nose bob, capping her teeth, and liposuction. Through the modern miracle of cosmetic surgery, Jessica Hahn had become Pinocchio in reverse.

*   *   *

At a time when all seemed to be lost, I received a phone call in the middle of the night from an Assemblies minister who had remained my friend. He had a story to tell me that would surely lift my spirits. "It all happened during the time that Brother Zimmerman was giving you the most trouble," he related. I could visualize the story perfectly as he recounted it.

A missionary couple in the Philippines were beside themselves with excitement. Brother Zimmerman would be coming there—to their home! "Brother Z" himself, and Mrs. Zimmerman!

The missionary couple had an extremely slim budget, but felt they must offer the Zimmermans something to eat during the royal visit. They decided to make a pizza for their honored guests. They prepared the pizza with exquisite care, topped it off with anchovies from a can they had been saving for a long time, and baked it to perfection. The couple placed the pizza on the kitchen counter to cool and hurried to the airport to meet the Zimmerman's plane.

When they returned to their modest house, the missionary wife went to the kitchen. She found to her dismay that the family cat had eaten the anchovies off the pizza, leaving tell-tale footprints in the sauce and dough. Lacking the time and ingredients to make another pizza, and in a panic, she dusted the footprints off the pizza, retopped it with the rest of the anchovies from the can, and put it in the oven for a few extra minutes. Praise God, there were enough anchovies and the pizza could take a bit more baking! Nobody would know the difference.

After the repast, the Zimmermans graciously praised their hosts for the good lunch and hospitality. The two couples then left for a sightseeing tour of the area. When they returned, the missionary couple were horrified to find the cat lying dead on the front porch. Good Lord! It must have been the anchovies the cat ate! The Zimmermans had eaten the same tainted anchovies.

The couple quickly realized that their duty to save the lives of the Zimmermans would have to outweigh their reluctance to confess the embarrassing story of the cat, the pizza, and the footprints. Mustering up all his courage and fervently intoning a silent prayer, the missionary said, "Brother Zimmerman—we have to—tell you something. . . ."

Brother and Sister Zimmerman were rushed to the hospital, where they had to endure the gagging procedure of having their stomachs pumped. When the ordeal was finally over, Brother and Sister "Z" affected the utmost in stoic Pentecostal holiness and grace as they wobbled weakly to the airport for the long, miserable flight home.

The missionary couple rode back to their house in silence. As they pulled into the driveway, their neighbor called to them and rushed over. "I wanted to talk to you earlier today," he said breathlessly. "I'm sorry—

but I ran over your cat and killed him. I couldn't help it. I put him on the front porch and rang the bell, but nobody was home. I wanted to tell you about it before you found him."

Out of concern for the discomfort of Brother and Mrs. "Z" no doubt, the whole story was shared with only a small, select group of God's servants. The best part of the story is that "Brother Z" never found out "the rest of the story"—until this book.

I only wish I had heard about this at the time. Maybe I would have gone on believing that there is a just God in heaven after all.

XLII

A final puzzle remained unsolved. First of all, why did the Christians hate me so much? Why were they so determined to destroy me? Why had I been such a lightning rod, taking jolt after jolt of their hatred and jealousy? It seemed that whenever some other minister failed, no matter how serious the offense or how bizarre the circumstances, he would be treated with compassion and forgiveness, and given the benefit of every doubt. I had not committed any of the innumerable offenses attributed to me. My only "sin" had been an imprudent marriage in my youth, which had ended in a painful divorce. Yet, at the hands of the Christians I received only merciless condemnation.

Key missing pieces of the puzzle had to do with the FBI. I knew where that had started. I had knowledge about the relationship between Marilyn Monroe and the United States Government, and the reports of her alleged murder and her sexual relationship with John and Robert Kennedy. It seems that the object of the game was to discredit me so thoroughly that, if I ever chose to talk, my testimony would carry no weight. When my popularity as a public personality increased, so did the fear of disclosures by me, in official circles.

I availed myself of the Federal Freedom of Information Act (FOIA) to see what was in FBI files about me. The Government did everything it could to avoid complying with my request, stalling me and demanding unnecessarily precise descriptions of the documents I sought. While my Freedom of Information proceeding was pending, the FBI renewed its harassment efforts against me.

One day an FBI agent pounded on the door of my friend's house in San Francisco, where I planned to resettle. Unintimidated, my friend who lived in the house had the presence of mind to ask the agent for his card, a request a G-Man is obligated to fulfill. From that, I got the name of Special Agent Mickey Degnan of the San Francisco office of the FBI. I immediately phoned the number on the card.

"Well," Degnan exclaimed, "this is quite unusual, to get this kind of immediate cooperation from someone we want."

"Why are you surprised, Mr. Degnan? I'm not the criminal. You people are. Now I want to ask *you* a question. What is it you want out of me? You bastards have bugged my telephone, and my friends' telephones, intercepted my mail, and interfered with every area of my life!'"

"Why, I am surprised at you, Mr. Miles," Degnan countered smoothly, "using such language, and you having been a churchman."

Suddenly it all came together. "The church! You know all about the church! Of course! Why did it take me so long to realize it? I felt all along that even the *Christians* couldn't be *that* bad. Now I understand it. *You* people were involved! The last thing you wanted was for me to be in the ministry, have access to the public, and possibly tell the truth about Marilyn Monroe! You were the ones instigating everything, stirring up hatred against me! I understand *everything* now. Thank you, Mr. Degnan."

I wrote a letter to President Reagan to ask his help in obtaining the documents, attaching copies of the previous correspondence on the matter. Within two weeks—in January 1988—the documents arrived.

I sat in shock, going through the papers on me the FBI had kept in their files. There were numerous blackings-out and deletions, allegedly for "national security" reasons and to protect the "privacy" of the informants against me. The FBI clearly had no legitimate reason for a criminal investigation of me. I had once, under great provocation, threatened to punch out a lawyer. Under that pretext, they had started a file on me for "extortion." They continued "investigating" under the file for many years, without any prospect of developing more information on the old incident and long after the U.S. Attorney had rejected the case as trivial and refused to prosecute. In their endless investigations of me, they came up with intimate details about everything in my life, and then distorted the facts for effect.

For example, the file contained the statement, "[blacked out name] STATES SUBJECT POSSIBLY RECEIVED PSYCHIATRIC DISCHARGE FROM ARMED SERVICES." That is *not* what my military records state, and not the case. Rather, that kind of flimsily supported, contrived conclusion is what FBI agents casually but deliberately "confide" to people connected with someone on their character assassination "hit list." I learned how this is done from Jack Ryan, who was fired from the FBI after twenty-three years as an agent because he refused to continue using these tactics on innocent citizens. These practices are still used. They are no mere McCarthy era fossils!

Other tidbits in the file, undoubtedly used to plant rumors about me, had it that I was suspected of anti-American activities, specifically of being a German sympathizer in the early forties. Since I was born in 1933, this would have made me eight or nine years of age. The files made it clear that these stories were to be widely spread. One document proposed ". . . to take this to every logical area of show business." These assaults hobbled my show business career, and completely killed any chance for me to have a film career.

My rage grew when I learned how regularly they had harassed Rose Marie and her friends. They had even gone to Rose Marie's place of employment. She had never told me.

Over the years, there had been three attempts on my life. The documents revealed that the FBI knew entirely too much about those events not to be involved. Although much of the FOIA information on that topic had been blacked out, and seventeen pages were deleted altogether, enough remained for me to piece it together. (A witness has since come forward linking the attempts to a famous Mafia hit man, who worked on several such assignments for both the FBI and CIA, including an assassination attempt on Fidel Castro.)

I learned for the first time why my biological father never wanted to see me. The documents indicated that he had been contacted by the FBI. A phone call to my half-sister in March 1988 clarified the matter somewhat. She learned of it for the first time from me. She called our father, who confirmed that the FBI had convinced him he should have nothing to do with me. She broke down crying as she told me. My father still refuses to see me.

The FBI had managed to make most of the people who were important to me leery of me and afraid. The people contacted were told to be careful, to report anything out of the ordinary—as if I were some sort of nut, ready to go beserk at any moment. Most of the people they contacted simply never wanted to hear from me again. It explained why people would often be so open to me for a time, then suddenly turn hostile.

The FBI even paid Louie the doorman of my apartment building in Forest Hills to report on me. They did not have to pay the Christians anything. They are more than willing to take part in a slander campaign for free. Many nonchurch people had enough common sense to see through the ploy and stick with me despite these visits from the FBI. But the Christians' exaggerated respect for authority made them putty in the FBI's hands. The Christians nearly finished the job the FBI had begun.

Amazingly, my marriage to Rose Marie managed to survive the FBI harassment for ten years. Had I never stepped inside a church, our marriage would still be intact.

Years ago, I went to columnist Jack Anderson and reporter Brit Hume— now ABC News White House correspondent—in Washington, D.C. I gave Hume a diary that had fallen into my hands. It had been kept by the person who was closest to me during that time. That person had been witness to a conversation in the White House in which the participants plotted the murder of Marilyn Monroe. That diary, which had become a curse to me, contained explosive information, and there were no copies. Unfortunately, this diary has since disappeared.

In 1988 a startling book, *Dangerous Dossiers* (Donald F. Fine, Inc.), by *New York Times* reporter Herbert Mitgang appeared. It documents many instances of FBI harassment of individuals, with the same modus operandi as in my case. It also tells how Ronald Reagan and his wife at the time, Jane Wyman, were FBI informants known by the code names "Confidential Informant T-10" and "T-9." That was when Reagan was president of the Screen Actors Guild, whose members he was supposed to help protect, but whose careers he helped to wreck instead.

I have been refused any kind of legal assistance to help with my FBI problems. An attorney named Howard Tobin pursued the matter for a while, but bowed out without a satisfactory explanation. My Congressman, George Miller III, refused to acknowledge my letters requesting his assistance in these matters. Former Congressman Paul N. ("Pete") McCloskey, Jr., now practicing law, coldly told me that "the FBI has a perfect legal right to investigate anyone they wish as many times as they wish. This is necessary for the protection of this country." Apparently the FBI's interest in me makes me a menace to the country *ipso facto* in the eyes of "Pete" McCloskey, George Miller, and others too comfortable with "the system."

Stories corroborating my own, about horror stories of religious involvement and sinister abuses of the FBI, are surfacing, making my experiences no longer seem so incredible. The legal machinery it would take to curtail FBI harassment of blameless citizens under the fiction of "criminal" investigation is still not in place. There is plenty left to do.

*   *   *

I looked at my face in the lighted dressing room mirror. My hair had all turned silver gray. The squat chin I had never liked was transformed for the better by a beard. My new look of maturity wore well. I had gained some wisdom at great cost, and I was happy with my life again.

After a final brush of my hair, I adjusted my bow tie, got up, slipped on the tux jacket, took a final glance in the mirror, and walked out to begin the performance. A man stood behind the curtain with a Lipizzaner horse.

"Are you the new rider?" I asked him.

"Yes," he replied. "My name is Michael Jaeger."

"What did you do before coming to us?"

"I had just graduated from seminary. I was going to be a priest."

"What happened?"

"I got right to the ordination, then realized that once I took those vows I would never be able to have a family. I felt it was better to make the decision before I took the vows than afterwards."

"Welcome to the show," I said, and started to walk toward the curtain. As an afterthought, I turned back to him and asked, "'Tell me something, Michael. Was it—a trauma for you to leave the Church?"

He looked at me with a twinkle in his eye. "Only *you* would know how much."

I turned to the lady who pulls the curtain. "How does it look out there, Beverly?"

"Looks like another full house," she answered, smiling. "I think as many people are interested in seeing you as they are the horses."

"Ironic, isn't it?" I said, while checking my cuff links.

I took my position behind the curtain as an unseen voice said, ". . . and here is your narrator—Austin Miles!"

The spotlight beam hit the curtain as it opened and I entered. A particularly receptive audience greeted me. As I looked the applauding crowd over, I began to think about my life.

"The church destroyed my marriage. But they could not destroy my life. If they think they've discouraged me to the point where I wouldn't go on, they've got another think coming. Why, I've got enough memories of Rose Marie and Lori to last me for the rest of my life." I could hear the music of Bach's "Let the Sheep Safely Graze" as I pictured Rose Marie the first time I saw her at the TWA counter, when she turned around briskly to greet me. The candlelight dancing across her face as she told me about the swans, the two of us happily walking out of the little steepled town hall in Massachusetts with Peter and Gisela tossing rice at us, Rose Marie snuggling her head on my shoulder by the Lake of Zurich, her frustration on the French ski slope, her inimitable gesture bidding me to talk to the crazy woman speaking in tongues at Glad Tidings Tabernacle. I thought of Lori, trick-or-treating on the plane to Rome, singing "Angels We Have Heard On High" as her Christmas present to me, winning the beauty pagent. "No, they cannot destroy my memories.

"Besides, all those things happened in my *first* fifty years. The *next* fifty years will be even better. I have a lot of life to live, and some dreams left to fulfill. The best from me is still ahead."

. . . In the meantime, far to the south of me, a Pentecostal televangelist reappeared on the airwaves. His network consisted of a handful of stations. But with his charisma and star quality, he could possibly rise rapidly—again.

Commentary

The Bible says that when Jesus Christ returns, He will come for the church, "that he might present it to himself a glorious church, not having spot, or wrinkle, or any such thing: but that it should be holy and without blemish" (Ephesians 5:27). This would explain why Christ has consistently been a no-show.

Ironically, one "prophet of God" who predicted that Christ would return in 1982 was none other than Pat Robertson, who represented the very "spot" and "blemish" that the Apostle Paul referred to. So positive was the Reverend Robertson of the timing of the Second Coming that he announced to the world that God had commissioned him to usher in the event!

In his excellent book, *Salvation for Sale* (Prometheus Books, updated paperback edition, 1988), Gerard Thomas Straub, a former producer of "The 700 Club," describes an incredible "top secret" meeting of Christian Broadcasting Network (CBN) staff as they made preparations to greet Christ. Calling the operation "God's Secret Plan" (GSP), their mission was to prepare a file of technical and logistical information to enable them to televise this event successfully. One serious technical discussion centered around the burst of light that would accompany Jesus when He landed and how the CBN television cameras would be able to handle it.

This author recommends that you read *Salvation for Sale,* especially since (former) Reverend Pat Robertson has hinted that he might make another run for the presidency. It was through Gerry Straub that I met the thoughtful psychologist, Edmund D. Cohen, Ph.D., who, with Gerry, can be credited with torpedoing Robertson's 1988 presidential bid. For this, we can all be grateful. Had it not been for the careful monitoring of Robertson's telecasts by Cohen, beginning in 1984, Robertson might well have succeeded in denying his extreme, sometimes frightening, views.

Cohen provided the video tapes to *Time* magazine and the *New York Times.* The tapes showing Robertson making the statements, along with the news accounts of him denying his own words, got a lot of coverage, burying Robertson's credibility along with his presidential plans.

I wish I had met someone like Ed Cohen before I allowed myself to become involved with the "born-agains." He too has gone through "the experience." He became so involved that he entered Westminster Seminary—for a third round of postgraduate study. He eventually caught on to the damaging mind-control that the church seeks to exert. He dropped out, but not without feeling hurt and disillusioned. None of us escape the church experience without deep sorrow and disappointment over the deception.

Intrigued by what he saw and experienced, Cohen wrote a fascinating book, *The Mind of the Bible-Believer* (Prometheus Books, updated paperback edition, 1988). It should be required reading for seminarians, and especially for mental health professionals called upon to repair the damage done by the militant church.

Cohen lays out clearly the methods of mind-control systematically practiced by the church. He also reveals and analyzes the "seven devices" that the church skillfully uses to ensnare its prey and then separate them from the world, including in many cases, their families. There is not one Christian or ex-Christian alive who cannot identify with each of Cohen's "devices." They were used on all of us.

For example, Device 1 is called "the benign, attractive persona of the Bible." Cohen describes this as "a colossal bait-and-switch sales pitch that is worked on the new believer" (p. 171). It is "the most external of the seven" devices. One thing represented on the surface becomes something entirely different in actual practice. "Always, the inarticulate meaning is more somber and intimidating than the *apparent* meaning that had helped attract the new recruit into participation. The new inductee is weaned away from the ordinary meaning of each key term, *baited and switched* to the 'deeper' meaning. Also, the terms come to have meanings so different for Christians than for others that they serve as stumbling blocks to Christians' and outsiders' attempts to communicate with one another" [my italics] (p. 187).

While reading the treatise, I understood better how the church subtly undermined my family and marriage. As Cohen states: "Accordingly, the constant big-lie repetition from the Evangelicals—an example of Device 1—that the biblical program is synonymous with family values, goes glaringly against the grain of the Bible. . . . As we shall see, Jesus and Paul did not hesitate to divide families over religion, and the biblical program for conduct within the family is unrelievedly hierarchical, militating much more strongly against than for spontaneous human give and take" (p. 174).

While the Christian church outwardly preaches the importance of family and marriage, it conveniently neglects to complete the limited endorsement with the disclaimer, "as long as *everyone* in that family is *totally* in agreement with the church and its pastor." If that condition is met, the family is preserved at any cost, and "retreats" and "biblical counseling" are offered to couples having problems. *But,* if a member of the family resists the control or financial demands of the church, or balks at the church generally, the church will do everything possible to separate the troublesome wife, husband, child, or parent from the family in order to protect the faith. This is precisely what happened to Rose Marie and me. There are countless others who have gone through similar experiences. I hope that they will come forward as a result of this book and tell their stories as well.

In Device 3, "logocide," Cohen asks the question, "How far is it possible to go in misusing words—planting them in contexts that distort their meanings and draw their feeling tones and connotations too far into the foreground—to mislead people, confuse them, and mount a campaign of disinformation against them?"

Then he gives this example: "Husbands are repeatedly told to love their wives (Ephesians 5:25; Colossians 3:19, and 1 Peter 3:7). But the commandment is always covered in a haze of mystical symbolism, burdening the relationship of husband and wife with the distracting spiritual task of typifying the union of Christ with His church. We gain more insight into the attitudes being coaxed into place by the things not said in the instructions. Fathers are never told to love their children, only not to provoke them (Ephesians 6:4 and Colossians 3:21). Interestingly, the talent for keeping his children in subjection is set out as one of the qualifications of a pastor (1 Timothy 3:4). Wives are never directly instructed to love their husbands" (p. 220). "Love" in biblical terms ends up having practically nothing to do with "love" in human terms. Notice how the church *controls* the so-called love in a family, on its own terms, so that it can be manipulated in any direction that will benefit the church.

Then Cohen explodes a scripture that meant something totally different to me the first time I heard it: "This is my commandment, That ye love one another, as I have loved you" (John 15:12). Cohen points out: "Note that the . . . statement commands only love . . . for other believers ('one another'). Unbelieving fathers, mothers, sons and daughters are not necessarily included in any of the other categories of persons the believer is commanded to love . . . , i.e., strangers, neighbors and enemies" (p. 221). Cohen's notes are more enlightening than Schofield's.

Clearly, the church destroys open, responsible human relationships and turns them into fantasy ones. Cohen puts it this way, "[t]he biblical pseudo-psychology premise has it that humans are incapable of truly caring for one another without a God-obsession in the forefront of consciousness, and what may seem like lovingkindness from an unbeliever is really God, unseen, jerking his [the unbeliever's] strings" (p. 212-213). It would appear that one does not necessarily have to be an emotional cripple upon entering the church to be transformed into one after a steady diet of church indoctrination. The somber reality of that transformation is covered in Device 5, "dissociation induction" (manipulating the recruit into fleeing "the world," and his own "carnal thoughts"), and Device 6, "bridge burning" (bringing the inductee to the point where there is no turning back). Add Device 7, "holy terror" (suggesting to the believers who have been softened up by the other devices, how horrible eternal life in God's concentration camp will be if they deviate), and the enslavement is completed.

Had Cohen's book been available to me before my conversion, most likely I would have avoided the experience that destroyed my family. Had someone shown me this book while I was living in the world of born-again Christianity, I would have taken vigorous offense at many of Cohen's conclusions. Despite the discomforting passages, there would have been for me enough material of obvious truth that even my born-again Christian mind would have had to acknowledge it. I would have understood what the Christian life was doing to me and to Rose Marie, and no doubt would have pulled out of the destructive fantasy in time to save my family, and a good portion of my life savings.

Knowledge can prevent us from making many mistakes. Any organization, theory, or theology that cannot stand up under examination is not legitimate, and can only cause harm.

Until now, we have been permitted only a one-sided, positive image of Christianity and the church. This must change. The history of religion and how it has affected civilization—for ill as well as for good—should be a mandatory subject in our schools. That knowledge would give those who might be attracted to Christianity, as leaders or as followers, the opportunity to make an intelligent decision instead of a blind or ignorant one. The result would be a stronger church, and possibly a real blessing, as religious leaders of the future could detemine never to repeat the horrible mistakes of the past.

An issue that demands reexamination is the church and taxes. Church property, church income, and returns on church investment are tax-free. The preachers, religious leaders, and televangelists live in tax-free homes and drive tax-free cars. We all subsidize their free ride by paying *much* higher taxes than we would if religion paid its fair share. This means that *all* of us actually *subsidize* the church with the money we have worked so hard to earn. We could put the money to better use in supporting our own families—among other ways. Since this tacit method of collecting for the church is forced upon all of us, there really is no separation of church and state—as both the churches and the government have so long misled us to believe.

Consider this example: If the state of Texas alone collected the fair amount of taxes on church-owned property in that state, the proceeds would come to billions of dollars annually! To add insult to injury, the church leaders whose enterprises pay no taxes seem to have more to say about how the government should be run than the citizens who pay the taxes to run it. Paying their fair share of taxes would in no way alter the right of any church to continue to worship without interference.

That the Christian church has done some measure of good to some individuals cannot be denied. But, as Cohen says, "Even a clock that has stopped is right twice a day." However, from my personal viewpoint, I do not feel that any number of publicized good deeds could make up for the destruction of my life and family, or even justify the church's existence. Even so, I will not endeavor to tell people not to become involved with the church, but just to be cautious.

Living in the agony of the eighties, where it appears that so many religious leaders are corrupt, a prophecy is being fulfilled: ". . . as that the day of Christ is at hand. Let no man deceive you by any means: for that day shall not come, except there come a *falling away first,* [from the church] and that man of sin shall be revealed, the son of perdition . . ." (2 Thessalonians 2:2-3) [my italics].

A backlash against Christianity began in the late eighties as the churches continued to disgrace themselves. While some churches boasted increasing memberships, thousands of their churchgoers and supporters were going out the back door in disgust. The churches are beginning to feel the pinch. Some are closing down altogether. Young people, seeing the church as a colossal failure, have turned to other avenues of life, not necessarily healthy ones. That is the big tragedy.

On a recent flight from New York to Chicago, my seat mate was Dr. David Larsen, Professor of Practical Theology at Trinity Evangelical Divinity School in Deerfield, Illinois. "In the face of the scandals," he told me, "morale is not good in the seminaries, and fewer and fewer young people are interested in the ministry as a vocation. Attendance is down." The "falling away" is evident.

At the moment, the church of Jesus Christ sits on a rotting foundation. All other churches built on the existing foundations will crumble as well. The only way for the church truly to serve God is to level completely what presently exists, rebuild the foundation, and start all over. This will require a total house cleaning, and church reform. At present, there are too many difficulties, too many people involved with wrong motives to insure a successful conclusion.

It may be that the church will be silenced altogether for a few years, with a total "falling away." God may see that as necessary, while He waits for a new generation to emerge: young people He can work through, a generation that will bring back honesty and integrity. As a new breed of ministers rise up, we may finally be able to hear what Christ *really* wanted to say, in a church without "spot" or "blemish."

In the meanwhile, I will remain on spiritual R and R while it all gets worked out. I lost God in church. Maybe by leaving the church, I will get back to God. If I do, it will be a private matter. I believe religion was meant to be private. When Jesus ministered to individuals in the fields and in the homes, all went well. It was only when He got involved in the synagogues—the organized church—and tried to minister there that He got into trouble. And so be it.

Concordance

257, 273, 275-280, 300, 308-310, 313, 314

Rosin, Robert W., 218

Roth, Wolfgang, 33

Royal Lipizzan Stallion Show, 111, 113, 118, 121, 124, 125, 126, 128, 134, 136, 137, 139, 140, 144, 145, 147, 150, 194, 282, 295, 296

Royal Rangers, 148

Ryan, Jack, 307

Ryan, Congressman Leo, 231

Sacrificial giving, 117, 193

St. Patrick's Cathedral, New York, 178

Salvation for Sale (Straub), 311

Sanders, Colonel Harland, 100, 266

Santa Claus, 55, 58, 178, 277-280

Sara, Aubrey, 142, 249, 291, 292

Satan, 48, 144, 149, 190, 232

Schmock, Winston, 261-262

Schofield's Notes, 315

Schuller, Robert, 250, 293-294

Schuller, Robert Vernon, 294

Schultz, E. R., 149

Schultz, Lee, 102, 103, 104, 109, 113

Scoutmaster, 24

Screen Actors Guild (SAG), 309

Selling Post, The, 69

Serro, Bridget, 219, 220, 221

Serro, Richard, 219

Servetus, Michael, 68

"700 Club," 9, 194, 218, 219, 220, 239, 240, 241, 248

Sex, 149, 166, 171, 262, 265, 267, 290, 292, 294-296, 305. *See also:* Adultery, Child molestation, Church sex, Foot fetish, Fornication, Jessica Hahn, Heterosexuality, Homosexuality, Lesbian, Lust, Massage parlor, Masturbation, Nude, Oral Sex,

Perversion, Prostitute(s), Steam room

Shanks, William, 20

Shanahan, Alice, 34

Sheen, Bishop Fulton, 178

Shell, Arthur, 145, 146, 237

Shelton, Don, 184, 185, 189

Short, Bridget Serro, 219, 220, 221

Shrine, 89

Shrine doctor, 53

Shriner(s), 26, 29, 51, 71, 84, 281

Siegel, Mr., 169

Slain in the Spirit, 193, 194, 222

Slezak, Walter, 76

Sloan-Kettering Memorial Hospital, New York, 177

Smiley, Dolores, 295

Smith, R. D. E., 118, 120, 121, 122, 123, 140, 165, 174, 204, 218, 225

Southern Indiana Gas and Electric, 19, 24

Spirit-filled church, 11

"Spirit Himself, The," 94

Springfield Leader and Press, 184, 185

Springfield News Leader, The, 184

Spurr, Thurlow, 238-239, 246, 247

Stanley, Otis, 296-298, 300

Stanton, Cameron, 167-170

Steam room, PTL, 12, 13, 182, 183, 192, 238, 245, 265

Steel Pier, Atlantic City, 39

Steffensen, Ernest, 118, 123

Sterling, Jack, 34

Stevens, Irving, 182, 183

Stewart, Boyd, 63

Stewart, Jim, 19, 21

Stewart, Melvin, 12

Stoehr, Chris, 229, 231

Straub, Gerard Thomas, 311

Stubbs, Judy, 128

Sutera, Joseph, 122